I0129421

Managing Alcohol, Tobacco and Other Drug Problems:

A Pocket Guide for Physicians and Nurses

Centre for Addiction and Mental Health
Centre de toxicomanie et de santé mentale

Addiction Research Foundation
Clarke Institute of Psychiatry
Donwood Institute
Queen Street Mental Health Centre

A World Health Organization Centre of Excellence

St. Joseph's
HEALTH CENTRE
TORONTO

Managing Alcohol, Tobacco and Other Drug Problems: A Pocket Guide for Physicians and Nurses

Edited by: Meldon Kahan, MD, and Lynn Wilson, MD; Development: Andrew Johnson, CAMH; Editorial: Sue McCluskey, CAMH; Design: Mara Korkola, CAMH; Creative consultation: Nancy Leung, CAMH; Formatting: J. Lynn Campbell; Print production: Christine Harris, CAMH, Annie Hart, CAMH; Marketing: Arturo Llerenas, CAMH; Permissions: Phil DiRosa, CAMH; Project support: Sandra Thomson, SJHC, Blanca Uriarte, CAMH

Printed in Canada
Copyright © 2002 Centre for Addiction and Mental Health

National Library of Canada Cataloguing in Publication

Main entry under title:

Managing alcohol, tobacco and other drug problems: a pocket guide for physicians and nurses / principal editors, Meldon Kahan and Lynn Wilson.

Includes bibliographical references and index.
ISBN 0-88868-413-4

1. Substance abuse—Treatment. I. Kahan, Meldon, MD II. Wilson, Lynn, MD III. Centre for Addiction and Mental Health.

RC564.15.M34 2002   616.86'06   C2002-902648-2

For information on other Centre for Addiction and Mental Health
resource materials or to place an order, please contact:
Marketing and Sales Services
Centre for Addiction and Mental Health
33 Russell Street
Toronto, ON M5S 2S1 Canada
Tel.: 1-800-661-1111 or 416-595-6059 in Toronto
E-mail: marketing@camh.net
Web site: www.camh.net

CAUTION: **An Important Note**
While the authors have made every effort to ensure accuracy, physicians and nurses should consult with the manufacturer's recommendations before prescribing or administering the medications mentioned in this guide.

NOTE: This pocket guide is intended as a companion to *Management of Alcohol, Tobacco and Other Drug Problems: A Physician's Manual.*† Consult the manual for additional information and references. Portions of this guide have been adapted or excerpted from the manual, and from the Project CREATE module series.††

†Brands, B., Kahan, M., Selby, P. & Wilson, L. (2000). *Management of Alcohol, Tobacco and Other Drug Problems: A Physician's Manual*. Toronto: Centre for Addiction and Mental Health.

†† Wilson, L., Kahan, M. & Midmer, D. (2000). *Project CREATE Module Series for Undergraduate Medical Education and Faculty Development*. Toronto: Undergraduate Education Committee of the Faculties of Medicine.

Managing Alcohol, Tobacco and Other Drug Problems:

A Pocket Guide for Physicians and Nurses

EDITED BY: Meldon Kahan, MD, and Lynn Wilson, MD

CONTRIBUTORS:
Bruna Brands, PhD
Carol Edwards, RN
Brian Chisamore, MD
Douglas Gourlay, MD
Ajay Kapur, MD
Bhushan Kapur, MD
Christine Koczmara, RN
David Marsh, MD
Peter Mezciems, MD
Michael McGuigan, MD
James Rankin, MD
Peter Selby, MD
Kay Shen, MD
Kingsley Watts, MD

Publication of this pocket guide was made possible through a grant from the Lawson Foundation and support from St. Joseph's Health Centre, Toronto, and the Centre for Addiction and Mental Health.

CONTENTS

vi   Preface

viii   Introduction

1   1   Definitions

5   2   Role of Nurses and Physicians

9   3   Screening and Assessment of Alcohol Problems

14   4   Screening and Assessment of Other Drug Problems

17   5   Identification of Substance Use in Older Adults, Women and Adolescents: Specific Recommendations

20   6   Laboratory Detection of Alcohol and Other Drug Use

30   7   Problem Drinking

35   8   Drinking and Driving

38   9   Alcohol Withdrawal

50   10 Pharmacotherapy for Alcohol Dependence

54   11 Alcoholic Liver Disease

62   12 Other Medical Complications of Alcohol Use

67   13 Nicotine and Smoking Cessation

76   14 Opioid Prescribing for Chronic Pain

85   15 Opioid Dependence and Chronic Pain

90   16 Opioid Withdrawal

92   17 Pharmacotherapy for Opioid Dependence

99   18 Benzodiazepines for Anxiety and Insomnia

105   19 Benzodiazepine and Barbiturate Dependence and Withdrawal

113   20 Polysubstance Use and Withdrawal

117   21 Cocaine

122   22 Cannabis

125   23 Other Drugs

141   24 Intoxication and Overdose: Alcohol, Opioids, Benzodiazepines, Cocaine,
          Methanol, Ethylene Glycol

153   25 Injection Drug Use and Infectious Disease

161   26 Pregnancy and Substance Use

183   27 Substance Use and Mental Illness

187   28 Surgery and Substance Use

193   29 Drug-Seeking

195   30 Psychosocial Treatment for Substance Use

199   31 Counselling and Motivational Interviewing

206   32 Physician and Nurse Impairment

211   Appendix: Substance Use Resources in Ontario

212   References

218   Index

PREFACE

SUBSTANCE dependence and the range of other issues that invariably accompany the misuse of alcohol and other drugs belong to all of us. Education, skill and understanding are needed to help overcome historical attitudes that prevent those who need help from accessing treatment.

This non-judgmental guide to the care of people with alcohol and other drug problems is an exceptionally useful tool that will help clinicians to recognize that substance use problems are medically treatable, and help their patients to accept this view as well. By focusing on management issues in a refreshingly accessible, concise manner, this guide will not only demystify the treatment of patients with substance use issues, but also lead to better treatment outcomes.

Drs. Kahan, Wilson and colleagues have my congratulations for assembling a particularly useful guide on a topic of concern to every clinician.

Marilyn J. Bruner

President and CEO
St. Joseph's Health Centre, Toronto

GROWING recognition of the extent, severity and sequelae of substance use has paralleled an increasing awareness of the broad determinants of health that physicians and nurses must understand in helping their patients. For a variety of moralistic, cultural, psychological and social reasons, health professionals have often paid little heed to substance use. The reasons do not include scientific evidence or clinical significance.

This pocket guide provides medical and nursing students, physicians and nurses with a highly synthetic distillation of both clinical pharmacology and clinical wisdom from a group of contributors working in the "real world" of clinical care. Challenging clinical presentations such as the woman who is pregnant and using substances, or the impaired physician, are addressed with practical steps for the clinician.

Answers—or at least the beginnings of answers—are contained within a couple of pages for most problems and are a healthy antidote to the therapeutic nihilism that can otherwise prejudice the care of people who have substance use problems. These patients are no less deserving of our efforts than anyone else.

David S. Goldbloom, MD, FRCPC

Physician-in-Chief
Centre for Addiction and Mental Health

Professor of Psychiatry
University of Toronto

INTRODUCTION

Advice and treatment by physicians and nurses can substantially reduce substance use and its associated morbidity and health care costs, yet physicians are often hampered by lack of training and knowledge in this area.

Fortunately, clear, well-researched protocols have been developed for identifying and treating substance use and its complications. This guide summarizes the simplest and most effective of these protocols, honed through our experience at the Centre for Addiction and Mental Health and the Addiction Medicine Service at St. Joseph's Health Centre in Toronto. The guide is intended as a quick reference for the busy physician and nurse.

The editors wish to acknowledge the following people for their contributions to this project: Marilyn Bruner, Dr. Karen D'Apolito, Dr. David Goldbloom, Dr. Lorretta Finnegan and Sheila Lacroix.

KEY

In this pocket guide the symbol **A** refers to screening and assessment information, and the symbol **P** refers to treatment protocols and other medical interventions that go beyond screening and assessment.

1

DEFINITIONS

Substance dependence

A syndrome characterized by the "3 Cs":
· **Compulsive** drug use (much time and effort spent acquiring and using the drug, and recovering from its effects)
· Loss of **control** (unable to stop use)
· **Consequences** of use (physical, social, psychological).

DSM-IV CRITERIA FOR SUBSTANCE DEPENDENCE†

A maladaptive pattern of substance use, leading to clinically significant impairment or distress, as manifested by 3 (or more) of the following, occurring at any time in the same 12-month period:

1. tolerance, as defined by either of the following:
   a) a need for markedly increased amounts of the substance to achieve intoxication or desired effect
   b) markedly diminished effect with continued use of the same amount of the substance
2. withdrawal, as manifested by either of the following:
   a) the characteristic withdrawal syndrome for the substance
   b) the same (or a closely related) substance is taken to relieve or avoid withdrawal symptoms
3. the substance is often taken in larger amounts or over a longer period than was intended
4. there is a persistent desire or unsuccessful efforts to cut down or control substance use
5. a great deal of time is spent in activities necessary to obtain the substance

(e.g., visiting multiple doctors or driving long distances), use the substance (e.g., chain-smoking), or recover from its effects

6. important social, occupational, or recreational activities are given up or reduced because of substance use

7. the substance use is continued despite knowledge of having a persistent or recurrent physical or psychological problem that is likely to have been caused or exacerbated by the substance (e.g., current cocaine use despite recognition of cocaine-induced depression, or continued drinking despite recognition that an ulcer was made worse by alcohol consumption).

†Reprinted with permission from *Diagnostic and Statistical Manual of Mental Disorders* (4th ed.). Copyright 1994, American Psychiatric Association.

Physical dependence on substances

Characterized by *tolerance* and *withdrawal*. Does not imply psychological dependence. Patients on high drug doses may experience tolerance and withdrawal without being psychologically dependent on the drug (e.g., individuals treated with high doses of opioids for chronic pain).

Substance tolerance

A neurological adaptation to the psychoactive effects of a substance; more of the drug is required to achieve the same effect. Tolerance develops quickly to the psychoactive effects of alcohol and opioids. Highly tolerant patients can behave almost normally after consuming opioid doses that would be fatal in non-tolerant patients.

Substance withdrawal

A constellation of symptoms and signs that occur within hours or days of cessation of the drug.

Substance abuse

This term is often used loosely to describe the problem use of an illicit drug or the medically unsanctioned use of licit drugs (e.g., taking codeine in amounts greater than prescribed, from unauthorized sources such as friends or the street, or to achieve euphoria rather than pain control).

DSM-IV CRITERIA FOR SUBSTANCE ABUSE†

A. A maladaptive pattern of substance use leading to a clinically significant impairment or distress, as manifested by 1 (or more) of the following occurring within a 12-month period:

1) recurrent substance use resulting in a failure to fulfill major role obligations at work, school, or home (e.g., repeated absences or poor work performance related to substance use; substance-related absences, suspensions, or expulsions from school; neglect of children or household)

2) recurrent substance use in situations in which it is physically hazardous (e.g., driving an automobile or operating a machine when impaired by substance use)

3) recurrent substance-related legal problems (e.g., arrests for substance-related disorderly misconduct)

4) continued substance use despite having persistent or recurrent social or interpersonal problems caused or exacerbated by the effects of the substance (e.g., arguments with spouse about consequences of intoxication, physical fights)

B. The symptoms have never met the criteria for Substance Dependence for this class of substance.

† Reprinted with permission from *Diagnostic and Statistical Manual of Mental Disorders* (4th ed.). Copyright 1994, American Psychiatric Association.

At-risk drinking

Consumption of alcohol above the recommended low-risk guidelines, with possible physical or social harm.

Problem drinking

Consumption above the recommended low-risk guidelines, causing 1 or more physical or social problems but without meeting the criteria for alcohol dependence.

Binge drinking

Consumption of excessive amounts of alcohol for days or weeks at a time, followed by periods of abstinence or reduced drinking.

Classification of substances of abuse

CLASS	EXAMPLES
Alcohol	
Sedative/hypnotics	Benzodiazepines: diazepam, lorazepam, oxazepam, chlordiazepoxide, triazolam, alprazolam
	Barbiturates: butalbital (in Fiorinal®), secobarbital
Opioids	Codeine, oxycodone, morphine, hydromorphone, hydrocodone, meperidine, heroin
Nicotine	
Inhalants	Glue, gasoline, solvents
Stimulants	Cocaine, amphetamine, MDMA (ecstasy)
Cannabis	Marijuana, hashish
Hallucinogens	Lysergic acid diethylamide (LSD), psilocybin, mescaline, phencyclidine (PCP)
Steroids	

Assessment†

Substance use assessment is the further investigation of patients whose screening results indicate that substance use is likely and whose screening results suggest compulsive use, impaired control and the presence of other psychosocial problems that render a brief intervention ineffective. Assessment:

· Examines problems related to use (e.g., medical, behavioural, social and financial)
· Provides data for a formal diagnosis of a possible problem
· Establishes the severity of an identified problem (i.e., mild, moderate, intermediate or severe)
· Helps to determine the appropriate level of care
· Guides treatment planning (e.g., whether specialized care is needed, components of an appropriate referral and eligibility for services)
· Defines a baseline of the patient's status to which future conditions can be compared.

† Adapted from: *A Guide to Substance Abuse Services for Primary Care Clinicians*. 1997. Substance Abuse and Mental Health Services Administration. Public domain.

2

ROLE OF NURSES AND PHYSICIANS

Nurses' responsibilities

IDENTIFICATION

Nurses on inpatient wards often identify alcohol and other drug problems before physicians, based on:
· Admission screening and assessment
· Observing drug-seeking behaviour
· Witnessing signs of withdrawal (particularly at night)
· Disclosures by patients and/or family members.

MANAGEMENT OF WITHDRAWAL

Nurses have an essential role in implementing symptom-based protocols for treating withdrawal from alcohol, opioids and benzodiazepines.

ADVICE AND TREATMENT REFERRAL

Nurses have a responsibility to:
· Advise patients that they may have a substance use problem.
· Inform the attending physician and other members of the health care team of nursing concerns and observations.
· Facilitate treatment referrals.

Physicians' responsibilities

· Screen for alcohol and other drug problems.
· Identify and treat medical complications of substance use.
· Treat withdrawal and its complications.
· Identify and treat psychiatric problems.

· Identify social problems; make appropriate referrals.
· Provide pharmacotherapy for preventing relapse (e.g., naltrexone).
· Prescribe potentially addicting drugs appropriately and safely.
· Provide advice and health information (e.g., brief advice for problem drinkers).
· Make appropriate treatment referrals (mutual aid, inpatient or outpatient programs).

Rationale for active intervention by nurses and physicians

Alcohol, tobacco and other drug problems are a major cause of morbidity and mortality. Controlled studies have demonstrated that advice and treatment by physicians and nurses reduces substance use and its associated morbidity and health care costs.

MORBIDITY AND MORTALITY CAUSED BY ALCOHOL, TOBACCO AND OTHER DRUG USE[1]

· Substance use accounts for 21% of all mortality, 23% of potential life lost, 8% of hospitalizations
· Canada, 1992: 6701 deaths attributed to alcohol, 33 498 deaths attributed to smoking

Economic costs of substance use: Canada, 1992*[2]

	TOTAL COST	HEALTH CARE COST	LAW ENFORCEMENT
Tobacco	9.56	2.68	—
Alcohol	7.52	1.3	1.36
Illicit drugs	1.4	.88	.4

*All figures are $billion Canadian.

Effectiveness of physicians' and nurses' advice for problem drinkers

At least 14 randomized controlled trials have demonstrated that advice from physicians/nurses to problem drinkers decreases alcohol consumption, ER visits and hospital admissions[3,4] (see also Chapter 7, Problem Drinking).

Treatment of alcohol dependence: Surgical patients

Identification and treatment of surgical patients with alcohol problems markedly reduces complication rates.[5-7] Patients who are dependent on alcohol and are treated for alcohol withdrawal and given disulfiram for 1 month prior to surgery have:

· Lower total complication rates
· Lower rates of MI and dysrhythmias
· Shorter stays in ICU.

Tobacco

· Leading cause of preventable death in Canada
· 30% of Canadian adults smoke; 34% of women aged 20–24 smoke

Proportion of deaths attributable to smoking:

· 30% of all heart disease deaths
· 85% of lung cancer deaths
· Among women, mortality from lung cancer exceeds that from breast cancer

Reversibility of adverse effects from smoking:

· Risk of MI, CVA drop within 24 h.
· Risk of CAD reduced by 20% in 1 year.
· Risk of CVA normalizes after 5 years.
· Risk of death equal to that of a non-smoker after 15 years.

Smoking-cessation intervention effectiveness (odds ratio):

· Nicotine patch: 2.9
· Counselling by clinician: 1.8

Treatment for substance dependence

SUCCESS OF INPATIENT REFERRALS TO TREATMENT PROGRAMS

Physicians who refer patients to a treatment program can expect that a large proportion (up to 60%) will accept the referral.[8]

Success rates and cost-effectiveness of formal treatment compare favourably with treatment of other chronic illnesses.

Treatment outcome at 6 months [9]

DRUG	SUCCESS RATE (%)*	RANGE (%)
Alcohol	50	40–70
Opioids	60	50–80
Cocaine	55	50–60
Nicotine	30	20–40

* > 50% ↓ in Addiction Severity Index

COST-EFFECTIVENESS OF TREATMENT

- One study found that the health care costs of a group receiving treatment for substance use was 1/3 that of matched waiting list controls over 1 year, because of decreased hospital admissions and ER visits. [10]
- In one trial, problem drinkers receiving brief physician advice had health care savings of $1150 per subject over a 1-year period because of decreased hospital admissions and ER visits. [11]

3

SCREENING AND ASSESSMENT OF ALCOHOL PROBLEMS

Physicians are poor at identifying alcohol problems,[7, 12] particularly in women and older adults. Detection rates can be improved by routine inquiry about alcohol use, and through use of screening questionnaires, laboratory tests, and knowledge of common clinical presentations.

ALCOHOL CONSUMPTION HISTORY

· Ask all patients about alcohol use.
· Ask about number of drinks per week.
· Convert response into standard drinks (see table below).
· Ask about maximum consumption on any 1 day in the past 3 months. (Patients often exclude heavy drinking days when asked only about typical or usual consumption.)
· Patients who drink wine or spirits at home often pour more than 1 standard drink in a glass. Ask these patients how many bottles (and what size) they consume per week.
· For patients who give vague responses:
  – Ask about previous week's drinking (this should be easily recalled).
  – Present them with a wide range of consumption: "Do you drink more like 8 drinks a week, or 40 drinks a week?"

Standard Drink Equivalents

| 43 mL (1.5 oz.) spirit (40% alcohol) | or | 142 mL (5 oz.) table wine (12% alcohol) | or | 341 mL (12 oz.) regular beer (5% alcohol) | or | 85 mL (3 oz.) fortified wine (18% alcohol) |

Detection of alcohol problems

While screening will identify a large proportion of patients with alcohol problems, many others will come to light only if the physician is alert to the various presentations of alcohol problems (see below).

Clinical presentations of alcohol problems

Cardiovascular	· Hypertension · Dysrhythmias · Cardiomyopathy
GI	· Fatty liver · Hepatitis · Cirrhosis · Gastritis · Pancreatitis · Dyspepsia · Recurrent diarrhea
Neurological	· Ataxia, tremor · Peripheral neuropathy · Cerebellar disease · Dementia · Korsakoff's syndrome
Behavioural	· Missed appointments · Non-compliance · Drug-seeking
Musculoskeletal	· Recurrent trauma · Myopathy
Reproductive	· Sexual dysfunction · Irregular menstrual cycles · Infertility · Low birthweight baby
Psychiatric	· Fatigue · Insomnia · Depression · Anxiety · Psychosis
Social	· Deterioration in social functioning · Spousal abuse · Violence, legal problems

Screening questionnaires
CAGE

The CAGE [13] is more sensitive than the alcohol consumption history or laboratory tests (75–85% for detecting consumption of 4 drinks per day or more). Sensitivity may be increased by using it *before* the alcohol history is taken (e.g., as part of a waiting-room questionnaire). The CAGE should be interpreted in light of information on the amount and frequency of alcohol consumption.

CAGE†

· Have you ever felt you ought to **C**UT DOWN on your drinking?
· Have people **A**NNOYED you by criticizing your drinking?
· Have you ever felt bad or **G**UILTY about your drinking?
· Have you ever had a drink first thing in the morning to steady your nerves or get rid of a hangover (**E**YE-OPENER)?

Males
2 "yes" responses suggests a current or past alcohol problem.

Females
1 "yes" response suggests a problem. [14]

†Reprinted with permission from *American Journal of Psychiatry*, 131(10), 1121-1123 ©1974.

T-ACE

The T-ACE is a useful screening questionnaire for pregnant women. (For questionnaire, see page 164).

🔊 Assessment of the patient with a suspected alcohol problem:
Detailed alcohol-related history

ITEM	COMMENT
Quantity–frequency of alcohol use	Consumption of over 14 drinks/week (men), over 9 drinks/week (women), or over 2 drinks/day suggests at-risk or problem drinking. Consumption of 40+ drinks/week suggests possible alcohol dependence.
Other drug use: benzodiazepines, opioids, street drugs (cannabis, cocaine), OTC drugs	Ask about prescribed, over-the-counter and street drug use. Ask about route (oral, inhalation, injection) and amount. Polysubstance use is common among people who drink heavily.
Alcohol withdrawal symptoms	Withdrawal symptoms are often not recognized as such by the patient or the physician. They typically present as anxiety, or morning/afternoon tremor quickly relieved by drinking or sedatives. Ask: "Do you ever drink during the day?" "Do you ever find that your hands shake when you reach for something?" "Does a drink make these shakes better?"
Consequences of use (social, occupational, financial, legal, physical)	Ask: "Has your spouse/partner expressed any concerns about your drinking?" "Has your drinking caused you any problems at home? "Has it caused any health problems?" "Legal or financial problems?" "Have you ever missed work because of drinking?" "Has drinking ever interfered with your work performance?"
Social situation	Ask about safety of children at home and spousal abuse.
Driving while impaired	See Chapter 8, Drinking and Driving.
Mental status	Ask about symptoms of depression, anxiety, psychosis. Ask specifically about suicidal ideation. Suicide is one of the main causes of death among alcohol-dependent patients.
Previous treatment attempts	This helps predict which treatment approach is likely to be most effective.
Readiness to change	See Chapter 31, Counselling and Motivational Interviewing.

Physical examination

ALL PATIENTS
· BP, heart rate
· Signs of intoxication (odour of alcohol, slurred speech)
· Signs of liver disease (hepatomegaly, spider nevae)
· Signs of withdrawal (tremor, sweating, ataxia)

PATIENTS WITH A LONG HISTORY OF HEAVY ALCOHOL USE (10+ YEARS)
· Cardiovascular (hypertension, cardiomyopathy)
· Mental status (dementia)
· Gait (cerebellar dysfunction)
· Peripheral sensation (distal polyneuropathy)

Laboratory investigations

· CBC, mean cell volume, AST, ALT, GGT
· If clinical evidence of cirrhosis: INR, albumin, bilirubin, electrolytes, creatinine, magnesium
· Hepatitis B, C serology (patients dependent on alcohol have a higher prevalence of viral hepatitis)
· HIV if current or past injection drug use or unsafe sexual practices
· β-HCG for women of childbearing age, if indicated
· Urine drug screen for cocaine, opioids, cannabis, benzodiazepines, barbiturates. Ask the patient's permission before ordering this test.

4

SCREENING AND ASSESSMENT OF OTHER DRUG PROBLEMS

⊘A SUBSTANCE USE HISTORY
- Ask all patients about prescription drug use (e.g., benzodiazepines, opioids) and OTC drugs (e.g., dimenhydrinate, acetaminophen with codeine).
- Ask all patients under 60 about street drugs (e.g., cocaine, cannabis, heroin).

Selected presentations of drug use
Physicians need to be aware of common clinical presentations of drug use.

⊘A Clinical presentations of drug use

Infections (injection drug use)	· Cellulitis, abscess
	· Hepatitis C (marker: elevated ALT)
Trauma	· Accidents, violence, suicide
Psychiatric	· Depression, anxiety, insomnia, psychosis (esp. cannabis, cocaine, hallucinogens)
Social	· Deterioration in social functioning
	· Spousal abuse, family violence
Other	· Weight loss
	· Loss of libido
	· Irregular menstrual cycles

Drug withdrawal symptoms*

DRUG	SYMPTOMS	ONSET/DURATION	COMPLICATIONS
Cocaine	· "Crash": increased sleep, eating · Withdrawal: depression, insomnia, irritability, drug-craving	· "Crash": 1–48 h · Withdrawal: 1–10 weeks	· Relapse, suicide
Opioids	· Depression, insomnia, drug-craving, myalgias, nausea, chills, autonomic instability (lacrimation, rhinorrhea, piloerection)	· Onset: 6–12 h · Peak: 2–3 days · Duration: 5–10 days · Insomnia, dysphoria, craving may last weeks/months	· Loss of tolerance (overdose on relapse) · Pregnancy: miscarriage, premature labour
Benzodiazepines, barbiturates	· Anxiety, insomnia, dysperceptions, autonomic, hyperactivity (less common)	· Onset: 1–2 days (short-acting), 2–4 days (long-acting) · Duration: weeks/months	· Above 50 mg diazepam or 500 mg butalbital/day: seizures, delirium, psychosis
Alcohol	· Tremor, vomiting, sweating, tachycardia	· Onset: 6 h · Duration: 7 days (usually peaks at 1–3 days)	· Seizures, delirium, psychosis, dysrhythmias

*Patients will often disclose their drug use if they feel they can get help for withdrawal symptoms.

ASSESSMENT OF THE PATIENT WITH A SUSPECTED DRUG PROBLEM

The assessment is similar to the assessment for alcohol problems. Ask about:
· Amount, pattern and route of use
· Withdrawal symptoms
· Other drug use. Poly drug use is common, therefore ask specifically about use of each class of drugs (alcohol, cocaine, opioids, benzodiazepines, cannabis)
· Consequences of use (physical, social, occupational, legal, financial)

- Social situation, including safety of children living at home
- Depression, anxiety, psychosis, suicidal ideation
- Spousal, child abuse
- Previous treatment attempts
- Injection drug use (if positive ask about sharing of injection equipment; history of hepatitis B, C and/or HIV)
- High-risk sexual activity (involvement in the sex trade, or sexual activity while impaired)
- Possibility of pregnancy

Physical examination
- Signs of intoxication or withdrawal (e.g., opioid intoxication: miosis, nodding off)
- Injection marks and bruising in arms, wrists, legs, neck, inguinal region; occasionally breasts, abdominal wall
- May also see ulcers or fibrosis in thigh or gluteal region from repeated im or sc injections
- Hepatomegaly, splenomegaly

Laboratory investigations
- Serology: hepatitis B and C, HIV
- MCV, GGT (to detect heavy alcohol consumption)
- AST, ALT (to detect alcoholic or viral hepatitis)
- Urine drug screen

5

IDENTIFICATION OF SUBSTANCE USE IN OLDER ADULTS, WOMEN AND ADOLESCENTS: SPECIFIC RECOMMENDATIONS

Physicians are less likely to identify substance use in older adults, women or adolescents. The strategies outlined below will increase detection rates.

OLDER ADULTS

· Ask about alcohol use when prescribing drugs with sedative properties. Older adults are often prescribed medications that interact with alcohol, such as benzodiazepines. They are more sensitive to the sedative effects of alcohol and other drugs.

· Give patients "permission" to acknowledge alcohol use. Older women are especially reluctant to admit to alcohol use because they fear disapproval. Ask: "Do you ever drink to help you sleep? Do you ever have a drink when visiting with friends? A lot of people do that."

· Be alert to non-specific presentations of alcohol dependence. Fatigue, depression, confusion, "failure to thrive," falls and other accidents may be incorrectly attributed to dementia or other causes.

· Ask a family member about a patient's alcohol use if you have any further concerns. Ask the patient's permission.

❀ WOMEN

Identification

Physicians need to use more sensitive screening instruments for women, such as the CAGE (with 1 as cut-off), or T-ACE (see page 164). Carefully screen for alcohol or drug problems if a woman presents with:

· Current or past history of physical, sexual abuse
· Regular use of benzodiazepines or opioids
· Substance-using partner
· Anxiety or mood disorder

❀ ADOLESCENTS

All adolescents should be screened for substance use. *Ensure confidentiality* to allay fears that you will tell their parents (review exceptions such as suicidality or disclosure of problem substance use in those under 16).

INITIAL HISTORY IN ALL ADOLESCENTS
Review with the adolescent each of these areas (HEADSS):

Home
Education
Activities
Drugs
Suicide
Sexuality

Ask about:
· Parental substance use
· Poor family relationships
· Abuse or neglect
· Psychiatric disorders, especially conduct disorder
· Early experimentation with substances

If the adolescent reports substance use:
· Avoid labelling or lecturing.
· Ask if the parents know about the substance use.
· Ask for clarification of slang terms.
· Ask about family history.
· Establish an agenda for further visits.

❧ Alcohol and other drug use history

SUBSTANCE USED	QUESTIONS FOR EACH SUBSTANCE
· Prescription drugs	· Age of first use
· Over-the-counter (OTC) medications, including herbal supplements	· Amount, frequency of present use
	· Most recent use
· Tobacco, alcohol, cannabis	· What the patient likes about the substance
· LSD, psilocybin, amphetamines, cocaine, heroin	· What the patient does not like (what problems, if any, the patient has had with the drug)
· Ecstasy (MDMA), ketamine, GHB	
· Inhalants (glue, gasoline)	
· IV drugs, steroids	
· "Any other substances used to get high"	

Clinical presentations of substance use in adolescents

Psychosocial	· Change in school performance
	· Involvement in illegal activities
	· Promiscuity, prostitution
	· Increased demand for money
	· Change in peer group
Medical	· Frequent injuries
	· Chronic cough, wheezing
	· GI symptoms (e.g., nausea, vomiting)
	· STDs
Psychiatric	· Anxiety, depression
	· Insomnia
	· Suicide attempts/gestures
	· Unexplained weight loss, anorexia, bulimia

6

LABORATORY DETECTION OF ALCOHOL AND OTHER DRUG USE

Alcohol: Direct measurements

Measurement of alcohol concentration in the serum or breath is indicated in the following circumstances:

· Suspected drinking and driving (Chapter 8, Drinking and Driving)
· Assessing decreased level of consciousness in a person who has been drinking (Chapter 24, Intoxication and Overdose)
· Determining causes of suspected alcohol and other drug overdose (Chapter 24, Intoxication and Overdose)
· Determining when to start diazepam loading for withdrawal (Chapter 9, Alcohol Withdrawal)

Breathalyser

Breathalysers are quick, convenient and accurate (alveolar concentration of alcohol correlates very closely with blood alcohol concentration), although not widely available in clinical settings.

Blood alcohol concentration (BAC)

FACTORS INFLUENCING BAC

BAC depends on body weight, gender and rate of metabolism. BAC is up to 20% higher in women than men for a given rate of alcohol consumption and same body weight, primarily because of a smaller volume of distribution. Other factors that can effect BAC include type of drink, current medications, general health and age (e.g., older adults have a higher BAC per unit consumed).

RATE OF DECLINE

BAC declines at a steady rate of 3.2–5.4 mmol/L per hour (15–25 mg/100 mL per hour, or approximately 1 drink/h). Heavy drinkers metabolize alcohol faster because of induction of liver enzymes.

CLINICAL INTERPRETATION OF BAC

Correlation between clinical presentation and BAC is greatly influenced by the patient's underlying tolerance. People who have high tolerance may be in withdrawal at levels that would cause intoxication in non-tolerant people:

BAC/Tolerance correlation: Clinical interpretation*

BAC (MMOL/L)	AMOUNT CONSUMED	NON-TOLERANT DRINKERS	TOLERANT DRINKERS
20	Men: 4 drinks in 1 h; Women: 2–3 in 1 h	Signs of intoxication	Normal or in withdrawal
30+	6+ drinks within preceding h	Obviously intoxicated, may be drowsy	Mildly intoxicated
60+	10+ drinks within preceding h	Stupor, irregular breathing. Death can occur from respiratory failure, aspiration.	Obviously intoxicated
90–120		Death can occur.	Death can occur.

*17.4 mmol/L = 80 mg% (legal limit in most jurisdictions). Divide mg% by 4.6 to calculate mmol/L.

BAC (mmol/L) per drink: Females and males*, **

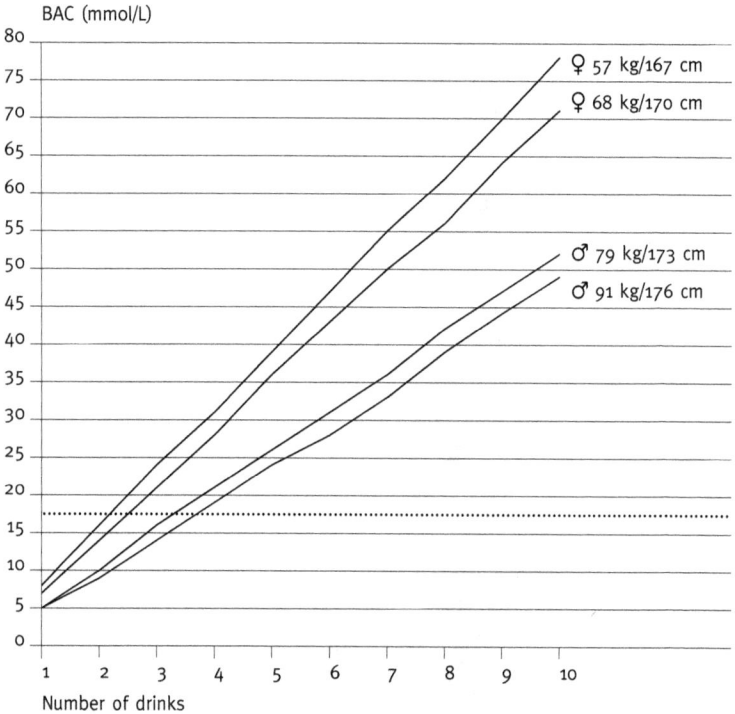

BAC (mmol/L)

♀ 57 kg/167 cm
♀ 68 kg/170 cm
♂ 79 kg/173 cm
♂ 91 kg/176 cm

Number of drinks

.... Legal limit in most jurisdictions: 17.4 mmol/L = 80 mg%

*Subtract 3.5 mmol/L for every h since first drink (heavy drinkers can metabolize up to 5.5 mmol/L per h). This assumes a constant rate of consumption. For example, a 57 kg woman consuming 8 drinks in 2 h would have a BAC of 55 mmol/L (62-3.5[2]).

**Note: The above calculations are based on averages and do not take into account any baseline BAC due to previous drinking.

Alcohol: Indirect measurements
Role of laboratory testing in diagnosis and treatment
· Abnormal GGT or MCV helps to confirm clinical suspicions, but normal values do not rule out an alcohol problem (low sensitivity).
· Repeated testing can be used to monitor response to treatment and provide feedback to patients. Typically GGT rises and falls in tandem with alcohol use. (The half-life of GGT is 4 weeks. The half-life of MCV is 3 months.)

Gamma glutamyl transferase (GGT)
Increased GGT has a sensitivity of 35–50% in detecting alcohol consumption of 4 drinks/day or more. GGT can be elevated by medications (e.g., phenytoin), non-alcoholic liver disease, diabetes and obesity.

Mean cell volume (MCV)
Increased MCV is somewhat less sensitive than GGT. MCV can be elevated by medications (e.g., valproic acid), folate and B12 deficiency, liver disease and hypothyroidism.

Other laboratory measurements
· Thrombocytopenia caused by alcohol-induced bone-marrow suppression is usually mild and resolves within weeks of abstinence.
· Thrombocytopenia caused by splenomegaly (secondary to portal hypertension) is more severe and does not respond as well to abstinence.
· High AST indicates alcohol-induced hepatitis.
· High bilirubin and INR and low albumin indicate hepatic dysfunction.

Other drugs: Direct measurements
Urine drug screening (UDS)
INDICATIONS
· Screening, assessment of drug use
· When considering prescribing opioids for chronic pain, to rule out illicit opioid and other substance use
· Monitoring compliance with treatment objectives (e.g., methadone treatment for opioid dependence)
· Legal reasons (child protection agency, suspension of driver's licence, parole)

PRECAUTIONS WITH UDS

Sensitivity, specificity

- UDS can have false positives and negatives, so care is needed in interpretation. Even simple clerical errors (e.g., assigning an incorrect name or date to a sample) can result in false positive test results.
- Detection is affected by many factors (e.g., protein binding, hepatic and renal clearance, tolerance and genetically determined rates of drug metabolism).
- Some of the factors that can make UDS difficult to interpret include time from ingestion to urine collection, in-vivo volume loading, addition of diluent (e.g., water) and urine pH.
- A negative result is generally more difficult to interpret than a positive one.
- Some drugs are difficult to detect (e.g., clonazepam); others may be detected for weeks after last use (cannabis). Alcohol is present in the urine only for a few hours, so generally is not detected.
- Passive inhalation of cannabis or cocaine smoke is not detectable by UDS (at typical cut-off thresholds).

CONSENT, LEGAL ISSUES

- Inform patients that you are ordering UDS (they have a right to refuse).

MONITORING COMPLIANCE AND DETECTING DIVERSION

- If you are ordering a UDS to monitor compliance with prescribed opioid drugs, carefully record the patient's last reported use, and the quantity used, *before* ordering the test. Otherwise, the patient might respond to a negative test by stating that he or she usually takes the drug but missed some doses prior to the UDS.
- Confirmatory testing is needed for UDS with forensic (legal) implications such as child protection, parole or transportation authorities (see below).

SCREENING AND CONFIRMATORY TESTING

If the patient faces serious consequences for even 1 positive UDS, the physician must ask the lab to do confirmatory testing on drug-positive samples. Usually, screening is done by immunoassay, and confirmatory testing is done using a more specific chromatographic method. At the present time, the gold standard for confirmatory testing is gas-chromotography/mass spectrometry (GC-MS).

WHAT TO ORDER

The physician must specify which drugs are to be analysed. The physician may order testing for one or more of:

· A general class of drugs (opioids, benzodiazepines, barbiturates, amphetamines), and/or
· A specific drug (oxycodone, cannabis, cocaine, methadone).

UDS for opioids

ENZYME IMMUNOASSAY (EIA)

EIA is a general screen that detects opioids for 2–4 days but does not distinguish specific types of opioids.

· EIA is very sensitive. It can detect oral ingestion of 5 mg of morphine for up to 48 hours.
· Poppy seeds and quinolone antibiotics can cause false positives for opioids.
· Oxycodone and meperidine can be missed with EIA.

FULL SCREEN (CHROMATOGRAPHY)

Chromatography detects opioids for only 1–2 days but is able to identify specific opioids (codeine, morphine, oxycodone, hydrocodone, meperidine).

· Chromatography is less sensitive than EIA. A UDS positive for opioids on EIA and negative on chromatography likely indicates poppy seed ingestion, use of opioids in low doses, or no opioid use in the past few days.
· Morphine is a metabolite of codeine, therefore the presence of both codeine and morphine on a UDS can occur with codeine use alone. It can also represent impurities found in heroin. Trace amounts of hydrocodone may be found if large amounts of codeine are ingested.
· Heroin is very rapidly metabolized to morphine. Heroin will show up as morphine or 6-mono-acetylmorphine (MAM), a metabolite of heroin. The latter must be ordered specifically. It can be detected by chromotography only if the sample is collected within several hours of use.

UDS for methadone

· Methadone does not show up as an opioid on immunoassay. A specific request must be made for methadone and/or its metabolite 2-ethylene-1,5-dimethyl 3,3, diphenylpyrrolidine (EDDP). (If EDDP is negative and methadone is positive the

patient may have added methadone to a clean sample.)
· If methadone is negative in a patient on methadone, this could reflect use of
  medications that speed methadone metabolism (e.g., phenytoin) or a highly
  alkaline urine (pH >7.5) causing methadone reabsorption (in which case EDDP
  will be positive).

Approximate UDS detection periods

DRUG	DETECTION PERIOD*	LIMITATIONS OF IMMUNOASSAYS
· Methamphetamine	· 2–3 days	· If EIA positive, confirmation by chromatography required because of high incidence of false positives (cross-reacts with phenylpropanolamine, ephedrine, psudeoephedrine, chlorpromazine, etc.).
. Amphetamine (metabolite of methamphetamine)	· 2–3 days	
. Methylenedioxy-methamphetamine (MDMA; "Ecstasy")	· 2–3 days	· MDA, MDMA will be positive for amphetamines on EIA but cross-reactivity poor. Low levels may not be detected.
		· Chromatography required to differentiate between amphetamine derivatives such as MDA and MDMA.
· Morphine (metabolite of heroin, codeine, hydromorphone)	· Opioids positive for 2–4 days (EIA), 1–2 days (chromatography)	· EIA does not differentiate between opioids and has poor sensitivity for oxycodone, meperidine.
		· Chromatography required to identify specific opioids (codeine, oxycodone, hydromorphone, hydrocodone etc.) but only 1–2 day detection period.
		· Even 1 poppy seed bagel will be detected on EIA.
· Heroin	· Minutes	· Heroin not detected in urine.
· 6-monoacetyl-morphine (MAM) (metabolite of heroin)	· < 12 h	· MAM detected by chromatography.
· Methadone	· 1–4 days	· Chromatography required to distinguish methadone from EDDP.
· Phencyclidine (PCP)	· 2–3 days	

· Cocaine	· Few h	· Cocaine detected by chromatography.
· Benzoylecgonine (metabolite of cocaine)	· 3–5 days	· Benzoylecgonine detected by EIA, chromatography.
· Δ9-tetrahydro-cannabinol (thc)	· 90% fall in 1 h (blood)	
· Δ9-tetrahydro-cannabinoic acid (marijuana metabolite in urine)	· Few days to many weeks depending on chronicity of use	
· Benzodiazepines . Diazepam · Flunitrazepam (Rohypnol®)**	· Days/weeks (depending on half-life) · 2 weeks or more after last chronic use of diazepam	· EIA does not differentiate between different benzodiazepines. Short-acting agents such as lorazepam, clonazepam, bromazepam have poor sensitivity and are often undetected. · Oxaprosin (Daypro®) can cause a false positive.
· Barbiturate (Phenobarbital)	· 1–2 weeks after last use	· Chromatography required to distinguish between barbiturates.
· Alcohol (Ethanol)	· 1.5 – > 12 h depending on the peak blood level · Urine typically positive for an additional 1–2 h	
· Gamma-Hydroxybutyrate (GHB)	· < 12 h	· Chromatography required.

*The detection period is dose-dependent. The larger the dose, the longer the period the drug/metabolite can be detected in the urine.
**Flunitrazepam is usually not detected with the generic EIA benzodiazepine procedure. Use HPLC to detect flunitrazepam. Many high potency benzodiazepines are missed in routine EIA screening.

Tampering with UDS

Patients can easily falsify UDS results by:

· Substituting another patient's urine
· Using their own previously stored sample
· Diluting their urine by water-loading, diuretics, or adding water directly to the sample
· Altering the pH of urine by consuming antacids or adding adulterants to the sample (Raising the alkalinity of urine with sodium bicarbonate or antacids can cause reabsorption of methadone, amphetamines and barbiturates from the urine, making these drugs more difficult to detect. The reabsorption also increases the half-life of the drug.)
· Elevating urinary sodium and chloride by adding adulterants such as table salt or bleach
· Adding proprietary compounds to the urine that are specifically designed to interfere with the screen or the confirmatory test. These compounds can often be purchased locally or are available through the mail or Internet.

DETECTION OF UDS TAMPERING

Supervision

If UDS results are important for legal or therapeutic purposes, then it is best to supervise the patient while obtaining the sample, or to temperature-test the sample.

Temperature testing

Temperature testing must be done immediately because urine temperature falls rapidly. Test with a rapid-response electronic thermometer or temperature strips. The normal range is 34–36° C within 1 minute of voiding, and 32–36° C within 4 minutes.

· When temperature testing, direct contact between the probe and sample must be avoided due to risk of cross-contamination with other potentially positive samples.
· A minimum of 40 mL is needed to avoid excessive ambient cooling of the sample.

Creatinine

Urine creatinine can be used to detect water loading. Tampering should be suspected if an average-sized patient has a urine creatinine of < 2–3 mmol/L. Creatinine is a better marker of dilution than specific gravity.

Sodium, chloride

Normal range: Na: 20–230 mmol/L; Cl: 15–250 mmol/L. Elevated urine sodium (> 280 mmol/L) and chloride (> 280 mmol/L) could indicate the presence of adulterants such as bleach or table salt.

Urine pH

Normal range 5.5–7.5. Urine pH < 5.0 or > 8.0 suggests adulteration, although urinary tract infections and certain diets can also elevate pH.

"Fingerprinting": Urine sodium, chloride, creatinine and pH

Two patients may attempt to submit the same "clean" urine sample or one patient may attempt to submit the same sample on two different occasions. This should be suspected if urine sodium, chloride and creatinine of two samples are within 2–3% of each other.

Note: pH is a less sensitive indicator because it is generally measured in increments of 0.5 units.

Other drugs: Indirect measurements
Injection drug use

Possible current or past injection drug use can sometimes be detected through measurement of ALT or hepatitis C serology.

Barbiturate use

Barbiturates cause elevations in GGT and MCV.

7
PROBLEM DRINKING

Low-risk drinking guidelines
· Maximum of 2 standard drinks per day (men and women)
· Maximum of 9 drinks/week (women)
· Maximum of 14 drinks/week (men)
· 0 consumption for special populations (see below)

STANDARD DRINK DEFINITION
One standard drink (13.6 g alcohol) = 12 oz (355 mL) beer, 5 oz (140 mL) wine or 1.5 oz. (40 mL) spirits (80 proof).

ABSTINENCE: WHEN TO RECOMMEND
· Pregnancy or breastfeeding
· On medications that may interact with alcohol, such as benzodiazepines or opioids
· Before and during operation of potentially hazardous machinery
· Medical conditions that may be aggravated by alcohol, such as cirrhosis of the liver, active viral hepatitis, active gastritis or peptic ulcer disease, pancreatitis, seizure disorder, unstable psychiatric illnesses
· Personal history of serious alcohol problems

Low-risk drinking guidelines: Rationale
CARDIOPROTECTION
Moderate alcohol consumption reduces mortality from cardiovascular disease by increasing HDL and inhibiting platelet aggregation. These effects are largely achieved with < 1 drink/day. Consumption of 3 or more drinks/day increases risk of hemorrhagic stroke, hypertension, cardiomyopathy and dysrhythmias in intoxication and withdrawal.

WOMEN

Lower limits are recommended for women because their blood alcohol concentration is higher for a given rate of consumption (see Chapter 6, Laboratory Detection of Alcohol and Other Drug Use). Moderate alcohol consumption marginally increases the risk of breast cancer. Risk increases by 70–80% in women consuming over 14 drinks/week.[15]

YOUNG ADULTS

Alcohol provides no protective effect on mortality in young people. Mortality increases linearly with increasing consumption (because of accidents, violence and suicide).

ADVICE TO ABSTAINERS

Abstainers should not be advised to start drinking to protect their heart. Other alternatives are at least as effective (e.g., increased exercise, improved diet, smoking cessation).

Management of problem drinking

Problem drinking is much more common than alcohol dependence (4:1 ratio), and is a major cause of alcohol-related morbidity and mortality.

Definition

A problem drinker:
· Drinks above low-risk drinking guidelines
· May have 1 or more physical or social consequences
· Does not meet the criteria for alcohol dependence (see next page).

Problem drinking versus alcohol dependence: Clinical presentations

KEY MEASURES	PROBLEM DRINKING	ALCOHOL DEPENDENCE
Withdrawal symptoms*	No	Often
Tolerance	Mild	Marked
No. of drinks consumed	More than 14/week (M), 9/week (F)	40–60/week or more
Drinks less than 4/day	Often	Rarely
Social consequences**	Nil or mild	Often severe
Physical consequences***	Nil or mild	Often severe
Socially stable	Usually	Often not
Neglect of major responsibilities	No	Yes

*In almost all cases, the presence of withdrawal symptoms indicates alcohol dependence
**Mild social consequence: Occasional argument with spouse, fatigue at work
Severe: Loss of family or job
***Mild physical consequence: Hypertension, insomnia, fatty liver
Severe: Cirrhosis, pancreatitis

Treatment

Whereas patients with alcohol dependence often require abstinence and formal treatment, many problem drinkers are able to achieve reduced drinking goals with advice from their physician. Problem drinkers may require abstinence and more intensive treatment if they fail to respond to simple advice, and their drinking is causing significant medical, psychiatric or social problems.

Treatment approaches: Problem drinking versus alcohol dependence

	PROBLEM DRINKING	ALCOHOL DEPENDENCE
Preferred treatment goal	Abstinence or reduced drinking	Abstinence
Treatment options	Physician advice +/– several counselling sessions	One or more of: Mutual aid groups (e.g., AA); inpatient or outpatient treatment programs; naltrexone, disulfiram; relapse prevention counselling

| If failure to respond to treatment | If drinking is causing significant health or social problems, recommend abstinence, formal treatment | Intensify treatment and/or recommend additional treatment options |

🅿 PROTOCOL FOR PROBLEM DRINKING: BRIEF ADVICE FOR PATIENTS

· Inform patient of low-risk drinking guidelines.

· Explain the health effects of alcohol, linking them to the patient's current health problems.

· Mention non-specific effects of drinking—fatigue, insomnia, low mood.

· Discuss the effects of alcohol (if any) on family and work. Ask if the spouse/partner has expressed any concerns about drinking.

· Monitor GGT and MCV at baseline and monthly. Give feedback to patient about progress.

   – *Note:* The half-lives of GGT and MCV are 4 weeks and 3 months respectively. Therefore these tests do not always accurately reflect recent changes in drinking pattern.

· Ask the patient to set a treatment goal: abstinence, or consumption within low-risk guidelines.

· If a reduced-drinking goal is chosen, ask the patient to specify the number of drinks/day, and the number of drinking days/week.

· Ask patient to keep a daily record of the number of drinks consumed and to bring it in the next office visit.

· Give the patient "tips" to reduce his or her rate of consumption and avoid intoxication (see next page).

· Provide motivational counselling as needed (see Chapter 31, Counselling and Motivational Interviewing).

· If time permits, encourage patient to analyse high-risk drinking situations (see next page).

· Arrange a follow-up visit.

Tips to avoid intoxication

· Aim for 1 drink per hour.
· Alternate alcoholic with non-alcoholic drinks.
· Dilute drinks with mixer.
· Set a 20 min "time-out" between the decision to drink and having the drink.
· Avoid drinking on an empty stomach.
· Sip drinks, do not gulp.
· Start drinking later in the evening.

🄐 ADVICE FOR COPING WITH HIGH-RISK DRINKING SITUATIONS

· Ask patients to describe when they drink. (e.g., "I drink with my friends at the bar on the weekend.")
· Ask them to identify triggers to drinking. Possible triggers include social events, coping with negative emotions or situations and habit (e.g., having a bottle of wine every night with dinner).
· Ask the patient to come up with solutions. (e.g., Avoid high-risk situations—stay away from those friends or that bar; Choose alternate activities—go out with spouse/partner; Develop alternate ways to cope with anxiety—go for a walk, call a friend.)

8

DRINKING AND DRIVING

Duty to report

All patients with alcohol problems should be asked if they drink and drive. Most jurisdictions require physicians to report patients suspected of driving while impaired (e.g., physicians in Ontario are required to report to the Registrar of Motor Vehicles, Ministry of Transportation).

SUGGESTED CRITERIA FOR REPORTING

Any of the following are reasonable grounds for reporting to the Registrar:

· Patient admits to drinking and driving.

· Family member informs physician that patient is drinking and driving.

· Patient drinks steadily throughout the day and regularly drives.

· Patient drove to your clinic while intoxicated.

· Patient regularly drives and has recently experienced withdrawal seizures.

· Patient has other alcohol-related medical complications that impair driving ability (e.g., cerebellar ataxia).

ASSESSING INTOXICATION

If you smell alcohol on the patient's breath and the patient drove to your clinic, determine the degree of the patient's intoxication:

· Ask how much the patient drank that day. Men who drink 4 drinks in an hour, and women who drink 3 drinks in an hour, may be above the legal limit.

· Document slurred speech, emotional lability or other signs of intoxication.

· Ask the patient to perform cerebellar tests (walking heel to toe, pointing finger to nose).

· Order a BAC test. Inform the patient why you're doing this (patients have the right to refuse).

INFORMING THE PATIENT OF YOUR DECISION TO REPORT
· Explain to the patient that you have a legal obligation to report (check with your jurisdiction).
· Explain that the decision to suspend the licence is made by the authorities, and the patient has the right to appeal that decision.
· Patients may ask you to give them a chance to abstain and attend treatment before deciding to report them. However, trusting the patient to comply with your instructions is not considered an adequate reason for failing to report.

After the suspension

While patients are often angry about being reported, physicians can use the opportunity to advise patients on the need for abstinence or reduced drinking, and the need for counselling and treatment. Sometimes the embarrassment and inconvenience of the suspension are powerful motivators for change.

POST-SUSPENSION MONITORING
The patient's license is reinstated once the authorities have received confirmation from the physician that the patient has attended treatment and maintained abstinence or low-risk drinking levels for a specified number of months. Monthly patient visits are recommended. At each visit:
· Ask about alcohol consumption.
· Monitor with GGT and MCV.
· Order urine drug screen if other drug use is an issue.
· Ask the spouse/partner or close family member (with the patient's permission) to corroborate the patient's reported alcohol consumption.
· Encourage the patient to attend aftercare.

Prevention

Inform all patients who drink regularly about the risks of driving while impaired. Even BACs well below the legal limit (0.08 g% or 17 mmol/L) can impair the ability to react quickly in complex driving situations.

Risk of fatal motor vehicle accident

NO. OF DRINKS IN 1 H (M)	NO. OF DRINKS IN 1 H (F)	BAC* (G%)	RISK
3	2	0.05	2x
4	3	0.08	4x

*Blood alcohol concentration

9
ALCOHOL WITHDRAWAL

Physicians must be proficient at identifying and treating alcohol withdrawal. Unrecognized and untreated withdrawal delays recovery and can lead to serious complications such as seizures, dysrhythmias or delirium. While withdrawal is usually mild and requires no pharmacotherapy, it can be severe and prolonged, requiring intensive treatment and hospital admission.

🅐 Alcohol withdrawal: Clinical features

CLINICAL FEATURES	TIME COURSE	COMMENT
Uncomplicated withdrawal: · Anxiety, insomnia, headache · Autonomic hyperactivity (tremor, sweating, tachycardia, hypertension, vomiting)	· Onset 6–12 h after last drink, duration up to 7 days	· At risk if 40+ drinks/week consumed · More severe and prolonged in the older adult
Seizures (complicated withdrawal): · Preceded by autonomic hyperactivity · Grand mal, non-focal, brief	· Typically 12–72 h, can occur up to 7 days	· 10–15% lifetime risk in alcohol dependence · 30–50% of recurrent seizure if past hx of seizure
Dysrhythmias: · Varies from occasional ectopic beats to atrial fibrillation, supraventricular and ventricular tachycardias	· 1–7 days	· Increased risk if underlying cardiomyopathy, hypokalemia, hypomagnesemia

Hallucinations:	· 1–7 days	· At risk: Underlying
· Usually tactile or auditory		psychotic disorder
· Patient oriented, usually aware they are not real		
Withdrawal delirium:	· Begins day 3–5	· At risk: Seriously ill inpatients (e.g., pancreatitis, pneumonia, post-operative)
· Confusion, disorientation, decreased level of consciousness		
· Florid visual, auditory hallucinations		· Mortality rates ~5%, from dysrhythmias and hypokalemia due to excess catecholamines
· Symptoms often worse at night		
· May have marked autonomic hyperactivity with fever, vomiting, diaphoresis and hypertension		

ASSESSMENT OF WITHDRAWAL
· Number of standard drinks per week: Risk of withdrawal increases with consumption above 40 drinks/week.
· Relief drinking: Ask if the patient has anxiety and tremors in morning or afternoon, and if the symptoms are quickly relieved by alcohol or sedatives.
· Seizures, dysrhythmias, hallucinations, delirium during previous withdrawal episodes: Patients with previous complications are at risk for similar complications during their current withdrawal.
· Other drug use, especially benzodiazepines, opioids and other CNS depressants: The diazepam loading protocol used for alcohol withdrawal is not effective for benzodiazepine withdrawal. Instead, diazepam tapering over days or weeks should be used.

PHYSICAL EXAMINATION
· Vital signs, hydration: Tachycardia and hypertension commonly accompany withdrawal. Dehydration is common, especially in severe withdrawal with vomiting and diaphoresis.

- General appearance, sweating: Patients in withdrawal are often diaphoretic and anxious—check for sweat on palms, forehead.
- Cardiovascular, respiratory, liver, spleen: Look for stigmata of chronic liver disease.
- Postural or intention tremor: Tremor is the most reliable sign of withdrawal. Patients often have no tremor at rest, so the tremor should be elicited by having patients hold their hands up and placing hands fingertip to fingertip. Elicit the intention tremor by asking patients to reach for an object. Walking can also elicit a "whole body tremor."
- Extraocular movements: Rule out Wernicke's.
- Gait: Ataxic gait suggests severe withdrawal, cerebellar disease, Wernicke's and/or subdural hematoma.
- CIWA-A: (see pages 41–43)
- Mental status: Level of consciousness, orientation; hallucinations; depression, suicidal ideation

LABORATORY INVESTIGATIONS

Consider ordering baseline bloodwork, particularly if the patient is vomiting, dehydrated, malnourished, has signs of liver disease, or has seizures, arrythmias, hallucinations, confusion.

Tests to order:
- CBC, glucose, creatinine
- Electrolytes (hypokalemia is common in withdrawal and may contribute to dys-rhythmias)
- Hepatic transaminases (GGT, AST, ALT)
- INR, albumin, bilirubin especially if hepatomegaly or other signs of liver disease
- Calcium, magnesium (see below)
- Other tests as indicated (e.g., ECG)

MAGNESIUM
- Magnesium is often low in alcohol-dependent patients who have liver disease.
- Hypomagnesemia is associated with a more severe withdrawal, and is a risk factor for Tourssaides du Pointes arrhythmia.
- Oral replacement should be considered (1500–3000 mg od-tid), although there is no clear evidence that it alters the course of withdrawal.

⊘ CLINICAL INSTITUTE WITHDRAWAL ASSESSMENT FOR ALCOHOL (CIWA-A)
- The CIWA-A scale is a valid and reliable instrument for monitoring withdrawal. It consists of 10 items, including tremor, sweating and vomiting. Each item is scored from 0 to 7.
- A total score of 10 or more indicates the need for benzodiazepine treatment.
- A score of 8–9 indicates the need for further observation and possible treatment with 10–20 mg of diazepam (especially if objective signs such as tremor are present).
- A score of < 8 on 2 consecutive occasions suggests treatment is complete. On completion of treatment the patient should be comfortable with minimal signs of withdrawal.
- If patient is still tremulous, consider benzodiazepine treatment even if the score is < 8.
- Do not base decision to treat solely on subjective items such as anxiety; physical signs should also be present. Awaken patient for scoring (sleep does not necessarily mean withdrawal has resolved). Do pulse and BP with each assessment.

⊘ Clinical Institute Withdrawal Assessment for Alcohol (CIWA-A)

NAUSEA AND VOMITING

Ask: "Do you feel sick to your stomach? Have you vomited?"

Observation:

0. no nausea and no vomiting
1.
2.
3.
4. intermittent nausea with dry heaves
5.
6.
7. constant nausea, frequent dry heaves and vomiting

AGITATION

Observation:

0. normal activity
1. somewhat more than normal activity
2.
3.
4. moderately fidgety and restless
5.
6.
7. paces back and forth during most of the interview, or constantly thrashes about

continued on next page

CIWA-A, continued

TREMOR

Arms extended and fingers spread apart

Observation:

0. no tremor

1. not visible, but can be felt fingertip to fingertip

2.

3.

4. moderate, with patient's arms extended

5.

6.

7. severe, even with arms not extended

TACTILE DISTURBANCES

Ask: "Have you any itching, pins and needles sensations, any burning, any numbness, or do you feel bugs crawling on your skin?"

Observation:

0. none

1. very mild itching, pins and needles, burning or numbness

2. mild itching, pins and needles, burning or numbness

3. moderate itching, pins and needles, burning or numbness

4. moderately severe hallucinations

5. severe hallucinations

6. extremely severe hallucinations

7. continuous hallucinations

PAROXYSMAL SWEATS

Observation:

0. no sweat visible

1. barely perceptible sweating, palms moist

2.

3.

4. beads of sweat obvious on forehead

5.

6.

7. drenching sweats

AUDITORY DISTURBANCES

Ask: "Are you more aware of sounds around you? Are they harsh? Do they frighten you? Are you hearing anything that is disturbing to you? Are you hearing things you know are not there?"

Observation:

0. not present

1. very mild harshness or ability to frighten

2. mild harshness or ability to frighten

3. moderate harshness or ability to frighten

4. moderately severe hallucinations

5. severe hallucinations

6. extremely severe hallucinations

7. continuous hallucinations

ANXIETY

Ask: "Do you feel nervous?"

Observation:

0. no anxiety, at ease

1. mildly anxious

2.

3.

4. moderately anxious, or guarded, so anxiety is inferred

5.

6.

7. equivalent to acute panic states as seen in severe delirium or acute schizophrenic reactions

VISUAL DISTURBANCES

Ask: "Does the light appear to be too bright? Is its colour different? Does it hurt your eyes? Are you seeing anything that is disturbing to you? Are you seeing things you know are not there?"

Observation:

0. not present

1. very mild sensitivity

2. mild sensitivity

3. moderate sensitivity

4. moderately severe sensitivity

5. severe hallucinations

6. extremely severe hallucinations

7. continuous hallucinations

HEADACHE, FULLNESS IN HEAD

Ask: "Does your head feel different? Does it feel like there is a band around your head?" Do not rate for dizziness or light-headedness. Otherwise, rate severity.

Observation:

0. not present

1. very mild

2. mild

3. moderate

4. moderately severe

5. severe

6. very severe

7. extremely severe

ORIENTATION AND CLOUDING OF SENSORIUM

Ask: "What day is this? Where are you? Who am I?"

Observation:

0. oriented and can do serial additions

1. cannot do serial additions or is uncertain about date

2. disoriented for date by no more than 2 calendar days

3. disoriented for date by more than 2 calendar days

4. disoriented for place and/or person

Total CIWA-A score: _____

A CIWA-A score of 10 or more indicates the need for benzodiazepine treatment.

Management of alcohol withdrawal

MANAGEMENT OF UNCOMPLICATED ALCOHOL WITHDRAWAL: ASSESSMENT

Most patients in alcohol withdrawal experience only anxiety, insomnia and mild tremor, and they do not require pharmacotherapy. To determine if patients may need medical treatment:

· Ask about previous withdrawal episodes. If they have had no difficulty or complications previously, and their pattern of drinking has not escalated, they may safely go through withdrawal either at home or in a withdrawal management centre.

· If in doubt, have them come into the office after abstaining from alcohol for 12–24 h and assess the severity of their withdrawal.

MANAGEMENT OF UNCOMPLICATED WITHDRAWAL: PROTOCOL FOR DIAZEPAM LOADING

· Diazepam 20 mg po q 1–2 h prn for CIWA-A ≥ 10. (Some patients require several hundred milligrams.)

· Observe for 2–4 h after last dose. Treatment completed when CIWA-A ≤ 8 on 2 measurements 1–2 h apart. The patient should appear comfortable, with minimal tremor or sweating.

· Take-home diazepam is generally not required. If uncertain about whether the load is completed and the patient is unable to remain in clinic, give no more than 2–3 10 mg tablets.

· Give thiamine 100 mg im then 100 mg po for 3 days.

RATIONALE

Diazepam loading and other symptom-triggered protocols are more effective and safer than scheduled benzodiazepine dosing. They avoid over- or under-treatment, reduce the likelihood of "cross-addiction" to benzodiazepines and alcohol, and allow for observation of response. Because of its long half-life, diazepam remains effective for the full duration of withdrawal. It is ideal for treatment in an out-patient clinic, ER or inpatient unit.

PRECAUTIONS TO DIAZEPAM LOADING

· Will not prevent seizures in patients taking large doses of benzodiazepines or barbiturates in addition to alcohol (see protocols on pages 115–116).

· If cannot tolerate oral diazepam, use lorazepam sl (see below), or diazepam 2–5 mg iv/min.—max. 10–20 mg q 1 h.

· Diazepam has a long half-life and is metabolized to active metabolites in the liver, leading to prolonged and excessive sedation in:
- Elderly and debilitated patients
- Significant liver dysfunction (cirrhosis, severe hepatitis)
- Low serum albumin
- Respiratory distress (e.g., severe asthma, COPD)

In these patients use lorazepam instead.

❷ MANAGEMENT OF UNCOMPLICATED WITHDRAWAL: PROTOCOL FOR SYMPTOM-TRIGGERED LORAZEPAM TREATMENT
Lorazepam sl, po 1–2 mg q 2–4 h prn for CIWA-A ≥ 10.

RATIONALE
Lorazepam is a useful alternative to diazepam because it has a shorter half-life and is not metabolized to active metabolites in the liver. However, lorazepam cannot be used as a loading protocol because symptoms may recur once it wears off. Therefore, the patient may continue to require doses over several days.

USE OF BAC TO DETERMINE WHEN TO INITIATE TREATMENT OF WITHDRAWAL
· Some highly tolerant patients go into withdrawal when BAC is < 20–25 mmol/L. Do not give diazepam until you estimate the BAC is within that range or lower.
· BAC declines by 4–5 mmol/h. Therefore a patient with a BAC of 60 mmol/L may go into withdrawal in 7–12 h.
Note: 17 mmol/L = 80 mg%

Management of complicated withdrawal: Alcohol and nicotine withdrawal

Nicotine withdrawal may add to the psychological distress of alcohol withdrawal. Hospitalized patients who are in alcohol withdrawal and are unable to smoke should be offered nicotine replacement therapy, even if they intend to resume smoking on discharge.

Management of complicated withdrawal: Mixed alcohol and other drug withdrawal

See Chapter 20, Polysubstance Use and Withdrawal.

Management of complicated withdrawal: Seizures, dysrhythmias, hallucinations and delirium

🅟 MANAGEMENT OF COMPLICATED WITHDRAWAL: PROTOCOL FOR PREVENTION AND TREATMENT OF WITHDRAWAL SEIZURES

If history of withdrawal seizures:

· Diazepam 20 mg q 1–2 h for at least 3 doses. Give diazepam even if CIWA-A < 10 (although some signs of withdrawal should be present).

· Additional doses as needed for CIWA-A ≥ 10.

· Anti-seizure medication is not necessary unless patient has a seizure disorder or multiple seizures (> 2) despite diazepam.

INVESTIGATION OF WITHDRAWAL SEIZURES

Investigate for structural or metabolic causes (CT scan, EEG, etc.) if:

· First seizure in patient > 40 years of age

· Focal features

· Abnormal neurological exam

· Outside the typical time frame for seizures (i.e., > 7 days since the last drink)

· Multiple seizures (> 2) or status epilepticus

🅟 MANAGEMENT OF COMPLICATED WITHDRAWAL: PROTOCOL FOR TREATMENT OF DYSRHYTHMIAS IN WITHDRAWAL

· Use diazepam-loading protocol.

· Correct fluid and electrolyte disturbances.

· Treat specific dysrhythmia using standard protocols.

· May require admission and cardiac monitoring.

INVESTIGATION OF DYSRHYTHMIAS

· Consider echocardiogram to detect underlying cardiomyopathy.

· Look for liver disease (association between cardiomyopathy and cirrhosis).

MANAGEMENT OF COMPLICATED WITHDRAWAL: PROTOCOL FOR TREATMENT OF HALLUCINATIONS

· Diazepam loading protocol
· Haloperidol 2–5 mg im/po q 1–4 h—max. 5 doses per day
  – *Note:* Haloperidol lowers seizure threshold. Use with caution in 1st 3 days; give 3 doses of diazepam 20 mg q 1–2 h as seizure prophylaxis.
· Newer antipsychotics may be used as alternatives to haloperidol (e.g., risperidol, olanzapine).

MANAGEMENT OF COMPLICATED WITHDRAWAL: PROTOCOL FOR TREATMENT OF WITHDRAWAL DELIRIUM

Delirium is a medical emergency and must be treated aggressively.

· Look for and treat underlying medical illness.
· Ensure vigorous fluid and electrolyte replacement—dehydration can be severe, and hypokalemia can trigger dysrhythmias.
· Order cardiac monitoring—may need ICU admission.
· Provide supportive nursing care—avoid restraints.
· Give diazepam as per loading protocol for autonomic hyperactivity—may require hundreds of milligrams.
· Give haloperidol or other antipsychotic for hallucinations.

Wernicke's encephalopathy

Patients who are malnourished and alcohol-dependent are at risk for thiamine deficiency because the metabolism of alcohol requires thiamine as a co-factor. Untreated Wernicke's encephalopathy can result in Korsakoff's syndrome: permanent, severe impairment of short-term memory.

CLINICAL PRESENTATIONS OF WERNICKE'S ENCEPHALOPATHY

· Triad of encephalopathy, ataxia, ophthalmoplegia (e.g., nystagmus, paralysis of upward gaze)
· Can occur in intoxication or withdrawal
· Often difficult to diagnose (not all features may be present; encephalopathy, ataxia difficult to assess in presence of intoxication or withdrawal)

(P) MANAGEMENT OF COMPLICATED WITHDRAWAL: PROTOCOL FOR PREVENTION OF
WERNICKE'S ENCEPHALOPATHY
· Give routine multivitamin supplementation to alcohol-dependent patients.
· Always give thiamine 100 mg im, then 100 mg po for 3 days to the patient
presenting with intoxication or withdrawal.
· Do not give large volumes of iv dextrose/glucose solutions until thiamine
administered. Glucose uses thiamine as a co-factor and excessive amounts can
trigger an acute thiamine deficiency.

Planned outpatient withdrawal management

Patients who experience daily or frequent withdrawal symptoms can have a
planned diazepam loading in the physician's office or emergency department:
· Advise them to have their last drink the night before their scheduled morning
appointment.
· If the patient shows up intoxicated, reschedule or admit to the appropriate withdrawal management unit.
· Use the CIWA-A scale to monitor withdrawal, and use the diazepam loading protocol as described above.
· Follow up in 1 to 2 days.

Criteria for hospital admission

· Patient remains in significant withdrawal despite 80 mg or more of diazepam
given in the office or ER
· Delirium, recurrent dysrhythmias or multiple seizures (> 2)
· Unsafe to discharge home or to withdrawal management because of ataxia, con-
fusion, dehydration
· Serious medical or psychiatric illness

Follow-up and advice on discharge

(see also Chapter 30, Psychosocial Treatment for Substance Use)
· Express concern about the patient's drinking.
· Review treatment options: Outpatient and inpatient programs, mutual aid groups
(e.g., AA), pharmacotherapy.
· Give patient information on treatment facilities.

· Recommend follow-up with family physician and/or addiction medicine specialist.

· Discharge to withdrawal management centre (detox centre) if patient lacks a supportive home environment.

P PROTOCOL FOR HOME TREATMENT OF WITHDRAWAL

Treating withdrawal with take-home prescriptions of benzodiazepines is not recommended unless:

· The patient is in withdrawal at the time of the visit.

· The patient refuses or is unable to remain in your office for diazepam loading.

· The patient is not in severe withdrawal, and has no history of severe withdrawal (e.g., seizures).

· The patient agrees not to drink alcohol while taking the diazepam.

If these conditions are met:

· Prescribe diazepam 10 mg q 4 H PRN, no more than 6–10 tabs.

· Advise the patient to go to emergency if symptoms are getting worse.

· If possible, have a family member dispense the medication.

· Have the patient follow-up with you in the next 1–2 days.

10

PHARMACOTHERAPY FOR ALCOHOL DEPENDENCE

Naltrexone (ReVia®)

ACTION

Alcohol consumption causes endogenous endorphin release. Naltrexone, a competitive opioid antagonist, blocks the action of endorphins, thus reducing the pleasurable and reinforcing effects of alcohol. Controlled trials have shown that naltrexone is moderately effective in reducing craving for alcohol and the frequency and intensity of alcohol binges.

INDICATION

Treatment of alcohol dependence, in conjunction with supportive counselling and a treatment program.

🅟 PROTOCOL FOR NALTREXONE
· Dose: 25 mg for 3 days, then 50 mg per day (as a single daily dose). If 50 mg is ineffective, dose may be increased to 100 mg; max. dose, 150 mg per day.
· Duration of treatment: If effective, treatment should be continued for 3 to 6 months, or longer if no adverse effects and patient continues to derive benefit.

PRECAUTIONS AND CONTRAINDICATIONS
· Will trigger severe opioid withdrawal if patient is physically dependent on opioids. Opioids should be discontinued for 10 days before starting naltrexone.
· Discontinue naltrexone 3 days prior to elective surgery.
· If urgent need for anaesthesia or analgesia, use non-opioid analgesics and anaesthetics, and consult with anaesthetist.

· Patient should be treated for alcohol withdrawal during or prior to initiation of naltrexone (patients will find it hard to reduce drinking if they are having ongoing withdrawal symptoms).

HEPATOTOXICITY

· Several studies have demonstrated improvement in liver enzymes in patients on naltrexone due to reduction in alcohol consumption.[16, 17] However, naltrexone can cause reversible elevations in transaminases, particularly at high doses (i.e., 300 mg/day).
· Safety in cirrhosis is not known. Use only if other treatment options have failed; monitor closely.
· Contraindicated in acute hepatitis and liver failure.

Monitoring protocol for hepatic transaminases

BASELINE LEVEL	ACTION
< 1.5 times normal	Monthly monitoring for 3 months, less frequent monitoring thereafter
1.5–3 times normal	Repeat level in 2 weeks
> 3 times normal	Do not prescribe medication, repeat in 2 weeks
Elevated bilirubin	Do not prescribe medication

Disulfiram (Antabuse®)

ACTION

Covalently binds to acetaldehyde dehydrogenase, causing a toxic buildup of acetaldehyde if alcohol is consumed.

INDICATION

Treatment of alcohol dependence. Probably most effective in older, socially stable individuals who take disulfiram under the daily supervision of a spouse/partner or pharmacist.

🅟 PROTOCOL FOR DISULFIRAM
- Dose: 125–250 mg hs
- Duration of action: 7 days (range 2–10 days)
- Duration of treatment: If effective, continue for 3 to 6 months, or longer if no adverse effects and patient continues to derive benefit.

WARNING FOR PATIENTS
- The patient should be warned that consumption of alcohol within 7 days of a dose of disulfiram could cause a potentially fatal reaction.
- If the patient discontinues disulfiram and relapses to alcohol, upon abstaining wait at least 48 h before resuming disulfiram.
- Avoid alcohol-containing cough medicines and food.

MONITORING
Liver transaminases at baseline, 2 weeks, then monthly for 3 months.

ADVERSE EFFECTS WITH DRINKING
Reaction is dependent on dose of alcohol consumed.

Common effects include:
- Flushed face, vomiting, headache, chest pain, palpitations.

Serious effects include:
- Seizures
- Hypotension
- Vagally-induced dysrhythmias.

ADVERSE EFFECTS WITHOUT DRINKING
- Fatigue (often resolves in a few weeks)
- Garlic taste in mouth
- Acne
- Toxic hepatitis
- Peripheral neuropathy
- Erectile dysfunction
- Depression
- Psychosis

PRECAUTIONS AND CONTRAINDICATIONS
Cardiovascular
Patients with CAD or CHF and patients on antihypertensive agents are less able to tolerate disulfiram-induced hypotension.
· Contraindicated in unstable angina, recent MI.
· Use with caution in patients with stable CAD, hypertension and CHF.

Psychiatric
· Contraindicated in schizophrenia and other psychotic states; can exacerbate psychosis.
· May exacerbate a primary mood disorder although alcohol-induced depression often improves with disulfiram-facilitated abstinence.

Reproductive
Contraindicated in pregnancy; may cause congenital defects

GI
Contraindicated in severe cirrhosis of the liver; can cause toxic hepatitis

Acamprosate
Chronic alcohol use causes an up-regulation in excitatory neurotransmitters such as glutamate, which in turn causes alcohol withdrawal and craving. Acamprosate (not yet available in Canada) antagonizes glutamate, thus reducing withdrawal symptoms and craving. Randomized controlled trials have found that acamprosate increases abstinence rates in alcohol-dependent patients. [18]

Ondansetron
Ondansetron, a selective 5-HT3 receptor antagonist, was found in one RCT to reduce drinking in patients who became alcohol-dependent before age 25. [19] Ondansetron is presumed to act by attenuating dopamine release in the mesolimbic reward centre. The effective dose in this trial was 4 µg/kg bid. Further research is needed on this medication, and it is not yet indicated for use in alcohol dependence.

11

ALCOHOLIC LIVER DISEASE

🔵 Clinical features of alcoholic liver disease

CLINICAL FEATURES	COMMENTS
Fatty liver	· Usually asymptomatic, with enlarged, firm liver on examination.
Alcoholic hepatitis	· Often asymptomatic; sometimes causes typical symptoms of hepatitis (fatigue, anorexia, weight loss, vomiting, jaundice, right upper quadrant pain). · The most severe cases present with fever, jaundice, ascites, hyperdynamic circulation and encephalopathy. · Severely decompensated patients have a mortality rate of up to 50%.
Cirrhosis	· Presents with hepatomegaly or small, shrunken right lobe and hypertrophied left lobe (palpable in epigastrium). · Stigmata of chronic liver disease may be present (gynecomastia, testicular atrophy, spider nevi, palmar erythema, splenomegaly, ascites). · Complications include encephalopathy, ascites, bleeding varices and subacute bacterial peritonitis.
Cirrhosis with hepatitis	· Patients with cirrhosis sometimes develop a super-imposed alcoholic hepatitis. · Can precipitate liver failure if severe. · Chronic or recurrent hepatitis accelerates the progression of cirrhosis.

Investigations
GGT, MCV, PLATELETS
· Elevated GGT, macrocytosis and mild thrombocytopenia suggest continued alcohol use but not necessarily liver disease.
· Macrocytosis with target cells can occur in cirrhosis.
· Persistent or severe thrombocytopenia suggests splenomegaly.

AST, ALT
In alcoholic hepatitis AST > ALT often in a 2:1 ratio. ALT > AST in viral hepatitis.

HEPATITIS B, C
People who drink heavily have a higher prevalence of viral hepatitis, which worsens the prognosis of alcoholic liver disease.

INR, ALBUMIN, BILIRUBIN
↑ INR, ↓ albumin, ↑ bilirubin indicates liver dysfunction caused by cirrhosis or severe alcoholic hepatitis.

ULTRASOUND
· Often normal even in cirrhosis.
· Nodularity indicates cirrhosis.
· Splenomegaly suggests portal hypertension.
· Ultrasound can be used to detect ascites and to screen for hepatomas.

ENDOSCOPY
Detects varices and measure portal pressures in patients with cirrhosis. Also detects gastritis, esophagitis and ulcers.

LIVER BIOPSY
Rules out other causes of liver disease and determines the extent of cirrhosis prior to long-term treatment.

Treatment
Fatty liver
Reversible with alcohol abstinence or reduction to low-risk levels.

Alcoholic hepatitis—mild to moderate

· Reversible with abstinence or reduction to low-risk levels.
· Even if patient is a problem drinker and not alcohol-dependent abstinence should be recommended if the patient is symptomatic or if transaminases are ≥ 3X normal.

Alcoholic hepatitis—Bad prognostic indicators

· Encephalopathy
· Low serum albumin
· Elevated serum bilirubin above 340 µmol/L
· Prolonged prothrombin time to more than 8 seconds above control value

Alcoholic hepatitis—severe

Prednisolone improves short-term survival in alcoholic hepatitis with spontaneous hepatic encephalopathy, or a discriminant-function value > 32, [20] as follows:

Discriminant function EQ

Discriminant function =
4.6 x (prothrombin time—control time [in seconds])
+ (serum bilirubin [in µmol/L] ÷ 17)

P PROTOCOL FOR PREDNISOLONE
40 mg/day for 4 weeks, then 20 mg/day for 1 week, then 10 mg/day for 1 week. Contraindicated in renal failure, GI bleed, infection.

Cirrhosis of the liver

RISK OF CIRRHOSIS
Patients have a 10–20% risk of developing cirrhosis if they consume:
· (Men) 80 g of alcohol (6 drinks) per day for 10–20 years (cumulative dose 300–600 kg).
· (Women) 40 g (3 drinks) per day for 10 years (cumulative dose 150–300 kg).
Other factors that affect risk are genetic predisposition and viral hepatitis.

MEASURES TO PREVENT PROGRESSION

· Abstinence (even moderate alcohol consumption can accelerate liver damage). Five-year survival in cirrhosis with complications: abstainers, 60%; still drinking, 34%.
· Avoid regular use of acetaminophen (2.5–4 g/day can cause hepatotoxicity).
· Use hepatotoxic medications with caution and careful monitoring.
· Hepatitis A, B immunization, if indicated.
· Treatment of hepatitis B, C.

LONG-TERM TREATMENT: PROPYLTHIOURACIL (PTU)

One large randomized controlled trial demonstrated a decrease in mortality in patients prescribed PTU for alcoholic hepatitis, with or without cirrhosis.[21] Despite this study, PTU is not widely used for liver disease associated with alcohol consumption.

PTU induces subclinical hypothyroidism, decreasing the metabolic rate and oxygen demand. This decreases hypoxia in the portal triads, an intermediate step in hepatic injury.

Patients who abstain from alcohol experience the greatest benefit.

P PROTOCOL FOR PTU

· **Dose:** 300 mg/day
· **Duration:** Useful both in the acute phase and as a long-term treatment

PRECAUTIONS

Monitor with CBC and TSH, as PTU can cause hypothyroidism and (rarely) bone-marrow suppression.

LONG-TERM TREATMENT: LIVER TRANSPLANT

Patients who receive liver transplants have low relapse rates and good long-term survival.[22]

Transplants are indicated for patients in liver failure who have low risk of relapse:

· Abstinent for 6 months to 2 years
· Participated in treatment
· Strong psychosocial supports

Management of complications of cirrhosis

🅟 PROTOCOL FOR ESOPHAGEAL VARICES

Prevention of bleeding and rebleeding
· Endoscopy yearly.
· Nadolol or propanolol reduces risk of bleeding in portal hypertension and confirmed varices.
· Nadolol dose: 40–80 mg/day. Aim for 25% decrease in resting pulse.
· Isosorbide-5-mononitrate increases the effectiveness of beta-blocker therapy. [23, 24]

Acute bleeding
· Stabilization (ABCs, iv, blood products)
· May need ICU admission, Blakemore or Linton tube
· Endoscopic banding (preferred over sclerosing injections)
· Octreotide (Sandostatin®) if endoscopic banding failed or unavailable: 50 mg iv bolus, then 25–50 mg/h x 2 days (max. 5 days in patients with high risk of rebleeding). Octreotide is a synthetic analogue of somatostatin, with a prolonged duration of action.
· Other options: somatostatin; terlipressin
· Transjugular intrahepatic portosystemic shunt if frequent rebleeding despite the above measures

Hepatic encephalopathy [25]

CAUSES
· Altered nitrogen load to GI tract (e.g., increased dietary protein, constipation, GI bleed)
· Sedating drugs (e.g., benzodiazepines, opioids)
· Metabolic causes (e.g., hypoxia, hypokalemia, azotemia, dehydration, hypothyroidism, hypoglycemia, anemia)
· Infections (e.g., spontaneous bacterial peritonitis)
· Surgery and/or anaesthesia

PREVENTION
· Low-protein diet
· Avoid sedating drugs, especially long-acting benzodiazepines. Patients in alcohol or other drug withdrawal should only be given benzodiazepines if their withdrawal

is severe. Only use small doses of a benzodiazepine that does not form active metabolites in the liver (e.g., lorazepam).

· Judicious use of diuretics to avoid dehydration, electrolyte imbalance

Clinical features of hepatic encephalopathy

Grade 1	· Subclinical with normal mental status examination except for subtle changes on psychometric tests
	· Patient experiences fatigue, day-night reversal, personality/mood changes, poor work and driving performance
Grade 2	· Asterixis, lethargy
Grade 3	· Somnolence, confusion, disorientation, hypoactive reflexes, muscle rigidity
Grade 4	· Coma

Laboratory investigations: new onset of encephalopathy

Hepatic encephalopathy is a diagnosis of exclusion.

· Monitor CBC, electrolytes, hepatic transaminases, bilirubin, INR, albumin

· EEG

· Blood ammonia (increase from baseline suggests worsening encephalopathy)

· CXR, blood cultures if infection suspected

· CT scan if structural abnormalities suspected

· If ascites present, paracentesis and culture of ascitic fluid to rule out subacute bacterial peritonitis

P PROTOCOL FOR TREATMENT OF CHRONIC, LOW-GRADE ENCEPHALOPATHY (GRADE 1,2)

· Treat precipitating cause

· Low-protein diet (usually 60 g/day), preferably with vegetable protein

· Avoid sedating drugs, especially benzodiazepines

· Lactulose (an osmotic laxative) dose: 30–45 mL tid-qid until 2–3 soft stools daily

P PROTOCOL FOR TREATMENT OF DEEP ENCEPHALOPATHY (GRADE 3,4)

General measures
· NG tube
· Consider tracheal intubation

Medication
· Lactulose orally or via nasogastric tube, retention enema (less effective).
  Oral dose: 30–45 cc hourly until stool present, then 15–45 mL tid-qid until
  2–4 soft stools/day.
· Consider neomycin oral solution 500–1000 mg qid if no response to lactulose
  and patient is in grade 4 (coma). Neomycin can cause nephrotoxicity, ototoxicity,
  neuromuscular blockade. Use lowest effective dose, monitor serum concentration,
  avoid prolonged use of diuretics.
· Flumazenil if benzodiazepine use (but can precipitate withdrawal seizures in
  patients physically dependent on benzodiazepines).

Nutrition
· Withhold oral intake and give iv glucose for 24–48 h
· If not able to eat after 24–48 h, start enteral nutrition
· Protein intake of 0.5 g/kg per day, increase to 1–1.5 g/kg per day as encephalopathy
  clears
· Oral branched-chain amino acids if unable to tolerate protein

Surgical or radiological interventions
· Sometimes needed if unresponsive to therapy (e.g., radiologic occlusion of
  spontaneous portal-systemic shunts)
· Liver transplantation should be considered

Monitoring response to therapy
· Asterixis
· Ability to write name or execute simple drawing (e.g., 5-pointed star)

Ascites
DIAGNOSIS
· Patients notice increased abdominal girth
· Confirmed with clinical examination, ultrasound

P PROTOCOL FOR TREATMENT OF ASCITES
· Low-sodium diet (0.5–2.0 gm/day)
· Avoid NSAIDs
· Diuretics (spironolactone, furosemide; however, aggressive diuresis can cause encephalopathy and other complications). Use furosemide with caution (avoid use if no pedal edema). Monitor electrolytes, renal function.
  – Initial dose of spironolactone: 75 mg od; increase or add 2nd diuretic if little response after 5 days (furosemide 40 mg od)
· Paracentesis, albumin infusion if severe

Spontaneous bacterial peritonitis (SBP)

SBP occurs in patients with ascites. E coli, Klebsiella and Streptococcus pneumoniae are the most common organisms, although no organism is found in 30–50% of cases. The clinical presentation of SBP can be subtle:

Clinical features of spontaneous bacterial peritonitis (SBP)
· Malaise, encephalopathy
· Fever, abdominal pain and tenderness
· Leukocytosis, deterioration in liver function

DIAGNOSIS
Paracentesis and culture of ascitic fluid. > 250 neutrophils/mm^3 is diagnostic.

P PROTOCOL FOR TREATMENT OF SBP
Intravenous cephalosporin (e.g., cefotaxime 1–2 g iv q 6–8 h, or ceftriaxone 500–1000 mg iv q 12 h for 5–7 days). Recurrences are common (norfloxacin 400 mg/day can be used as prophylaxis).

12

OTHER MEDICAL COMPLICATIONS OF ALCOHOL USE

Neurological complications

BLACKOUTS

An acute, reversible amnestic syndrome. The patient cannot remember events that occurred during the heavy-drinking episode. The patient is conscious during a blackout, but may behave in an uncharacteristic or dangerous manner.

PERIPHERAL NEUROPATHY

Symmetrical, distal, sensorimotor neuropathy, affecting the legs more than the arms. Early signs include loss of the ankle reflexes and vibration sense. Patients with neuropathy may experience long-term weakness and neuropathic pain.

CEREBRAL ATROPHY

Can cause cognitive impairment ranging from subclinical deficits detectable on neuropsychological testing to severe dementia requiring long-term care. Impairment may be partially reversible with abstinence.

CEREBELLAR DEGENERATION

Ataxic, wide-based gait. Peripheral coordination (e.g., finger–nose test) is relatively preserved.

SUBDURAL HEMATOMA (ACUTE AND CHRONIC)

Can result from minor head injury (stretched subdural veins in patients with cortical atrophy). Clinical features may be non-specific (decreased level of consciousness, ataxia); may be confused with intoxication.

Note: Order CT scan if patient's ataxia or decreased level of consciousness is inconsistent with the BAC.

PSEUDO-PARKINSONISM

Parkinsonian symptoms (e.g., tremor, rigidity, bradykinesia); resolves sponta-neously with abstinence.

See page 47 for Wernicke-Korsakoff Syndrome and for cerebrovascular disease.

GI complications

Treatment for the complications listed below consists of abstinence plus stan-dard protocols.

ALCOHOLIC GASTRITIS AND ESOPHAGITIS

Causes dyspepsia and acute and chronic blood loss.

MALLORY-WEISS TEAR

Longitudinal tear at the gastroesophageal junction; presents with vomiting followed by hematemesis.

PANCREATITIS

Heavy alcohol use is one of the most common causes of acute, recurrent and chronic pancreatitis.

RECURRENT DIARRHEA

Caused by effects of alcohol on small bowel motility.

Cardiovascular complications

CARDIOMYOPATHY

Suspect cardiomyopathy in heavy drinkers presenting with LV dysfunction or dysrhythmia. Women are at greater risk. The cardiomyopathy is often associated with liver disease.

Treatment: abstinence, plus standard protocols. Patients should be advised that their cardiac function might improve significantly with abstinence.

DYSRHYTHMIAS

Atrial and ventricular tachydysrhythmias can occur in both intoxication and withdrawal and can cause sudden death.

If the tachydysrhythmia occurs while patient is in withdrawal:

· Admit or closely observe in ER, and treat with diazepam loading protocol plus standard protocols (see page 46).

· Ask about other substances that can cause dysrhythmias (e.g., cocaine, cannabis; consider urine drug screen).
· Echocardiogram to detect underlying cardiomyopathy.

HYPERTENSION
Three or more drinks per day increases risk of hypertension. All patients presenting with hypertension should be asked about alcohol use. Alcohol-induced hypertension is more refractory to antihypertensive treatment. However, it responds within days to weeks of abstinence or reduced drinking.

ISCHEMIC HEART DISEASE
Refer to Low-Risk Drinking Guidelines (see page 30).

CEREBROVASCULAR ACCIDENTS
People who drink heavily are at increased risk of hemorrhagic stroke (decreased platelet aggregation, hypertension) but reduced risk of embolic stroke (decreased platelet aggregation, improved lipid profile).

Respiratory complications
OBSTRUCTIVE SLEEP APNEA
Obstructive sleep apnea may contribute to hypertension, dysrhythmias.

Hematological complications
ANEMIA
Anemia requires full investigation. Possible causes include:
· Iron deficiency: Caused by acute or chronic blood loss from the GI tract (Alcohol-induced macrocytosis can mask a microcytic anemia from iron deficiency.)
· Folate deficiency: Caused by poor diet, interference with folate metabolism
· Sideroblastic anemia: Caused by inhibition of pyridoxal phosphate by alcohol
· Hypersplenism: Shortens survival of blood components, resulting in anemia, leukopenia and thrombocytopenia.

LEUKOCYTOSIS
Can be caused by alcoholic hepatitis or infection

Reproductive complications

ERECTILE DYSFUNCTION

Liver dysfunction causes abnormal production and metabolism of estrogens and androgens, resulting in testicular atrophy and erectile dysfunction. Even in males with normal liver function, intoxication can cause erectile dysfunction through an acute decline in testosterone levels.

OLIGO-, AMENORRHEA

Caused by depressed ovarian function

INFERTILITY

In both males and females, due to depressed testicular and ovarian function

FETAL EFFECTS

See Chapter 26, Pregnancy and Substance Use, for fetal alcohol syndrome, complications of pregnancy.

Malignancies

Epidemiological studies suggest alcohol is a carcinogen or co-carcinogen (with smoking) for several malignancies:

BREAST CANCER

Epidemiological studies suggest even moderate drinking marginally elevates risk. [15]

GI MALIGNANCIES

Esophageal, stomach, colon, rectal, hepatoma

ENT MALIGNANCIES

Mouth, pharynx, larynx

Endocrine and metabolic complications

DIABETES

Caused by chronic pancreatitis

HYPERURICEMIA

Alcohol (particularly beer) increases uric acid production and decreases renal excretion precipitating gout in susceptible patients.

HYPOGLYCEMIA
Caused by starvation, impaired gluconeogenesis, catecholamine excess in withdrawal

KETOACIDOSIS
Hypoglycemia induces counter-regulatory hormones that mobilize free fatty acids, causing an anion gap metabolic acidosis; responds to refeeding

DERANGEMENTS IN MINERAL METABOLISM
Low levels of magnesium, phosphate

Infections

Alcohol depresses the immune system, and people who drink heavily often live in crowded conditions, are malnourished and smoke heavily. They may ignore warning symptoms, so they present at a more severe stage of illness.

PNEUMONIA
· Usually Streptococcus and other common organisms
· At greater risk for Klebsiella, anaerobes, aspiration pneumonia, tuberculosis

OTHER INFECTIONS
· Subacute bacterial peritonitis
· Post-surgical wound infection

13

NICOTINE AND SMOKING CESSATION

Nicotine is a "chameleon drug," acting as a stimulant when the person is fatigued and as an anxiolytic when the person is tense. Its psychoactive effects are in part caused by the release of norepinephrine and dopamine. Inhaled nicotine reaches the CNS within 7s, making it a potent reinforcer.

Clinical features of nicotine withdrawal

Symptoms	Cravings for cigarettes, dysphoria, irritability, difficulty concentrating, insomnia, dreams of smoking, hunger, GI upset, headaches, lightheadedness, jaw clenching
Duration	Physical symptoms peak at 2–3 days, and resolve within 1 week. Cravings and difficulty concentrating may last for weeks or months.
Severity	More severe in patients smoking 20 cigarettes per day or more, or requiring a cigarette within 20 min of awakening.

SMOKING CESSATION COUNSELLING AND PHARMACOTHERAPY

In an adult population over 1 year, approximately 3–4% of people who smoke will quit without formal treatment, another 6–8% will quit with a brief counselling intervention (2–5 min) and 12–16% will quit with an intensive intervention (15–30 min in 4–8 sessions). A dose-response curve exists between quit rates and the intensity of counselling. Quit rates approximately double with the addition of appropriate pharmacotherapy.

🅐 MINIMUM INTERVENTION FOR ALL SMOKERS
· Ask all patients older than 9 years of age about smoking.
· Strongly urge all people who smoke to quit.
· Inform people who smoke about the health effects of smoking. Mention cardiores-
  piratory disease, cancer, adverse reproductive effects, erectile dysfunction.
· Ask people who smoke if and when they would like to quit.
· Offer assistance when they are ready to quit.

REMINDER SYSTEMS
Identify patients who smoke through reminder systems such as stickers or com-
puterized reminders. This will prompt you and your health care staff to address
the patient's smoking on an ongoing basis.

SMOKING-CESSATION CLINICS
Smoking clinics and other treatment programs should be considered for people
who have relapsed to smoking after brief physician advice, esp. if they are at
high risk medically.

Counselling patients: The stages of change
See also Chapter 31, Counselling and Motivational Interviewing.

Precontemplation
Approximately 50–60% of people who smoke are not interested in quitting.
· Periodically ask them about their smoking and their level of interest in quitting.
· Ask them how they feel about their smoking—benefits and concerns. You may
  use the motivational intervention described below.
· Continue to point out the health effects of smoking.
· Offer assistance for future quit attempts.

Contemplation
Approximately 30–40% of people who smoke are ambivalent about quitting—
they are thinking about it but not yet committed. The following motivational
intervention may be used:

Contemplation: Motivational intervention†

THE 5 Rs	CLINICIAN'S ROLE	EXAMPLES/COMMENT
Relevance	· Ask patients to indicate why quitting is *personally* relevant to their health status or family situation.	· Greater impact if health reasons linked to patient's current health status or risk factors
Risks	· Ask patients to identify potential negative consequences of smoking. · Suggest and highlight those that seem most relevant.	· Acute: asthma, impotence · Long-term: heart attack, lung disease · Environmental: children at home
Rewards	· Ask patients to identify benefits of quitting; suggest and highlight those most relevant.	· Health; improved taste and smell; financial benefit; better example for children; less wrinkling
Roadblocks	· Ask patients to identify barriers to quitting; discuss solutions.	· Weight gain · Depression · Loss of enjoyment
Repetition	· Repeat intervention every visit.	

†Adapted from: Fiore, M.C., Bailey, W.C., Cohen S.J. et al. *Treating Tobacco Use and Dependence. Clinical Practice Guideline*. Rockville, MD: U.S. Department of Health and Human Services. Public Health Service. June 2000.

Preparation

Of people who smoke, 10–15% are ready to quit. Use the motivational intervention described above, as well as the brief intervention strategy below.

WEIGHT GAIN

Address concerns about gaining weight (average gain is 5–7 pounds). Advise patient not to diet because of increased risk of relapse. Discuss other means of weight control (e.g., regular exercise decreases relapse rate in women).

Preparation: Brief intervention strategy†

STRATEGY	COMMENT
Ask patient to set a quit date.	Ideally within 2 weeks.
Ask for support of family and friends in quit attempt.	Social support is crucial.
Avoid exposure to tobacco, esp. at home.	Throw out tobacco products. Ask spouse/partner to quit with the patient.
Anticipate triggers and challenges, e.g., stress, boredom, post-meal, work break.	Ask patient, "What are you going to do instead of smoking?" Work with patient to develop strategies for each trigger.
Advise patient to reduce alcohol use.	Alcohol is a major trigger for relapse.
Educate about withdrawal.	
Recommend pharmacotherapy.	NRT, bupropion
Provide supplementary materials.	Provide literature and information about self-help programs.

Schedule follow-up visits. At each visit:
· Congratulate success.
· If slip or relapse: review circumstances, alter strategy, renew commitment to abstinence.
· Review pharmacotherapy.
· Refer to a smoking clinic if counselling has failed, esp. if the patient is at high risk medically.

† Adapted from: Fiore, M.C., Bailey, W.C., Cohen S.J. et al. *Treating Tobacco Use and Dependence. Clinical Practice Guideline.* Rockville, MD: U.S. Department of Health and Human Services. Public Health Service. June 2000.

Common smoking-cessation strategies

· The night before the quit date, have a farewell ceremony to "say goodbye" to the cigarettes.
· Quit together with a spouse or close friend who smokes.
· Carry a pocket reminder of reasons for quitting.
· If having strong urges to smoke, look at the pocket reminder, or call a friend who has agreed to act as a "sponsor."

· If possible, avoid situations that trigger strong urges to smoke (e.g., a smoke-filled restaurant).
· Avoid or reduce alcohol and coffee consumption if it triggers cravings.
· Spend money saved by not smoking on a weekly reward.
· See doctor regularly for support.

Smoking and mental health

· Ask patients what situations or moods trigger an urge to smoke. Patients often smoke to cope with situational stress or symptoms of anxiety or depression.
· Untreated mental health problems make it more difficult for patients to quit. Smoking-cessation counselling should be accompanied by treatment of anxiety, mood and adjustment disorders, and substance use disorders.

Smoking cessation and alcohol and other drug dependence

70–80% of patients dependent on alcohol are also dependent on nicotine.

Active drinking

· Patients who currently drink heavily are rarely able to quit smoking, although they should be encouraged to try if they wish to quit.

Initial phases of abstinence from alcohol

· Patients who are attempting to stop using alcohol should be asked if they also wish to quit nicotine. Most patients will decline, preferring to tackle one issue at a time.
· Patients who do wish to quit nicotine while attempting to stop using alcohol should be offered counselling and nicotine replacement therapy or bupropion. (*Note:* Bupropion is contraindicated in patients in acute alcohol withdrawal because of seizure risk.)

Patients who have undergone treatment for alcohol dependence and are now abstinent

· Smoking cessation rates among patients who are now abstinent from alcohol are about the same as for the general population. For this population, success rates per quit attempt are actually higher although they make fewer quit attempts, perhaps because they are not encouraged to do so by their physicians, addiction counsellors or families.

· Patients attempting to quit smoking should be encouraged to use the same strategies that helped them to stop using alcohol (e.g., avoidance of triggers).
· Smoking cessation attempts are associated with a small risk of relapse to alcohol use. Advise patients to have supports in place to prevent relapse (e.g., regular contact with AA sponsor).

Smoking cessation and dependence on other substances
· While the connection between smoking cessation and dependence on other substances has been less studied, the same principles most likely apply. Patients who have undergone treatment and are now abstinent should be encouraged to quit smoking.

Pharmacotherapy

Bupropion SR or the nicotine patch and gum should be routinely offered to all patients attempting to quit smoking, unless medically contraindicated. They should generally be used in conjunction with counselling; the combination of medication and counselling is more effective than either modality alone.

Bupropion SR (Zyban®)

Bupropion, an antidepressant, is believed to act by blocking dopamine and nor-epinephrine reuptake, thus relieving withdrawal symptoms and cravings.

ⓟ PROTOCOL FOR BUPROPION DOSING
· Start 1–2 weeks before patient's quit date.
· Maintain 2–3 months or longer.
· Give 150 mg per day for 3 days, then 150 mg bid.
· Doses should be at least 8 h apart to minimize risk of seizures.

COMMON SIDE-EFFECTS
Insomnia, headache, dry mouth, jitteriness. Insomnia can be minimized by taking medication on arising and in the early evening (e.g., 8 a.m. and 4 p.m.).

SERIOUS SIDE-EFFECTS
Seizures, rare reports of liver failure

CONTRAINDICATIONS
· Seizure disorders
· Acute alcohol, benzodiazepine, barbiturate withdrawal (seizure risk)
· Current or past bulimia or anorexia
· Patients taking Wellbutrin®, MAOIs or thioridazine

PRECAUTIONS
Patients at high risk for seizures:
· Dependent on alcohol, benzodiazepines, barbiturates or cocaine
· On medications that may lower seizure threshold (e.g., antidepressants, antipsychotics, quinolones, steroids)
· Diabetics on insulin or hypoglycemics
· Severe hepatic dysfunction.

MONITORING
· Monitor BP if used with NRT.
· Check liver (transaminases, INR, albumin, bilirubin) if patient has known liver disease or is at high risk (e.g., long-term heavy drinker or hepatitis C carrier).

Nicotine replacement therapy (NRT)

The nicotine patch and gum relieve withdrawal symptoms and reduce cravings by maintaining a steady serum level of nicotine.

P PROTOCOL FOR NICOTINE PATCH DOSING
· Initial dose: 20+ cigarettes/day, 21 mg patch; < 20/day, 14 mg patch.
· Patients who complain of withdrawal can have an extra 7 mg patch added to the 21 mg patch.
· If the patient is unable to cut down on his or her smoking within 4 weeks of starting the patch, treatment should be reassessed.
· Maintain on the higher dose for 6 weeks, then taper to the 14 mg patch for at least 2 weeks, then the 7 mg patch for 2 or more weeks.
· Treatment is usually completed within 2–3 months, but some patients require longer.
· Nicotine gum should be used as a supplement for strong cravings or high-risk situations.

PRECAUTIONS

NRT and continued smoking

Advise patients not to smoke while on the patch. If they do smoke, consider a dosage increase.

Coronary artery disease

NRT is not an independent risk factor for acute cardiovascular events, and is safe in patients with stable angina. However, it is not recommended in patients with serious dysrhythmias or unstable angina, or in the early post-MI period (i.e., first 2 weeks).

Pregnancy

The patch should be used in pregnancy only if counselling has failed. The lowest effective dose should be used for the shortest possible time. Consider the 16-h patch in pregnant patients (Nicotrol®) or take the 24-h patch off at night.

Using the patch: Patient advice

· Apply on a non-hairy part of the skin (upper arm or outer thigh).
· Smooth down to ensure adequate adherence.
· Onset of action may take up to 30 min.
· Chew a 2 mg piece of nicotine gum for strong urges or withdrawal symptoms.
· If you experience nightmares while using the patch, remove it before going to bed or use a 16-h patch.
· If the withdrawal is severe on awakening, apply the patch before retiring for the night.

Nicotine gum

Nicotine gum may be used alone (as a scheduled medication) or in combination with the patch (as a prn medication).

🅟 PROTOCOL FOR NICOTINE GUM

· Dose: Available in 2 mg and 4 mg strengths. The 2 mg strength is recommended for patients who smoke < 1 pack per day (ppd) or are on the patch (see below); 4 mg is recommended for > 1 ppd.

- Scheduled dosing: At least 1 piece every 1–2 h for 1–3 months. Most patients need 10 pieces/day. Do not exceed 20 (2 mg) or 10 (4 mg) pieces/day.
- PRN dosing: In combination with patch. Use prn for urges to smoke. Use for anticipated triggers such as after a meal.
- Chew and park: To ensure adequate buccal absorption of nicotine, instruct patients on proper chew and park techniques: Chew on the gum a few times until a "minty" taste appears, then let the gum sit between the teeth and the buccal mucosa. Repeat for 30 min or until taste is gone.

  Patients who chew nicotine gum like regular gum will swallow the nicotine and may complain of GI upset.
- Combination pharmacotherapy: The effectiveness of NRT is enhanced when the patch is used with prn therapy such as gum. Patients may be offered the patch and gum at the beginning of therapy or after failure of the patch alone. The nicotine inhaler and nicotine nasal spray (not yet available in Canada) are also effective prn medications.

Second-line treatments

Nortryptiline and clonidine may be used if NRT or bupropion has failed or is contraindicated.[26] Controlled studies suggest that nortriptyline may be effective for both depressed and non-depressed smokers.[27, 28]

P PROTOCOL FOR NORTRIPTYLINE
- Initiation: 10–28 days before quit date
- Dosage: 75–100 mg/day for 12 weeks

P PROTOCOL FOR CLONIDINE
- Initiation: 1–3 days before quit date
- Dosage: 0.1 mg bid, increase by 0.1 mg/day per week as needed (max. 0.75 mg/day), for 3–10 weeks

14

OPIOID PRESCRIBING FOR CHRONIC PAIN

Opioids have an important role to play in the treatment of many patients with chronic non-malignant pain. While chronic pain patients without preexisting risk factors are at low risk of opioid dependence, opioids should be used with caution in patients with a current or past history of a substance use disorder.

Effectiveness

RCTs of opioid treatment in chronic nociceptive and neuropathic pain document average decreases in subjective pain ratings of 20–30% or higher. [29-31]

DOSE-RESPONSE CURVE

Opioids have greatest incremental benefit at lower doses with gradual plateauing of response (but no ceiling dose). In the narcotic naïve patient, if partial analgesia is not achieved with dose increases, the pain may not be responsive to opioids.

MAXIMUM DOSE

Equianalgesic doses of greater than 300 mg/day of morphine are usually not necessary and should only be prescribed after obtaining a second opinion.

Indications for opioid analgesics

TYPE OF PAIN	EXAMPLE	FIRST LINE	EFFECTIVENESS OF OPIOIDS	COMMENT ON OPIOID USAGE
Somatic pain	Severe degenerative disk disease	Follow WHO analgesic ladder: NSAIDs or acetaminophen, then opioids	Effective	Document significant organic pathology before long-term treatment

Indications, continued

Neuropathic pain	Diabetic neuropathy	TCAs, anticonvulsants (e.g., gabapentin)	Not very effective, but helpful in selected cases	Higher doses may be required; dosing limited by side-effects
Visceral pain	Chronic pancreatitis	Condition-dependent	May be needed for severe visceral pain (e.g., Crohn's disease)	Not indicated for common GI problems (e.g., irritable bowel)

OPIOIDS NOT INDICATED FOR
· Fibromyalgia
· Irritable bowel syndrome
· Isolated tension headache

OPIOIDS AND MIGRAINE
Meperidine should be used only as a last resort for severe migraine. First-line medications include 5-HTI receptor agonists such as naratriptan, intranasal or intravenous DHE, metochlopromide, chlorpromazine, NSAIDs.

Acute complications of opioid therapy
· Respiratory depression, increased airway resistance
· Hypotension
· Confusion, delirium
· Neurotoxicity (meperidine):
  –Repeated parenteral doses of meperidine causes accumulation of normeperidine, a neurotoxin, resulting in seizures, hallucinations, delirium, hypertension.
· Hallucinations (all opioids)
· Coma, convulsions (MAOIs in combination with meperidine)
· Exacerbation of seizure disorders, supraventricular dysrhythmias
· Increased intracranial pressure in head trauma patients

PATIENTS AT HIGH RISK FOR ACUTE COMPLICATIONS
· Non-tolerant to opioids
· Receiving large or repeated doses of potent parenteral opioids

· On other medications with sedative properties, e.g., antihistamines, benzo-
diazepines
· Concurrent alcohol or other substance use
· Elderly, debilitated, volume-depleted
· Hepatic, renal insufficiency (especially morphine)

Chronic adverse effects of opioids

General
· Sweating
· Fatigue

Respiratory
· Exacerbation of obstructive sleep apnea, COPD (especially early in therapy or
excessive doses)

GI
· Constipation, nausea
· Narcotic bowel syndrome: pseudo-obstruction with dilated loops of bowel on
x-ray; diagnosis of exclusion; resolves on discontinuing opioid

Neurological
· Sensitization to pain, hyperalgesia
· Medication-induced headache:
  – Occurs in migraine patients who frequently use short-acting analgesics such as
    NSAIDs or acetaminophen-codeine combinations
  – Becomes much more frequent, with features similar to tension headaches
  – Usually resolves within weeks of discontinuing analgesic

GU, Reproductive
· Hypogonadism
· Erectile dysfunction
· Menstrual irregularities
· Urinary retention

Psychiatric
· Confusion in the elderly
· Depression, dysphoria
· Small risk of dependence (see Chapter 15, Opioid Dependence and Chronic Pain)

🔒 ASSESSMENT OF THE CHRONIC PAIN PATIENT
· Previous records
· Full history
· Current, past or family history of alcohol and/or other substance use
· Psychiatric history to identify mood and anxiety disorders
· Social history including supports at home and stressors
· Current coping strategies
· Physical examination
· Investigations to document organic pathology

🔒 SCREENING FOR SUBSTANCE DEPENDENCE
All patients should be screened for a current, past or family history of substance use or dependence. Opioids should be used with extreme caution, if at all, if:
· Positive CAGE (see page 11)
· Drinks above low-risk drinking guidelines (> 14/week [men], > 9/week [women];
  > 2 per drinking day)
· Regular use of illicit drugs
· Previous long-term, heavy prescription opioid or benzodiazepine use

Prior to starting opioids
· Carefully assess and document pre-opioid function and level of pain.
· Remember this is a *trial*. Most patients with chronic pain *do not* require opioids.
· Focus on improved functioning, not complete pain relief (complete pain relief is generally an unattainable goal in chronic pain).
· Give comprehensive trial of non-opioid alternatives:
  –Lifestyle adjustment: exercise, change in work tasks
  –Supportive counselling, cognitive-behavioural therapy
  –Physiotherapy
  –First line medications (see table on pages 76–77).
· Use team approach: involve pain specialist, physiotherapist, psychologist.
· Titrate opioids cautiously, esp. in those at risk (e.g., elderly, COPD).
· Avoid benzodiazepines and other sedating drugs.
· Warn patients about combining opioids with alcohol, and about driving, esp. early in therapy or during dose changes.

· Obtain informed consent.
· Before long-term opioid prescribing: review risk of physical dependence, potential adverse effects.

During opioid titration

· Identify 1 prescribing physician to avoid inadvertent double-doctoring in patients with several physicians.
· Use verbal or signed treatment agreement. While treatment agreements may seem legalistic, they do spell out patient responsibilities, and they are helpful if the patient misuses your prescription.

Items in a treatment agreement

· Maximum amount of opioids dispensed per week
· Only 1 prescriber
· Only 1 pharmacy
· Do not use opioids contained in OTC preparations
· Do not use opioids acquired from friends
· Do not give opioids to others
· Take opioid only as directed
· No early dispensing
· Keep regular appointments
· UDS will be requested
· Opioid treatment will be reassessed periodically, and discontinued if ineffective or adverse effects
· Consequences of breaking the contract: Physician may cease prescribing

· Keep a narcotic prescription flow chart. Record date, name of drug, dose and amount dispensed.
· Use urine drug screens periodically, particularly for patients on high doses of potent opioids, such as morphine or oxycodone. Diversion, double-doctoring and non-authorized drug use cannot be reliably detected in any other way.

Note: Order a full UDS (chromatography) that will identify cannabis, cocaine, benzodiazepines and the different types of opioids. When ordering a UDS, always enquire about medication use in the past few days or weeks, including quantity, frequency and time of last use (see also Chapter 6, Laboratory Detection of Alcohol and Other Drug Use).

Urine and blood drug screens: Clinical example—patient prescribed 4 Tylenol® #3 per day*

SCREEN RESULT	CONCLUSION
· Oxycodone in UDS	· Double-doctoring or buying illicit oxycodone
· UDS negative for codeine and morphine	· Non-compliant; possibly selling the drug
· Serum acetaminophen negative	

*Note: Serum acetaminophen or ASA levels will identify excess doses or diversion in patients taking combination preparations.

Tamper-proof your prescriptions.

· Keep prescription pads in a secure location.
· Write amount in words and numbers.
· Put double lines through the unused section of the script.
· Keep phone repeats to a minimum.
· Use numbered or non-reproducible scripts.

· Avoid short-acting opioids with high dependence liability (e.g., oxycodone, hydromorphone, meperidine). These agents have a more potent psychoactive effect, and their short half-life means more frequent administration and more severe withdrawal.
· Avoid chronic use of self-administered, parenteral opioids. These agents are rarely indicated, and they carry a greater risk of complications, overdose, dependence and withdrawal.
· Switch to sustained-release opioids (e.g., MS-Contin®, OxyContin®, Codeine Contin®, Duragesic® patch). Advantages of sustained-release opioids:
  – More consistent pain relief
  – Less intoxication, withdrawal
  – May be less reinforcing.

Note: Sustained-release opioids can be abused. Patients who open, crush or bite the capsules can ingest or inject large amounts of potent, fast-acting opioids.

🄿 PROTOCOL FOR OPIOID TITRATION
- If first-line medications (see table on pages 76–77) are ineffective, add acetaminophen/codeine combinations.
- Do not exceed 4 g acetaminophen per day. Use extra caution with heavy alcohol use, liver disease.
- If codeine helps, consider switching to sustained-release codeine (Codeine Contin®).
- Add short-acting morphine if codeine combinations fail; titrate cautiously.
- Be cautious about exceeding 300 mg of morphine per day.
- Once stable morphine dose is achieved, switch to sustained-release opioid (e.g., MS Contin®, fentanyl patch [Duragesic®]).
- Titrate over 3–6 weeks, using pain scale of 1–10 (1 for very mild pain, 10 for extreme pain) to assess degree of pain relief (e.g., a sustained-release opioid would be considered very effective if it reduced a patient's pain from 8/10 to 4/10 over 12 h).
- Except during titration phase, try to minimize use of prn ("breakthrough") doses.

END-POINT OF TITRATION
- Optimal dose: modest pain relief without drowsiness or other adverse effects.
- Reassess frequently (at least every 8 weeks), monitoring level of pain, functioning and adverse effects.
- Discontinue opioids if no pain relief, major adverse effects or interference with function.
- Dose should be reassessed periodically (patient may not need as much if pain diminishes over time).
- Where possible, seek corroborative evidence of functional status. Family members and other health care professionals can often provide useful, otherwise unattainable information to aid in this determination.

Clinical uncertainty
Physicians are often faced with situations of clinical uncertainty about the need for opioids and, if indicated, the optimal type and dose.

Patients on higher opioid doses

If uncomfortable with the dose of opioid prescribed, refer the patient to a consultant. Ask the consultant specifically about opioid use, e.g., "In your experience, do patients with this pain condition require opioids in this amount?"

Patients on moderate doses

If the patient is on a small or moderate dose of an opioid but you are uncertain about whether it is still needed, consider a trial of tapering. If the patient feels more alert and the pain remains the same, continue the taper. If the patient's pain worsens, return to the original dose.

Patients who are unresponsive to high doses but whose pain worsens when dose is reduced

Patients whose pain has responded poorly to opioids sometimes report a worsening of pain when their opioid dose is tapered. This does not mean that their pain is opioid responsive; they may be experiencing withdrawal-mediated pain, particularly if they are on high doses of opioids, or they are opioid-dependent. Many patients with withdrawal-mediated pain improve after managed withdrawal.

Features of withdrawal-mediated pain

Onset:

4–12 h after last dose, depending on opioid's duration of action. Most severe in morning.

Symptoms:

Myalgias ("pain all over"); underlying pain (e.g., back) greatly increased; nausea, sweating, anxiety, dysphoria (see Chapter 15, Opioid Dependence and Chronic Pain for description of opioid withdrawal). Symptoms quickly relieved with opioid use.

Management of withdrawal-mediated pain

The clinician must decide whether the pain is opioid-responsive or not. With opioid-responsive pain, dosage increases consistently decrease the severity of pain and increase the duration of pain relief, to the point where pain control is adequate (e.g., 30–50% better than baseline, with analgesia lasting at least 2 h/dose [short-acting] or 5–6 h/dose [long-acting]).

Managing withdrawal-mediated pain

TYPE OF PAIN	RECOMMENDED ACTION
Withdrawal-mediated, opioid-responsive	Adjust dose or frequency of scheduled long-acting opioids.
Withdrawal-mediated, not opioid-responsive	Managed withdrawal (slow tapering with long-acting opioids, including methadone or buprenorphine) (see Chapter 15, Opioid Dependence and Chronic Pain).
Withdrawal-mediated, psychologically dependent	Discontinue opioids; switch to methadone or buprenorphine.

15

OPIOID DEPENDENCE AND CHRONIC PAIN

Psychological dependence on opioids appears to be relatively uncommon in chronic pain patients. Tolerance to the analgesic effects of opioids develops slowly—patients are often able to remain on the same dose for months or years. Most patients do not experience euphoria with opioids.

Patients who do become dependent usually have a current or past history of dependence on alcohol or other drugs. They use opioids for their psychoactive effects. Because tolerance to these effects develops rapidly, they are forced to quickly escalate their dose.

Unfortunately, opioid dependence does not preclude the coexistence of a chronic pain problem. In those individuals with both pain and substance dependence, consultation with other practitioners more experienced in this area is advised.

Behaviours suggesting opioid dependence*

· Running out of opioids early, continually asking for more
· No clear pattern of graded analgesic response**
· Concern expressed by spouse/partner, previous physician
· Double-doctoring, prescription forgery
· Unauthorized drugs in the UDS
· Drowsiness, "nodding off"
· Doses far in excess of what is normally required for patients with similar condition
· Refusal to try other treatments

*Look for a pattern of behaviour, not an isolated incident.

** Graded analgesic response: Dose increases either cause improvements in subjective pain ratings by 1–2 out of 10 or the duration of analgesia lasts a little longer. (In those who are on regular doses and are opioid-tolerant a graded analgesic response is not observed until the base opioid requirements have been met, even in opioid-responsive pain.)

★ ASSESSMENT OF PATIENTS SUSPECTED OF OPIOID DEPENDENCE

Complete the assessment outlined on page 15. In addition, complete patient history by asking about:

· Analgesic effectiveness of opioids. Patients dependent on opioids may give dramatic or implausible responses: "With the higher dose, my pain went away completely for 2 days, now it is just as bad" or "When I take it, the pain goes to 0/10 but only for 15 min. then it is back to 10/10."
· Psychoactive effects of opioids (e.g., decreased anxiety, greater sense of well-being)
· Withdrawal symptoms (such as myalgias, dysphoria—see page 90)
· Pattern of use (binge use suggests opioid dependence, e.g., taking the entire daily dose at once)
· Accessing opioids from other sources (doctors, friends, the street)

★ LABORATORY INVESTIGATIONS

· Urine drug screen, blood drug screen for ASA and acetaminophen
· Hepatitis B and C serology, ALT

★ CORROBORATING INFORMATION

Independently ask spouse/partner and previous physician if they have any concerns about patient's opioid use. Spouses are often the first to notice signs of opioid dependence. The previous physician's experience with the patient can be of help because it may take months before a pattern of behaviours suggesting dependence becomes apparent.

Pseudoaddiction

Patients with inadequately treated pain sometimes adopt drug-seeking behaviours (pseudoaddiction). The diagnosis of pseudoaddiction in the patient with a preexisting addictive disorder is best made by a practitioner experienced in both addiction assessment and pain management.

Clinical features of opioid dependence versus pseudoaddiction

	DEPENDENCE	PSEUDOADDICTION
Response to dosage increase	Inconsistent, unpredictable	Graded analgesic response
Drug-seeking behaviour	Continues	Patient satisfied with a dose that is reasonable for his or her source of pain

Management of opioid dependence and chronic pain

Try to determine which issue (dependence or pain) is dominant, and address that issue first. In some cases pain must be managed concurrently with the assessment and stabilization of the addictive disorder.

Patients with opioid dependence do best with comprehensive treatment. Consider referral to a pain specialist, addiction medicine specialist, mutual aid group, treatment program, cognitive therapy and/or other treatment modalities.

Prescribing opioids to patients who are dependent

If the patient's pain should not normally require opioids (e.g., fibromyalgia, tension headaches, irritable bowel syndrome, musculoskeletal pain with minimal findings):

· Discontinue opioids, ideally by tapering. Consider first switching to a sustained-release opioid.
· Treat withdrawal with clonidine (see page 91).
· Consider methadone treatment if above treatment approaches fail.

If the patient has organic pain requiring opioids:

· Consider methadone treatment.
· If methadone unavailable or unacceptable, taper opioids to a lower, more stable dose (see below). Avoid immediate-release opioids.
· Careful boundary-setting, frequent follow-ups and dispensing at short intervals all improve outcomes.

Methadone for opioid dependence and chronic pain

If the patient has organic pain for which opioids are indicated, methadone may be the treatment of choice. This should only be undertaken in consultation with an addiction medicine specialist and pain specialist.

BENEFITS OF METHADONE TREATMENT

· In the appropriate dose, methadone relieves drug craving and symptoms of withdrawal for up to 24 h, without inducing sedation or euphoria.

· Methadone is usually dispensed several times per week under a pharmacist's supervision. The patient is expected to provide supervised urine drug screens (UDS) and should be encouraged to engage in ongoing counselling (see Chapter 17, Pharmacotherapy for Opioid Dependence).

· Double-doctoring is difficult, because UDS can detect methadone and its metabolite separately from other opioids. Also, only a small number of physicians have a licence to prescribe methadone.

· While methadone's duration of analgesic action is only 6–8 h, once-daily administration may be adequate if opioid dependence dominates the clinical picture. This may also be true in those cases where withdrawal-mediated pain dominates.

Opioid tapering

Often patients who are opioid-dependent feel more alert and energetic when they are tapered, and their pain remains the same or even improves. In withdrawal-mediated pain the patient's pain may worsen initially with the taper, then improve as the withdrawal resolves. The patient should be encouraged to attend a formal alcohol and drug treatment program and to try other pain management modalities.

Note: Do not attempt an outpatient taper unless you know the patient well and you feel the risk of double-doctoring is minimal.

Tapering and pregnancy

Tapering is contraindicated in pregnancy because of risk of spontaneous abortion or preterm labour. If available, refer the patient to an addiction medicine specialist.

🅟 PROTOCOL FOR OPIOID TAPERING

Initiation

· If patient is on relatively small amounts of milder analgesics (e.g., codeine), taper with codeine or Codeine Contin®.

· If on large doses of potent opioids (e.g., hydromorphone, oxycodone):

– Calculate equianalgesic dose of long-acting morphine (see table, page 89).

– Start patient on 1/2 this dose (tolerance to one opioid not fully transferred to another opioid).

–Use frequent, smaller doses rather than infrequent, large doses (patients often
 overestimate their drug use, and therefore may be less tolerant than expected).

Taper

· Adjust up or down as necessary to relieve withdrawal without inducing sedation.
· Taper by 10% every 4–7 days.
· Provide frequent follow-up and supportive counselling.
· Monitor with UDS.
· Avoid sedative-hypnotic drugs, especially benzodiazepines.

Completion of the taper

· Complete taper in 2 weeks to 3 months.
· Patients who are unable to complete the taper may be maintained at a lower dose
  if their mood and functioning improve and they follow the treatment agreement.
· Clonidine may be used near the end of the taper if the patient is having difficult
  withdrawal symptoms (see Chapter 16, Opioid Withdrawal).
· If ongoing use of unauthorized drugs or the patient refuses to taper:
  –Stop prescribing opioids and offer treatment for withdrawal.
  –Consider referral for methadone treatment (see Chapter 17, Pharmacotherapy for
   Opioid Dependence).
  –Consider discharging the patient from your practice. If the choice is made to dis-
   charge the patient, the physician must inform the patient of the need for treatment
   and acknowledge the risks of continued opioid use.

Equianalgesic opioid doses†,*

OPIOID	EQUIVALENT ORAL ANALGESIC DOSE (mg)
Morphine	20–30
Codeine	200
Hydromorphone	7.5
Oxycodone	10–15
Meperidine	300

†Adapted from: *Compendium of Pharmaceuticals and Specialties*, Canadian Pharmacists Association, 1999.

*Based on analgesic equivalence, not psychoactive effect. Doses are approximate with large indi-
vidual variation. The listed doses do not apply to patients with renal or hepatic insufficiency or
other conditions affecting drug metabolism and kinetics.

16

OPIOID WITHDRAWAL

Opioid withdrawal has no serious medical complications in otherwise healthy individuals, except in pregnant women and neonates. Patients treated for withdrawal should be referred to a treatment program. Medical staff must understand that with opioid withdrawal there is a serious risk of flight, suicide or overdose (because of loss of tolerance).

Opioid withdrawal is usually mild and transient in patients taking moderate doses for analgesia. However, patients taking higher doses for their psychoactive effects experience intense anxiety, dysphoria and drug craving. Physical symptoms are like a bad case of the flu affecting the respiratory and GI tract.

Clinical features of opioid withdrawal

Physical symptoms	· Myalgias, chills · Abdominal cramps, diarrhea, nausea
Psychological symptoms	· Intense anxiety and dysphoria · Craving for opioids · Restlessness, insomnia, fatigue
Signs	· Lacrimation, rhinorrhea, yawning · Dilated pupils · Retching, vomiting · Sweating, chills, piloerection · Tachycardia, hypertension (usually mild)
Time course	· Begins 6–24 h after last use · Peaks at 2–3 days · Physical symptoms of acute withdrawal largely resolve by 5–10 days · Insomnia and dysphoria may last weeks to months

Major complications
Suicide: Caused by anxiety, dysphoria
Pregnancy: Spontaneous abortion, preterm labour
Neonatal withdrawal: Seizures, death if not identified and treated
Overdose: Patients lose their tolerance to opioids within 3–7 days after last use, and may overdose if they relapse.

WARNINGS AND PRECAUTIONS
· Ask all patients about suicidal ideation.
· Screen for pregnancy.
· Warn patients about overdose if they resume use at previous doses.

Clonidine treatment
While less effective than methadone in the treatment of opioid withdrawal, clonidine is more readily available and is rarely a drug of abuse.

Note: Because it can cause postural hypotension, it should be used with caution in patients with pre-existing heart disease or patients on antihypertensives. Patients should be warned to avoid activities leading to vascular pooling (e.g., hot tubs, baths, etc.)

PROTOCOL FOR CLONIDINE DOSING
· Test dose: 0.1 mg po
· Check BP 1 h later; do not prescribe further if BP < 90/60
· Give 0.1 mg tid-qid for 5–7 days
· If 0.1 mg ineffective, increase to 0.2 mg tid-qid prn (watch for hypotension)
· Inpatient: Increase to 0.3 mg tid-qid; check BP prior to each dose
· Warn about postural symptoms, drowsiness, driving; no hot showers or baths
· Combine with:
  – Antinauseants (e.g., dimenhydrinate)
  – Antidiarrheals (e.g., loperamide)
  – Analgesics for myalgia (e.g., NSAIDs)
  – HS sedation, (e.g., trazodone; insomnia is often the most uncomfortable symptom of withdrawal). Only prescribe HS benzodiazepines for 5–7 days.

Mixed opioid and other drug withdrawal
See Polysubstance Use and Withdrawal, Chapter 20.

17

PHARMACOTHERAPY FOR OPIOID DEPENDENCE

Opioid dependence can be treated with methadone, buprenorphine or naltrexone.

Methadone

Note: Physicians in Canada need a special exemption from the *Controlled Drugs and Substances Act* (1996) to prescribe methadone for opioid dependence (contact the provincial licensing authority or the Bureau of Drug Surveillance for further information). This section is intended for physicians who do not have a methadone licence but who occasionally provide care for patients on methadone. For further information, see *Methadone Maintenance: A Physician's Guide to Treatment* (Toronto: Centre for Addiction and Mental Health, 1998, 2002).

RATIONALE FOR METHADONE TREATMENT IN OPIOID DEPENDENCE

In the appropriate dose, methadone relieves drug cravings and withdrawal symptoms for 24 h, without inducing sedation or euphoria. Because of cross-tolerance, patients on methadone experience less euphoria with opioid use, diminishing the reinforcing effects of illicit opioids. Methadone retains patients in treatment; patients must attend the clinic if they are to receive the medication. Methadone programs monitor drug use and should provide counselling. Treatment is often long-term (months or years).

EFFECTIVENESS

A number of controlled trials and large cohort studies have demonstrated that methadone is a highly effective treatment for opioid dependence.

Pre- and post-results from 2 cohort studies of methadone treatment for heroin dependence [32, 33]

VARIABLES	PRE	POST
Socially productive	36%	76%
Arrest rate/100 person-years	201	1.2
Injection drug use	81%	29%
Mortality rate		Decreased by factor of 11

INDICATIONS
· Physical and psychological dependence on high daily doses of potent opioids (e.g., heroin, hydromorphone)
· Long history of opioid dependence (usually 1 or more years)
· Failed at or unwilling to try other forms of treatment, or unlikely to succeed given chronicity of use or other factors

PHARMACOLOGY
· Route: Oral (mixed with orange juice to prevent iv use)
· Half-life: Average 24 h (range 16–55 h)
· Absorption: Fully absorbed within 30 min
· Peak serum level: 2–4 h
· Duration of action: Up to 24 h for relief of withdrawal symptoms; 6–8 h for analgesia
· Side-effects: Similar to other opioids (see pages 77–78). Initial titration carries greater risk of overdose than other oral opioids because its long half-life leads to bioaccumulation (see page 94).

COMPONENTS OF METHADONE PROGRAMS
· Daily methadone dispensing supervised by a pharmacist
· Take-home doses ("carries") if doing well (to a max. of 6 carries/week in Ontario; this varies with jurisdiction)
· Regular supervised urine drug screening (UDS)
· Individual or group counselling

P PROTOCOL FOR METHADONE DOSING
- Initial dose: Methadone 15–30 mg po od. Consider the lower range for older patients and those on prescription opioids; the higher range for people physically dependent on heroin (who typically inject or smoke 1/10 to 1/4 g per day).
- Titration: Increase by 10–15 mg po od every 5–7 days according to symptoms. Titration can take several weeks or longer.
- Usual effective dose: 50–120 mg

PRESCRIBING PRECAUTIONS
Initial titration
- Before prescribing methadone, confirm the diagnosis of opioid dependence, through history, physical, UDS. Non-dependent patients given methadone are at greater risk for overdose and quickly become dependent on methadone.
- See the patient regularly: twice per week for first 2–3 weeks, then weekly until a stable dose is achieved.
- *Do not exceed the dosing guidelines. Onset of methadone overdose can be slow and insidious. Because of bioaccumulation a patient may appear normal on the first day of an excess dose, and be comatose by the 4th day.*
- Do not prescribe other opioids or benzodiazepines concurrently.
- Warn the patient to avoid alcohol.
- Do not dispense methadone if the patient appears drowsy or intoxicated.
- Decrease the dose if you observe drowsiness or the patient or his or her spouse/partner reports drowsiness 2–4 h after taking dose.

Missed methadone doses
If the patient presents having missed his or her methadone dose:
- Contact the patient's pharmacy to verify dosage and time last dispensed.
- Patients who have missed methadone for 3+ days must be given a reduced dose because their tolerance has decreased. Check with the physician prescribing methadone.
- If methadone is not available, offer clonidine (not opioids) for withdrawal. *However, pregnant patients must be given methadone (not clonidine) to avoid complications induced by withdrawal.*

Vomited doses
Methadone is fully absorbed within 1/2 hour of ingestion. If the pharmacist or nurse witnessed the patient vomiting the dose within 15 min. of ingestion, half the dose may be replaced.

Hospitalized patients taking methadone
· Contact the patient's pharmacy to verify dosage and time last dispensed. *This is* **mandatory** *to prevent double-dosing.*
· Prescribe the usual methadone dose.
· Use caution in prescribing CNS and respiratory depressants such as benzodiazepines.
· Decrease the dose by 50% if 3 days of methadone are missed (see above); if 5 days missed, start at 30 mg for 3 days. Ask methadone prescriber for advice.

Acute pain management in the patient taking methadone
Long-term methadone is not effective for acute pain control because patients have developed tolerance to its effects.
· If the patient is on a stable methadone dose for a long period of time, prescribe opioids for pain control in usual dose. May need more frequent administration than usual because of tolerance (e.g, acetaminophen–codeine every 3–4 h rather than 4–6 h).
· Opioids should be used with considerable caution and at a lower dose with patients in the initial titration phase of methadone (first few weeks). Since they have not yet developed tolerance to methadone, additional opioid doses may cause drowsiness.
· For all patients taking methadone, avoid partial agonists such as pentazocine, butorphanol or buprenorphine (can trigger withdrawal).
· Do not prescribe opioids or benzodiazepines for longer than 1–2 weeks to patients taking methadone without first discussing with the methadone-prescribing physician.
· If "NPO" patient on methadone, have the patient take methadone mixed in sterile water rather than orange juice, or provide parenteral morphine. The patient should be returned to an oral dose as soon as practical. The methadone dose may initially have to be adjusted downward (due to loss of tolerance).

● PROTOCOL FOR INPATIENT OPIOID WITHDRAWAL MANAGEMENT USING METHADONE
Methadone can be used to treat opioid withdrawal with patients who are not
candidates for methadone maintenance and for whom clonidine is ineffective or
contraindicated. Its use should be reserved for patients taking high daily doses
of potent opioids (e.g., parenteral heroin or hydromorphone).

· Day 1: Methadone 5–15 mg q 6 h prn, to a max. dose of 40 mg. Hold and closely
monitor if drowsy.
· Days 2 and 3: Maintain on 1st day's total dose (up to 40 mg) plus 5 mg tid prn.
Hold if drowsy.
· Subsequent days: Taper by 5–10 mg per day.

Note: Hold or use lower doses in patients who have altered mental status, are
on sedating drugs, have respiratory compromise (e.g., pneumonia, COPD) or are
seriously ill.

See also Chapter 26, Pregnancy and Substance Use.

Buprenorphine

Buprenorphine, not yet available in Canada, is an alternative to methadone in
the treatment of opioid dependence. [34–36] As with methadone, buprenorphine
should be dispensed once per day in conjunction with UDS and ongoing counselling. (Carry privileges should be granted as with methadone.) The lab per-
forming the UDS must have an assay for detecting buprenorphine.

COMPARISON WITH METHADONE
· Much lower risk of death from overdose
· Milder withdrawal during tapering
· Can titrate to optimal dose in days (vs weeks on methadone)
· As effective as methadone 20–60 mg in relieving withdrawal symptoms and
decreasing illicit opioid use. Further research is needed on the comparative effi-
cacy of buprenorphine and methadone in doses above 60 mg.

PHARMACOLOGY
· Receptor activity: μ-opioid receptor partial agonist, k-receptor antagonist
· Route: Sublingual (poor oral bioavalability)
· Peak serum level: 60–90 min.

· Duration of action: 24+ h
· Analgesic duration of action: 6–8 h
· Overdose risk: Does not cause severe respiratory depression in overdose (bell-shaped dose-response curve). Due to high receptor affinity, naloxone or naltrexone does not effectively antagonize buprenorphine.
· Opioid antagonist effects: Partially blocks effects of other opioids, and can precipitate withdrawal in opioid dependence
· Adverse effects, drug interactions: Similar to other opioids
· Pregnancy: Safety in pregnancy not established

P PROTOCOL FOR BUPRENORPHINE DOSING

· Initial dose: should not be given until the patient is in mild to moderate opioid withdrawal.
  – Heroin dependence—wait at least 6 h after last heroin use before giving first dose of buprenorphine
  – Methadone dependence—taper to 30 mg od, then wait at least 24 h before giving first dose of buprenorphine

· Initial dose 2 mg sl od
· Titration: Increase daily by 2–4 mg/day
· Effective dose: Usual maintenance dose 8 mg sl od; can titrate to 16 mg sl od.

Naltrexone

Naltrexone is a competitive opioid antagonist (see Chapter 10, Pharmacotherapy for Alcohol Dependence). It binds very tightly to opioid receptors, completely blocking the effects of opioids for 24–72 h. Patients taking naltrexone know it is pointless to use opioids.

EFFECTIVENESS

There is little evidence of effectiveness of naltrexone among people who are heroin-dependent and socially unstable. It may be useful with socially stable patients as part of a comprehensive program. As with disulfiram, taking it under supervision of a spouse/partner or pharmacist may enhance compliance.

INDICATIONS

Adjunct treatment for patients who are opioid-dependent and who wish to remain abstinent from all opioids, including methadone and buprenorphine.

PROTOCOL FOR NALTREXONE
· Duration of therapy: ≥ 3–6 months
· Dose: 50 mg per day. If the naltrexone ingestion is supervised, administer 100 mg Monday, 100 mg Wednesday and 150 mg Friday (more convenient and equally effective schedule).

PRECAUTIONS

Naltrexone will precipitate a severe withdrawal syndrome in patients physically dependent on opioids. Therefore:
· See page 51 for hepatotoxicity.
· Patients must be opioid-free for at least 7–10 days.
· Their UDS should be negative for opioids.
· They should be free of any physical withdrawal symptoms. If in doubt, administer a naloxone challenge test.

NALOXONE CHALLENGE TEST
· Naloxone 0.4 mg iv or 0.8 mg sc
· Observe for 20 min (iv) or 45 min (sc)
· Do not prescribe naltrexone if the patient has any signs or symptoms of withdrawal. Repeat the test in the next 1–2 days, using a higher dose (naloxone 1.6 mg iv).

DISCONTINUATION AND OVERDOSE RISK
· Patients should be cautioned about increased opioid sensitivity after discontinuation of naltrexone. Recent reports have shown an increased mortality due to overdose in patients who discontinued long-term naltrexone and then used opioids.

18

BENZODIAZEPINES FOR ANXIETY AND INSOMNIA

Anxiety

Physicians must diagnose the cause of the patient's anxiety symptoms before prescribing benzodiazepines. Benzodiazepines are not the first–line treatment for any of the conditions listed below (e.g., SSRIs are a more appropriate initial treatment for panic disorder, and counselling is indicated for anxiety that has psychosocial causes).

Causes of anxiety

CAUSE	EXAMPLES
Psychiatric	· Panic Disorder
	· Obsessive-Compulsive Disorder
	· Major Depressive Disorder with prominent anxiety features
	· Psychosis
	· Substance-Induced Anxiety Disorder
	· Post-Traumatic Stress Disorder
Organic	· Dementia
	· Cardiorespiratory conditions
	· Hyperthyroidism
	· Medications (e.g., beta agonists, xanthines)
Psychosocial	· Work and family difficulties
	· Abuse

ASSESSMENT OF ANXIETY

The assessment should identify the causes of anxiety (listed above) and should include:

· Medical history
· Psychiatric history
· Alcohol and drug history
· Psychosocial history
· Physical exam

Management of anxiety: Non-medical

· Cognitive/behavioural therapy
· Progressive muscle relaxation, deep breathing, meditation
· Counselling for psychosocial issues

Lifestyle changes to reduce anxiety

· Exercise
· Obtain adequate sleep
· Avoid excess coffee and alcohol
· Modify work and other responsibilities
· Spend more time with family, friends
· Increase leisure activities

Medical management of anxiety: Alternatives to benzodiazepines

Buspirone

ADVANTAGES

Not addictive and causes little or no sedation. May be as effective an anxiolytic as diazepam.

LIMITATIONS

· Takes 1-2 weeks to work
· Will not help benzodiazepine withdrawal
· Patients who are used to benzodiazepines often do not like buspirone (no immediate "mellowing" effect).

SIDE-EFFECTS
Dizziness, nervousness, nausea, headache. Rare extrapyramidal symptoms.

P BUSPIRONE PROTOCOL
· Initial dose: 5 mg bid-tid

SSRIs and other antidepressants
ADVANTAGES
These agents are effective, non-addicting and generally safe even with alcohol and/or drug use. Most patients should have a trial with these agents before long-term benzodiazepine prescribing. Examples include paroxetine (Paxil®), sertraline (Zoloft®), nefazodone (Serzone®), venlafaxine (Effexor®), fluoxetine (Prozac®).

INDICATIONS
· Panic Disorder
· Social Phobia
· Depression with prominent anxiety symptoms
· Obsessive Compulsive Disorder
· Generalized Anxiety Disorder

Insomnia
CAUSES
Psychiatric causes: Anxiety disorders, mood disorders

Organic causes: Alcohol abuse, medications, cardiorespiratory conditions, sleep apnea, restless leg syndrome, prostatism, chronic pain

A ASSESSMENT
Assess as for anxiety (see page 100). In addition, a careful sleep history is essential. Patients may complain of insomnia, even though total sleep time is adequate. This occurs among older adults who go to bed early and wake up early, or among patients who do not work a nine-to-five schedule, going to bed late and waking up late. A sleep history may help prevent unnecessary prescribing.

🕭 Assessment of insomnia

SLEEP HISTORY	COMMENT
Sleep pattern	Bedtime, time asleep, time awake
Total hours of sleep	
Timing of difficulty	Trouble falling asleep, early wakening, etc.
Bedtime activities	Listening to radio, reading, etc.
Reason for awakening	Pain, worry, etc.
Daytime naps	

Management of insomnia: Non-medical

· Cognitive/behavioural therapy
· Progressive muscle relaxation, deep breathing, meditation
· Counselling for psychosocial issues

Sleep hygiene

· Avoid excess alcohol, coffee, cola.
· Exercise regularly, but not before bedtime.
· Do not overeat before bed.
· Use bedroom for sleep and sex only.
· Do not take daytime naps or go to sleep before 9–10 p.m.
· Minimize noise, excess heat and light.
· Relax before going to bed.
· If trouble sleeping, get up, do something else for 20 min., and then try to sleep again (but do not watch TV because of the photic stimulation).
· Do not sleep too late in the morning.

Management of insomnia: Medical

For patients who are at risk for benzodiazepine dependence, consider prescribing other medications with sedative properties. Examples include tryptophan, low-dose tricyclic antidepressants, trazodone and sedating SSRIs such as sertraline.

Benzodiazepines

CLASSIFICATION BY HALF-LIFE
· Long-acting (> 24 h): Diazepam, chlordiazepoxide, clorazepate, flurazepam
· Intermediate-acting (6–24 h): Oxazepam, lorazepam, nitrazepam, temazepam, alprazolam, clonazepam
· Short-acting (< 6 h): Triazolam, midazolam

INDICATIONS
· Short-term treatment of severe insomnia
· Severe acute anxiety
· Generalized Anxiety Disorder unresponsive to other treatments
· Panic Disorder (SSRIs are first line)
· Alcohol withdrawal
· Anticonvulsant, muscle relaxant, pre-procedure sedation
· Adjunctive treatment of Depression, Bipolar Affective Disorder and Schizophrenia

Note: Benzodiazepines can worsen depression. Use only if prominent anxiety symptoms and avoid high doses.

PRESCRIBING PRECAUTIONS
While benzodiazepines are generally safe, they should be prescribed with caution in the following circumstances:
· Problem drinking or other substance dependence (risk of dependence)
· COPD, sleep apnea
· Psychiatric disorders: Depression, Personality Disorders, Schizophrenia
· Patients on other psychoactive drugs (e.g., barbiturates, opioids, antidepressants, sedating antihistamines).

OTHER CONSIDERATIONS
· Avoid benzodiazepines with a high dependence risk (e.g., diazepam, alprazolam).
· Avoid use for longer than 3 weeks if possible. Whereas benzodiazepines retain their anxiolytic effectiveness for long periods, their effectiveness as hypnotics diminishes after several weeks. Furthermore, rebound insomnia can develop after several weeks of daily use, convincing patients that they continue to need the drug.

· Avoid long-acting benzodiazepines (e.g., diazepam, chlordiazepoxide, flurazepam) if possible, esp. in older adults, due to hangover effect, falls.
· Consider alternatives. Commonly used alternatives include trazadone, tryptophan, low-dose TCAs, and sedating SSRIs such as sertraline.

Benzodiazepines: Adverse effects

EFFECT	INCREASED RISK
Depression	High doses
Falls, hip fractures	In older adults and with long-acting agents
Confusion, worsening dementia	In older adults and with long-acting agents
Motor vehicle accidents	Early in therapy
Decreased respiratory drive	Early in therapy, in combination with other sedating drugs, in severe respiratory disease
"Floppy baby syndrome"	High doses during labour or late third trimester
Disinhibition	Personality disorders, psychosis
Rebound insomnia (vivid dreams, fitful sleep on cessation of benzodiazepines)	Occurs after 3+ weeks of daily therapy

WARNINGS TO PATIENTS ABOUT BENZODIAZEPINES
· Warn patients about combining benzodiazepines with alcohol, opioids or other sedating drugs.
· Caution patients not to drive if they experience a decrease in alertness, especially during initial days/weeks of treatment.

DURATION OF THERAPY
· Initial prescribing: Prescribe for no more than 3 weeks.
· Patients on long-term benzodiazepines: Periodically attempt to taper to lower dose (see pages 106–109)

19

BENZODIAZEPINE AND BARBITURATE DEPENDENCE AND WITHDRAWAL

Benzodiazepine dependence is uncommon—most patients take the medication as prescribed. Benzodiazepines probably carry a lower risk of dependence than alcohol, barbiturates, opioids or stimulants. Patients with a current or past history of dependence on other substances are at greatest risk for becoming dependent on benzodiazepines. The treatment approach is similar to other substance dependence. Concurrent treatment for anxiety disorders is often required (see pages 99–101).

Risk of dependence with different benzodiazepines

All benzodiazepines can cause dependence and withdrawal. Zopiclone (Imovane®), although not a benzodiazepine, is clinically similar to benzodiazepines and can cause dependence and withdrawal. Benzodiazepines with a rapid entry into the CNS and a more potent effect on CNS receptors will have a greater psychoactive effect and therefore a greater risk for dependence.

HIGHER RISK
Diazepam, lorazepam, alprazolam, triazolam

LOWER RISK
Oxazepam, chlordiazepoxide, clonazepam

Benzodiazepine withdrawal

Patients may experience withdrawal if they suddenly discontinue benzodiazepines after daily use for 2 months or more. Withdrawal can occur even with therapeutic doses, although it is more severe with high doses, short-acting agents, long duration of use and underlying anxiety disorder.

Serious complications can occur with abrupt cessation of doses equivalent to 50+ mg of diazepam/day, especially agents with short half-lives (e.g., alprazolam).

Clinical features of benzodiazepine withdrawal

ONSET	DURATION	SYMPTOMS	SIGNS	COMPLICATIONS
· 1–2 days (short-acting) · 2–4 days (long-acting)	· Several weeks to months	· Anxiety-related: Panic attacks, insomnia, irritability · Neurological: Dysperceptions (harsh sounds, blurry or distorted vision), tinnitus, depersonalization, déjà vu	· Autonomic hyperactivity (sweating, tremor, tachycardia, hypertension) · Autonomic signs less common than in alcohol withdrawal	· Seizures · Psychosis · Delirium · Cardiovascular complications (dysrhythmias, hypertension)

Benzodiazepine tapering

If benzodiazepines are discontinued, tapering is recommended over abrupt cessation unless the patient has only been taking the medication intermittently or for a few weeks.

INDICATIONS
· No benefit from benzodiazepine treatment
· No evidence of anxiety disorder
· Benzodiazepine dependence
· At risk for adverse effects—elderly, underlying depression or problem substance use

RATIONALE FOR TAPERING PATIENTS ON THERAPEUTIC DOSES
Periodic attempts to taper are warranted even for patients taking therapeutic doses with no apparent adverse effects. Patients sometimes find that they:
· No longer need the drug
· Feel more alert, energetic
· Experience more positive emotions such as enthusiasm
· Are better able to engage in counselling.

A PRIOR TO TAPERING

Assess for underlying mood or anxiety disorder, or psychosocial problems.
Tapering works best if patient and physician are committed to developing alternative coping strategies for anxiety.

P APPROACH TO TAPERING

· Slow tapers work better than fast tapers.
· Emphasize need for scheduled rather than prn doses.
· Halt or reverse taper if severe anxiety or depression.
· Follow-up q 1–4 weeks depending on response to taper.
· Ask patient about the benefits of tapering (e.g., more energy, increased alertness).

Outpatient vs inpatient tapering

Outpatient tapering is preferred for patients taking < 50 mg/day diazepam equivalent (see page 109 for equivalence table).

Inpatient tapering should be considered for patients taking 50–100 mg/day diazepam equivalent, but outpatient is possible if:
· Not physically dependent on other drugs
· Medically, psychiatrically stable
· Unlikely to access benzodiazepines from other sources.

Consider hospitalization and addiction medicine consult if *typical* daily use over past 2 months is equivalent to diazepam 100 mg or more.

P PROTOCOL FOR OUTPATIENT BENZODIAZEPINE TAPERING

Initiation
· Taper with a longer-acting agent such as diazepam or clonazepam (may have smoother taper).
· Convert to equivalent dose of diazepam (max. 80–100 mg/day) in divided doses (see page 109 for equivalence table).
· Adjust initial dose according to symptoms (equivalence table is approximate).

Tapering
· Taper by no more than 5 mg per week (or 5 mg per 3–4 days at doses above 50 mg of diazepam equivalent).
· Adjust rate of taper according to symptoms.

- Slow the pace of the taper once dose below 20 mg of diazepam equivalent (e.g., 2–4 mg per week).
- Dispense daily, twice weekly or weekly depending on dose and patient reliability.
- Another approach is to taper according to the proportional dose remaining:
  - Taper by 10% of the dose every 1–2 weeks until the dose is at 20% of the original dose, then taper by 5% every 2–4 weeks.

℗ PROTOCOL FOR INPATIENT BENZODIAZEPINE TAPERING
- Start taper at 1/2–1/3 the equivalent diazepam dose, administered tid-qid.
- If significant withdrawal on this dose, increase next day's total dose by 10–30 mg.
- May give diazepam 10–15 mg tid prn for acute withdrawal during taper.
- Hold diazepam and decrease daily dose if drowsiness or sedation.
- Taper by 5–15 mg per day as inpatient (no more than 10% of daily dose; slow taper as dose decreases).
- May switch to outpatient protocol at doses less than 50 mg.

PRECAUTIONS FOR BENZODIAZEPINE TAPERING
- If patient on alprazolam or triazolam, taper with alprazolam and triazolam, or equivalent dose of clonazepam. (Diazepam may not be effective for alprazolam or triazolam withdrawal.)
- If patient is an older adult or has severe liver disease, severe asthma or respiratory failure, or low serum albumin, diazepam may cause excessive and prolonged sedation. Taper with intermediate-acting benzodiazepine (such as lorazepam or clonazepam).
- Watch for mixed anxiety/depression. Patients with an underlying depression may experience increased anxiety and suicidal ideation during the taper. Taper slowly and halt or reverse taper if necessary.

Benzodiazepine equivalence table†

BENZODIAZEPINE	EQUIVALENCE TO 5 mg DIAZEPAM (mg)*
Alprazolam (Xanax®)**	0.5
Bromazepam (Lectopam®)	3–6
Chlordiazepoxide (Librium®)	10–25
Clonazepam (Rivotril®)	0.5–1
Clorazepate (Tranxene®)	7.5
Flurazepam (Dalmane®)	15
Lorazepam (Ativan®)	0.5–1
Nitrazepam (Mogadon®)	5–10
Oxazepam (Serax®)	15
Temazepam (Restoril®)	10–15
Triazolam (Halcion®)**	0.25

†Adapted from: Kalvik A., Isaac P, Janecek E. *Pharmacy Connection* 1995, 20–32; *Compendium of Pharmaceuticals and Specialties*, Canadian Pharmacists Association, 1999.

*Equivalences are approximate. Careful monitoring is required to avoid oversedation, esp. in older adults and those with impaired hepatic metabolism.
**Equivalency uncertain.

Mixed benzodiazepine and other drug withdrawal

See Polysubstance Use and Withdrawal, Chapter 20.

Barbiturate withdrawal

Fiorinal® (butalbital 50 mg + ASA, +/- codeine), the main barbiturate of abuse in Canada, is an analgesic for migraine headache. There is no evidence that barbiturates have analgesic properties,[37] and their use can cause dependence and other adverse effects. Therefore some authorities have recommended that Fiorinal® not be prescribed. Withdrawal can occur from discontinuation after daily use of 3–4 doses of Fiorinal® for 4 or more weeks. Complicated withdrawal can occur with abrupt cessation of doses equivalent to 500+ mg of butalbital (10+ tablets daily of Fiorinal®) for 1 month or more.

Clinical features of barbiturate withdrawal

ONSET	DURATION	SYMPTOMS	SIGNS	COMPLICATIONS
1–3 days	7–14 days	Similar to but more severe than alcohol withdrawal	Similar to alcohol: autonomic hyperactivity (sweating, tremor, tachycardia, hypertension)	Similar to alcohol: seizures, delirium, psychosis, dysrhythmias, hypertension

Phenobarbital loading

INDICATIONS

Daily doses of > 500 mg of a short-acting barbiturate such as butalbital for at least 1 month (10+ Fiorinal® capsules)

🅟 PROTOCOL FOR PHENOBARBITAL LOADING

· Admit.
· Order addiction medicine consultation if available.
· Begin loading when patient begins to go into withdrawal (tremor, tachycardia, sweating, etc.).
· Dispense phenobarbital 120 mg po q 1 h.
· Discontinue phenobarbital when patient exhibits 3 or more of the following signs of barbiturate intoxication:
  – Emotional lability
  – Nystagmus
  – Slurred speech
  – Ataxia
  – Slight drowsiness.
· Discharge when no longer drowsy and a reliable person is at home to monitor patient.

Note: The objective is to cause mild intoxication without compromising patient safety. Use caution and consider phenobarbital tapering rather than loading in older adults and those with liver or respiratory disease.

Outpatient tapering

INDICATIONS

Phenobarbital tapering is indicated for patients who are taking ≥ 200 mg/day and ≤ 500 mg/day of a short-acting barbiturate such as butalbital for at least 1 month.

🅟 PROTOCOL FOR PHENOBARBITAL OUTPATIENT TAPERING

· Convert to equivalent phenobarbital dose (dose will be ≤ 150 mg per day).
· Taper by 30 mg phenobarbital q 2–5 days.
· Adjust initial dose and rate of taper as needed (equivalences are approximate).

PRECAUTIONS FOR PHENOBARBITAL TAPERING

Precautions are similar to those for benzodiazepine tapering (see page 108). A lower initial phenobarbital dose is recommended in patients who have:

· Severe liver disease
· Older adults
· Respiratory disease.

Short-acting barbiturate and sedative/hypnotic equivalence table†

DRUG	EQUIVALENCE TO 30 mg PHENOBARBITAL (mg)*
Amobarbital	100
Butabarbital	100
Butalbital	100
Pentobarbital	100
Secobarbital	100
Chloral hydrate	500
Ethchlorvynol (Placidyl®)	500
Meprobamate (Equagesic®)	1,200

† Adapted from: D. Smith & D. Wesson. *Pharmacologic therapies for sedative-hypnotic addiction.* American Society of Addiction Medicine, 1994.

* Equivalences are approximate. Upward or downward titration is often required. Careful monitoring is required to avoid toxicity, esp. in older adults.

Barbiturate tapering with Fiorinal®

Tapering with phenobarbital is preferred over Fiorinal®, because phenobarbital is seldom a drug of abuse and its long half-life makes for a smoother and safer taper. Tapering with Fiorinal® itself should only be considered if:

· The patient is taking less than 8 tablets (400 mg butalbital) per day.

· The physician knows the patient well and has found no evidence of double-doctoring.

· The patient is unlikely to take more than prescribed or run out early (this could cause severe withdrawal [38]).

🅟 PROTOCOL FOR TAPERING WITH FIORINAL®

· Have pharmacy dispense medication q 1–7 days, depending on patient reliability.

· Prescribe on a tid-qid schedule.

· Complete the taper over 6–12 weeks.

20

POLYSUBSTANCE USE AND WITHDRAWAL

Polysubstance use is extremely common. Patients dependent on more than one substance generally have a poorer prognosis.

Assessment

A comprehensive drug history is required on all patients. Patients do not always view their polysubstance use as problematic; for example, people who use cocaine might feel that their diazepam use is beneficial or harmless. As a result, they may be forthcoming about their use of cocaine but minimize their use of diazepam.

Treatment goal

Abstinence from all substance use is generally the preferred treatment goal. Even apparently moderate use of the "secondary" drug may trigger cravings for the main drug, cause nonspecific problems such as depression or anxiety and contribute to the severity of withdrawal.

Management of polysubstance withdrawal

GENERAL PRINCIPLES

· Use the management protocols outlined in individual chapters for alcohol, benzo-diazepines, barbiturates and opioids.
· The substance posing the greatest risk of serious withdrawal should receive priority (barbiturates > alcohol > benzodiazepines > opioids).
· Alcohol withdrawal should be treated first because onset is earlier than benzo-diazepine or barbiturate withdrawal (if all substance use ceases at the same time).

- Phenobarbital is generally effective for acute barbiturate, alcohol and benzodi-azepine withdrawal.
- Benzodiazepine withdrawal has a prolonged subacute phase so tapering with benzodiazepines is generally indicated after completion of a phenobarbital or diazepam load (but wait until the patient is awake and alert).
- Equivalent doses are approximate, titrate carefully.
- When combining drugs such as phenobarbital, diazepam and clonidine, watch for oversedation and use conservative doses. When in doubt, consult with an addiction medicine specialist.

Comparison of withdrawal syndromes for different drug classes

SUBSTANCE	ONSET OF WITHDRAWAL SYMPTOMS	RISK FACTORS FOR COMPLICATIONS	COMPARATIVE RATING OF RISK	TREATMENT PROTOCOL
Alcohol	6–12 h	Hx of seizures, delirium etc.	High	· Diazepam loading
Barbiturates	1–3 days	≥ 500 mg/day short-acting barbiturate/day	High	· Phenobarbital loading
Benzodiazepines	1–2 days (short-acting); 2–4 days (long-acting)	Dose ≥ 50 mg diazepam equivalent/day	Intermediate	· Benzodiazepine tapering (diazepam, clonazepam, etc.)
Opioids	6–24 h	Pregnancy	Low	· Clonidine · Methadone · Opioid tapering

🅟 Protocol for polysubstance withdrawal

CO-OCCURRING SUBSTANCES		PROTOCOL
Alcohol withdrawal and...	· benzodiazepine withdrawal	· *Day 1:* diazepam loading (for alcohol withdrawal)* · *Day 2 and on:* diazepam tapering (for benzodiazepine withdrawal).
	· barbiturate withdrawal (daily dose 500 mg or more)	· Phenobarbital loading.
	· barbiturate withdrawal (daily dose 200–450 mg)	OUTPATIENT: · *Day 1:* diazepam loading (for alcohol withdrawal) · *then:* phenobarbital tapering (after diazepam load completed and patient alert). INPATIENT: · Phenobarbital loading.
	· opioid withdrawal	· *First:* diazepam loading · *then:* clonidine after loading completed (for alcohol withdrawal).
Benzodiazepine withdrawal and...	· barbiturate withdrawal (daily dose 500 mg or more)	· *Day 1:* phenobarbital loading · *then:* diazepam tapering when load completed and patient alert (start at 1/3 to 1/2 the equivalent diazepam dose).
	· barbiturate withdrawal (daily dose 200–450 mg)	· *If diazepam equivalent < 50 mg/day:* phenobarbital tapering. · If patient has significant withdrawal symptoms, physician may need to titrate dose upwards or add small dose of diazepam, e.g., 5 mg tid.
	· barbiturate withdrawal (daily dose 200–450 mg)	· *If diazepam equivalent > 50 mg/day:* diazepam tapering as per high-dose protocol. · If patient has significant withdrawal symptoms, physician may need to titrate dose upwards or add small dose of phenobarbital, e.g., 15 mg bid.

continued on next page

Polysubstance withdrawal, continued

Benzodiazepine withdrawal and...		· If barbiturate dose 350–450 mg, consider phenobarbital tapering concurrently but use conservative doses and watch for oversedation (see example**).
	· opioid withdrawal	· Diazepam tapering and clonidine (lower doses may be required—both diazepam and clonidine are sedating).
Opioid withdrawal and...	· barbiturate withdrawal (daily dose 500 mg or more)	· Day 1: phenobarbital loading · then: clonidine when load complete, patient is alert and has symptoms of opioid withdrawal.
	· barbiturate withdrawal (daily dose 200–450 mg)	· Phenobarbital tapering and clonidine (watch for sedation).

*Diazepam should be used with caution in elderly patients, debilitated patients and those with a low serum albumin. The half-life of diazepam can be prolonged in these patients, leading to oversedation. Lorazepam is a safe and effective alternative for these patients because it has a shorter half-life and is not metabolized to an active metabolite in the liver. Therefore, it is less likely to cause oversedation. Lorazepam is given in a dose of 1–2 mg every 2 to 4 hours for CIWA greater than 10. It can be administered orally, intramuscularly or sublingually. Because of its shorter half-life, it cannot be used as a loading protocol but must be administered for the full duration of withdrawal.

CLINICAL MANAGEMENT EXAMPLES

Consider a patient who takes daily doses of 20 mg lorazepam, 20 capsules of Fiorinal®, 12 Tylenol #3® and 6 alcoholic drinks. The following management would be recommended:

· Admit, initiate phenobarbital loading (will prevent withdrawal from butalbital, lorazepam and alcohol).
· When phenobarbital loading is complete and the patient is alert, add small doses of clonidine if necessary for opioid withdrawal symptoms.
· Initiate inpatient or outpatient tapering with diazepam, using an initial dose of 1/2 to 1/3 the equivalent lorazepam dose (i.e., 40–50 mg diazepam per day).

21

COCAINE

Mechanism of action
Inhibits the pre-synaptic reuptake of dopamine, norepinephrine and serotonin. Dopamine is responsible for the euphoria, norepinephrine for the cardiovascular effects.

Psychoactive effects
· First few uses: Euphoria, sense of well-being, power and increased energy
· Chronic use: Brief "rush," followed by anxiety, agitation, paranoid thoughts

Pharmacology
· Routes of adminstration: Intranasal (snorting), smoking (crack, freebase), intravenous
· Onset of action: Within seconds for smoking, injection; slower with snorting
· Duration of action: Euphoria lasts 20 min
· Dose: Usually 20–50 mg per use. People who use heavily typically consume 100–250 mg or more per day.

Pattern of use
· Some people take cocaine in small amounts only in specific social settings and never meet DSM-IV criteria for dependence.
· People who use heavy amounts tend to use cocaine in binges lasting hours to days, followed by a period of abstinence. They frequently suffer multiple adverse physical, psychological and social consequences.
· Often used in combination with other drugs (such as alcohol, cannabis, benzodiazepines, heroin). These drugs may be used to "come down" after a cocaine binge.

CLINICAL PRESENTATIONS OF COCAINE USE
- Insomnia
- Depression, suicidal ideation
- Loss of libido
- Social problems: financial, legal, job difficulties, family violence
- May be seeking opioids and benzodiazepines (to relieve cocaine withdrawal symptoms, or to sell)
- Missed appointments

PHYSICAL SIGNS OF USE
- Weight loss (often marked)
- Injection and track marks
- Nasal septal perforations
- Sinusitis, rhinitis

SCREENING FOR COCAINE USE
- Ask all patients under the age of 60 about street drug use, including cocaine.
- Ask about cocaine use in presentations listed above.
- If cocaine use suspected, look for injection and track marks, and bruising at injection site.

Laboratory screening
Urine drug screening
- The cocaine parent has a very short half-life and is detectable by chromotography for several hours after use.
- Cocaine's metabolite benzoylecgonine is detectable by immunoassay for 3–5 days after use.

Hepatitis/HIV
- Elevated ALT and/or positive HCV serology suggest injection drug use.
- HIV testing is indicated in all people who use cocaine, because of increased risk of unsafe sexual practices and injection drug use.

Management of cocaine withdrawal

The symptoms of cocaine withdrawal are primarily psychological. Management of withdrawal is largely supportive—pharmacotherapy for withdrawal has not been shown to be effective. Benzodiazepines may be used for agitation.

ABBREVIATED DSM-IV CRITERIA

Dysphoric mood with 2 or more of: fatigue, nightmares, insomnia, increased appetite, psychomotor agitation or retardation.

TRIPHASIC ABSTINENCE SYNDROME

A triphasic abstinence syndrome has also been described.
· Phase 1: "Crash" phase. Profound fatigue, sleepiness after a cocaine binge; resolves within a few days.
· Phase 2: Withdrawal dysphoria. Dysphoria, insomnia, irritability, strong drug cravings, vivid dreams with nightmares of drug use. Symptoms last for 1–10 weeks. Patients are at high risk for relapse.
· Phase 3: Extinction. Anhedonia and cravings gradually diminish over weeks/ months. Periodic cravings for cocaine may last years, leaving the ex-user chronically at risk for relapse.

COUNSELLING

· Express your concern and recommend abstinence.
· Look for and treat medical and psychiatric complications (depression, hepatitis, etc.).
· Refer for formal treatment.

Cocaine-induced psychiatric disorders

Depression

Very common in people who use cocaine heavily, and may lead to suicide. Depression usually resolves within weeks of abstinence. Severe and persistent depression may require antidepressants.

Hallucinations

Tactile hallucinations are most common (e.g., formication [the feeling of bugs crawling under the skin]).

Delirium

Transient aggression, agitation, impaired judgment, and psychosis, during acute intoxication

Psychosis

Paranoid delusions or hallucinations that often subside within 1–2 weeks after cessation of cocaine, but may persist for months

Cocaine-induced medical complications

Infections

· HBV, HCV, HIV, cellulitis, endocarditis
· Risk: With injection drug use, sharing straws or other equipment, and unsafe sexual practices while intoxicated

Cardiovascular

Proposed mechanisms for cardiovascular injury include vasoconstriction, platelet aggregation, accelerated atherogenesis, hypertension and LV hypertrophy. Complications are more likely in patients with underlying cardiovascular risk factors, but can occur in young, healthy people:

· Myocardial infarction
· Congestive heart failure
· Tachyarrhythmias (ventricular and supraventricular)
· Coronary and aortic dissection
· Myocarditis, pericarditis, endocarditis

Neurological

Acute:

· Intracerebral and subarachnoid hemorrhages caused by severe, acute hypertension and vasospasm.
· Seizures are very common. They are typically grand mal, occurring within minutes of use.

Chronic:

· PET scan studies suggest long-term cortical damage in chronic users.

ENT (from intranasal use)

Nosebleeds, nasal septal perforations, hoarseness, loss of sense of smell.

Respiratory
Pulmonary edema, respiratory failure from smoked cocaine.

GI
Bowel ischemia caused by ingested cocaine, e.g., smuggling by body packers.

Rhabdomyolysis, renal failure
Rhabdomyolysis causes myoglobinuria that can lead to acute tubular necrosis and renal failure.

Note: Cocaine users presenting with chest pain, myalgia and fever should be investigated with cardiac enzymes, creatinine, CPK, myoglobin in urine and ECG.

Hormonal irregularities
Irregular menses, infertility, galactorrhea, loss of libido.

Obstetrical complications
Spontaneous abortion, low birthweight, abruptio placentae, placenta previa, prematurity, intrauterine CVA in neonate (see also Chapter 26, Pregnancy and Substance Use).

22

CANNABIS

Cannabis (marijuana and hashish) is the most commonly used illicit drug in Canada. Its active ingredient is tetrahydrocannabinol (THC). While most people who use cannabis do not experience problems, a small proportion develop psychological dependence and adverse psychiatric effects.

Medical uses
Synthetic cannabinoid, in the form of dronabinol (Marinol®), is used to treat nausea and vomiting caused by chemotherapy. Other uses are under investigation.

Pharmacology
· Route: Usually smoked; may be ingested in food
· Duration: Several hours

Psychoactive effects
Symptoms are usually mild with no medical complications.
· Relaxation, feeling of well-being
· Visual, auditory perceptions more vivid
· Changes in sense of time
· Difficulty concentrating
· Increased appetite

Acute adverse effects
· Panic attacks
· Supraventricular dysrhythmias
· Impaired co-ordination and reaction time

Cannabis withdrawal

Mild withdrawal symptoms can occur with heavy use (irritability, insomnia, anorexia). These resolve within several days; medical treatment is rarely required.

People who use cannabis heavily and daily may experience anxiety and irritability if they discontinue cannabis abruptly. This may continue for several weeks or longer, until the patient adjusts to the absence of the mood-levelling effects of cannabis. This does not represent physiological withdrawal.

Chronic psychiatric effects

· May precipitate latent schizophrenia in predisposed patients [39]
· Can exacerbate psychotic disorders
· Can exacerbate depression and anxiety

CLINICAL FEATURES/PRESENTATIONS OF CANNABIS DEPENDENCE
· Depression, anxiety
· Less time spent with friends or family
· Other drug use accompanying cannabis use
· Financial or legal problems

SCREENING FOR CANNABIS USE
· History: Ask all patients < 60 years of age about street drug use, including cannabis.
· Physical signs: Conjunctival injection; smell of cannabis on clothes.
· Investigation: If confirmation testing is indicated, chronic cannabis use can be detected for up to 30+ days in UDS.

MANAGEMENT OF CANNABIS USE
· Discuss health risks with adolescents experimenting with cannabis use.
· Assess for mood, anxiety and psychotic disorders in people who use cannabis daily.
· Advise abstinence and consider referring to an alcohol and drug program if cannabis use is causing psychiatric or social problems. In particular, patients with schizophrenia, major depression or other significant psychiatric disorders should be advised to remain abstinent.

Medical complications

Respiratory

Chronic smoking (> 3 days/week, for 6–8 weeks) causes mild airway obstruction that may not be reversible with abstinence.

Cardiac

Supraventricular dysrhythmias and tachycardia can aggravate existing cardiac conditions.

Reproductive

Males: Decreased testosterone, sperm count and motility have been reported.

Females: Shorter menstrual cycles, galactorrhea.

Obstetrical

Low birthweight babies

23

OTHER DRUGS

Over-the-counter medications: Dimenhydrinate (Gravol®)

Dimenhydrinate is an antihistamine used in the treatment of nausea. Misuse and dependence are not common but do occur. Other sedating antihistamines may carry similar risks.

PSYCHOACTIVE EFFECTS
· Therapeutic doses: Mild sedation
· Higher doses: Hallucinations and confusion

TOLERANCE, WITHDRAWAL
Tolerance can develop to the psychoactive effects of dimenhydrinate. A withdrawal syndrome has been described, with anxiety and nausea lasting 7–10 days. Withdrawal is not common and has no serious medical complications.

Over-the-counter medications: Codeine preparations

The most commonly used over-the-counter (OTC) codeine preparations are Tylenol® #1 (acetaminophen + 8 mg codeine) and 222s (ASA + 8 mg codeine).

SCREENING FOR OTC DRUG USE
Ask about OTC drug use as part of the routine substance use history.

Anabolic steroids

Steroids are used to enhance athletic performance, increase muscle bulk and improve appearance. Doses used by weightlifters and bodybuilders are often 10–100 times higher than therapeutic doses. Steroids are taken orally,

intramuscularly or topically as a gel or cream. People who use steroids sometimes "stack" doses (combine different types of steroids) or "pyramid" doses
(cyclically increase then decrease their doses).

ADVERSE EFFECTS

Psychiatric
· Aggression ("steroid rage")
· Depression, anxiety, hypomania; frequently suicidal ideation
· Psychosis

Cardiovascular
· Elevates LDL, lowers HDL levels
· May be thrombogenic and directly toxic to the myocardium
· Case reports of MI, cerebrovascular accidents, pulmonary emboli

Endocrine
· Women: irregular menses, masculinizing effects such as acne, deep voice, hir-
sutism, male pattern-baldness
· Men: testicular atrophy and gynecomastia
· Endocrine effects not always reversible, particularly in women

Hepatic
· Elevations in liver transaminases, toxic hepatitis, hepatocellular carcinoma

Infections
· HBV, HCV, HIV if needle-sharing

STEROID DEPENDENCE
There are case reports of people who use steroids meeting criteria for dependence, including preoccupation with acquiring and using the drug, and escalat-
ing use. The prevalence of steroid dependence is unknown.

WITHDRAWAL
Fatigue, depression and craving for steroids have been reported in people who
use steroids heavily. Symptoms may resolve within days but there are case reports
of depression lasting for months.

SCREENING FOR STEROID USE

· Ask adolescents and young adults about steroid use if they are engaged in competitive sports such as weightlifting, football, competitive track or swimming.
· Ask female athletes about oral contraceptive use—sometimes used in huge doses for their anabolic effects.
· Start by asking about use of performance aids (e.g., protein supplements, creatine, growth hormone supplement) and/or androstenedione (a readily available steroid precursor) and if any acquaintances use steroids.
· Be alert to common symptoms, behaviours and physical signs (see below).

Clinical presentations of steroid use

COMMON SYMPTOMS AND BEHAVIOURS	PHYSICAL SIGNS
. Appetite changes	. Acne
· Menstrual abnormalities	· Striae, gynecomastia
· Muscle aches	· Marked increases in muscle bulk
· Changes in libido	· Needle marks
· Psychiatric: irritability, aggressiveness, depression, delusions, mania	· Hirsutism, deepened voice in females
· Requests for steroids, medications to combat side-effects, or tamoxifen (to reduce gynecomastia)	

ASSESSMENT OF STEROID USE: LABORATORY ABNORMALITIES

· Elevated liver transaminases (GGT unaffected)
· Elevated CPK
· Increased hematocrit and hemoglobin
· Decreased LH and FSH
· Testosterone levels: increased if exogenous testosterone is used; decreased if other steroids are used
· Abnormal sperm count test

Note: Intensive weightlifting can elevate ALT, AST and CPK even without steroid use.

⏽ MANAGEMENT OF STEROID DEPENDENCE
· Assess for adverse psychiatric and physical effects.
· Depression may require treatment with antidepressant medications and psychiatric care.
· Counsel on health effects of steroids.
· Address body image issues.
· Advise abstinence and avoidance of gyms where steroids readily available.
· Encourage the patient to develop alternative activities.
· Advise against needle-sharing.
· Refer for additional counselling if necessary.

Inhalants

Inhalants are volatile solvents such as gasoline or glue. They are used mainly by adolescents from disadvantaged groups, such as aboriginal youth, or in remote areas where other drugs are less available.

PHARMACOLOGY
· Route: Inhaled
· Onset: 3–5 min
· Duration: 3–6 h

PSYCHOACTIVE EFFECTS
Similar to alcohol intoxication: slurred speech, incoordination, aggression, agitation, disinhibition, euphoria. May cause transient psychotic symptoms including hallucinations and delusions. People may repeatedly inhale the solvent to prolong the intoxication. Intoxication is followed by fatigue and headache for several hours.

WITHDRAWAL
Chronic use can cause a withdrawal syndrome similar to alcohol: tremor, GI symptoms, malaise.

DEPENDENCE
Inhalants can cause dependence, with compulsive use and use despite harm.

ACUTE MEDICAL COMPLICATIONS
· Dysrhythmias related to catecholamine release

· Asphyxia, aspiration
· Acute encephalopathy (drowsiness, loss of consciousness)
· Trauma

(P) MANAGEMENT OF ACUTE INHALANT COMPLICATIONS
· ABCs, oxygen
· Monitoring and treatment of dysrhythmias
· Benzodiazepines for agitation

CHRONIC NEUROLOGICAL COMPLICATIONS
Similar to alcohol, but more severe with earlier onset:
· Cerebellar degeneration
· Peripheral neuropathy
· Cognitive deficits

OTHER COMPLICATIONS
· Hepatotoxicity
· Cardiomyopathy
· Fanconi-like syndrome

(A) SCREENING AND ASSESSMENT FOR INHALANT USE
· Ask adolescents from at-risk groups about solvent use.
· Assess for adverse psychiatric and physical effects.

(P) MANAGEMENT OF INHALANT USE
· Recommend abstinence and refer to treatment program.

Hallucinogens

Lysergic acid diethylamide (LSD), mescaline and psilocybins (a genus of mushrooms) are hallucinogens, i.e., they cause marked perceptual changes including hallucinations. Other drugs, such as cannabis and MDMA, also have hallucinogenic properties but are discussed in separate chapers.

PHARMACOLOGY
· Route: Oral
· Onset: 15–60 min
· Duration: Several hours

PSYCHOACTIVE EFFECTS
· Cognitive and sensory distortions
· Delusions, hallucinations
· Panic attacks and delirium
· Delusional patients may exhibit bizarre or dangerous behaviour

WITHDRAWAL
Psychoactive effects become less intense with daily use. No withdrawal syndrome
has been identified.

DEPENDENCE
Hallucinogens do not appear to cause dependence.

CHRONIC ADVERSE EFFECTS
Flashbacks
Brief episodes of hallucinations occurring months or years after last use; patient
has no hallucinations between episodes.

Persistent psychosis
Not clear whether hallucinogens cause a persistent psychosis, or unmask latent
schizophrenia.

🐦 ASSESSMENT FOR HALLUCINOGEN USE
· Ask all patients < 60 about street drug use including hallucinogens.
· Ask regular users of hallucinogens about symptoms of psychosis.

🅟 MANAGEMENT OF HALLUCINOGEN USE
· Advise abstinence; refer to alcohol and drug programs.

Stimulants: Amphetamines

Amphetamines include amphetamine, methamphetamine, crystal methamphetamine ("ice") and methylenedioxyamphetamine (MDA). Adverse cardiovascular
and psychiatric effects are similar to those of cocaine. (see also Chapter 21, Cocaine)

PHARMACOLOGY
Amphetamines stimulate the release of norepinephrine and dopamine. They act
on both alpha- and beta-adrenergic receptors.

· Route: Oral, intravenous, inhalation
· Onset: Within 30 min
· Duration: Several hours

PSYCHOACTIVE EFFECTS
Amphetamines cause euphoria similar to cocaine but with a slower onset and longer duration of action. As with cocaine, tolerance to these euphoric effects develops quickly.

ACUTE MEDICAL COMPLICATIONS
Cardiovascular
Like cocaine, amphetamines cause vasoconstriction and cardiac stimulation. This can result in hypertension, tachycardia, dysrhythmias, MI and cerebrovascular accident.

Psychiatric
Hyperactivity, agitation, paranoia, delusions, hallucinations

Neurological
Seizures, coma

Other
Hyperthermia

🝒 MANAGEMENT OF STIMULANT USE
· Approach similar to that for cocaine
· May use activated charcoal for an overdose of oral amphetamines

LONG-TERM PSYCHIATRIC EFFECTS
· Insomnia
· Depression
· Psychosis, esp. paranoid delusions
· Suicidal and/or homicidal behaviour
· Stereotypy
· Possible long-term neurological damage causing difficulties in memory and cognition

SCREENING

See Chapter 6, Laboratory Detection of Alcohol and Other Drug Use. Amphetamines are detectable on urine drug screen but cross-reacts with pseudoephedrine, chlorpromazine and other drugs.

Stimulants: MDMA ("ecstasy")

MDMA (3,4-methylenedioxymethamphetamine) is a "hallucinogenic amphetamine" with clinical effects similar to both stimulants and hallucinogens. MDMA is popular at "rave" parties and other social settings.

PHARMACOLOGY

MDMA stimulates release of dopamine, serotonin and, to a lesser extent, epinephrine and norepinephrine. It causes a variable, reversible depletion of serotonin.
· Route: Oral (tablets)
· Typical dose: 100 mg
· Onset of effects: 30–60 min
· Peak effects: 90 min
· Duration: 4–6 h (longer with higher doses)

PSYCHOACTIVE EFFECTS

People who use ecstasy experience euphoria, heightened sensuality and positive social effects: they feel less shy and more affectionate and empathic. Psychoactive effects are likely mediated by dopamine and serotonin.

LONG-TERM EFFECTS

Small studies on people who no longer use ecstasy suggest damage to neurons that release serotonin, which may lead to long-term memory impairment and other neuropsychiatric problems. [40]

DEPENDENCE

Most patients use ecstasy only intermittently. However, its pharmacological properties and case reports suggest the potential for abuse and dependence. While people quickly develop tolerance with regular use, they do not experience withdrawal symptoms on cessation of using the drug.

🔊 SCREENING FOR MDMA USE
· Ask all adolescents and young adults about illicit drug use, including ecstasy.

MDMA is detectable by urine drug screen but cross-reacts with other drugs (e.g., pseudoephedrine). See Chapter 6, Laboratory Detection of Alcohol and Other Drug Use.

MANAGEMENT OF MDMA USE
· Provide health information to people who use ecstasy occasionally (emphasize the need for hydration and rest when dancing).
· Recommend abstinence for patients with psychiatric problems such as depression.
· Recommend abstinence and refer to a treatment program for patients who have had medical, social or psychiatric problems related to ecstasy use.

ACUTE MEDICAL COMPLICATIONS
Pharmacological toxicity is caused by serotonin excess; sympathomimetic effects are generally mild. MDMA has greater toxicity in patients taking medications that increase serotonin concentrations, such as SSRIs or sumatriptan. MDMA also interacts with MAOIs and with ritonavir (Norvir®). Individuals who take MDMA at "raves" risk dehydration, electrolyte imbalance and other complications if they engage in prolonged physical activity without fluid replacement. Deaths due to malignant hyperthermia have been reported.

General
Hyperthermia, mydriasis, diaphoresis

Cardiovascular
Tachycardia, dysrhythmias, hypertension

Fluid and electrolyte
Dehydration, hyponatremia, hyperkalemia

Psychiatric
Anxiety, agitation, delirium, panic, dysphoria, hallucinations, paranoia

Cardiovascular
Chest pain, ventricular dysrhythmias

Neurological
· Hyperreflexia, myoclonus, jaw-clenching (bruxisms), rigidity, seizures
· Serotonergic syndrome: Altered mental status, agitation, fever > 38°C, myoclonus, hyperreflexia. Improves in 24 hours.

Other
· Hyperthermia and dehydration may lead to rhabdomyolysis, acute renal failure, disseminated intravascular coagulation.
· Cerebral/pulmonary edema and intracranial bleeds have also been reported.

Ⓟ MANAGEMENT OF MDMA OVERDOSE
· ABCs
· Supplemental oxygen
· Cardiac monitoring
· Specific treatment for hyperthermia, dehydration, rhabdomyolysis
· Serotonergic syndrome: symptomatic—cooling with wet blankets

Stimulants: Methylphenidate (Ritalin®)
PHARMACOLOGY
· Route: Usually oral; can be iv or snorted
· Dose: 60 mg/day max. therapeutic dose. Heavy users may take several hundred mg/day.
· Clinical effects and complications: Similar to cocaine, amphetamines

MANAGEMENT
Similar to cocaine, amphetamines

MISUSE POTENTIAL
Children with ADHD rarely become dependent on methylphenidate. Untreated ADHD appears to be a risk factor for problem substance use, and treatment reduces that risk. People who misuse methylphenidate are usually older adults with a history of polysubstance problems. Sometimes they misuse their children's methylphenidate.

PREVENTION OF MISUSE
Use alternatives to methylphenidate (e.g., bupropion, venlafaxine) for:
· Children whose parents have polysubstance use problems
· Older adolescents who have polysubstance use problems or who may be misusing methylphenidate
· Adults with a substance use disorder who claim to have adult ADHD.

Ketamine ("Special K")

PHARMACOLOGY

Ketamine is a short-acting general anaesthetic, producing dissociative anaesthesia followed by delirium. It is commonly diverted from veterinary sources.

· Route: Primarily oral, snorted, rarely parenteral
· Onset: CNS depression begins within 15–30 min., depending on route
· Duration of action: About 60 min. Amnesia may persist for 2 h following recovery from anaesthesia.

PSYCHOACTIVE EFFECTS

· Dissociation that can be pleasant, dreamlike or frightening. Some people report confusion, visual hallucinations, out-of-body experiences and an altered sense of time.
· Higher doses produce drowsiness, unconsciousness.
· Tolerance to the desired effects occurs relatively quickly, leading to dose escalation. No withdrawal symptoms have been reported.

SCREENING AND MANAGEMENT

See MDMA (see pages 132–133)

ACUTE MEDICAL COMPLICATIONS

Ketamine can cause dangerous respiratory depression when combined with other respiratory depressants such as alcohol, benzodiazepines or opioids.

Cardiorespiratory

Dysrhythmias, respiratory depression

Neurological

Seizures, myoclonus, polyneuropathy, increased intracranial pressure

Psychiatric

Delirium: Hallucinations, vivid dreams

Ⓟ ACUTE MANAGEMENT OF KETAMINE USE

Secure airway, maintain circulation, intubate if necessary.

Phencyclidine (PCP, "angel dust")

PHARMACOLOGY

Phencyclidine is a dissociative anaesthetic that affects a number of neuro-transmitter systems, including dopamine, serotonin, GABA and NMDA. It has anticholinergic effects, and it can cause hypertension and vasospasm due to catecholamine release or blockade of reuptake.

· Route: Intranasal, smoking
· Dose: 100 mg–1 g over 24 hours
· Onset: Minutes
· Duration of action: 4–6 hours

INTOXICATION

· Acute psychotic symptoms: Illusions and hallucinations, delusions, paranoia, catatonia, mutism, garbled speech
· Disorientation, confusion
· Violent or dangerous behaviour
· Sedative effects, increased by alcohol and other CNS depressants

CHRONIC EFFECTS

May cause memory impairment, depression

PHYSICAL SIGNS

· Fever
· Nystagmus (horizontal, vertical, rotary)
· Miosis
· Increased deep tendon reflexes
· Hypertension, tachycardia
· Blank stare

ACUTE MEDICAL COMPLICATIONS

· Seizures, focal or generalized (cerebral vasoconstriction)
· Hyperpyrexia (anticholinergic effects)
· Dose-dependent hypertension
· Hypoglycemia
· Rhabdomyolysis (seizure, trauma, muscle rigidity)
· Coma
· Death from seizures, trauma, cardiovascular collapse

🅟 MANAGEMENT OF PCP USE
· Quiet room if possible
· Activated charcoal (traps ionized PCP in stomach)
· Hydration; correct hypoglycemia
· Psychosis: Haloperidol 1–4 mg po, im q 2-4 h, or other antipsychotics (avoid phenothiazines because of anticholinergic effects)
· Seizures: Intravenous benzodiazepines
· Agitation: Diazepam or lorazepam; if severe, iv benzodiazepines; if venous access difficult, use im lorazepam or midazolam
· Other specific treatments: External cooling for hyperthermia, phentolamine or nitroprusside for severe hypertension; hydration, diuretics, urinary alkalinazation for rhabdomyolysis

IDENTIFICATION
Urine drug screen (cross-reactivity with dextromethorphan, diphenhydramine)

Gamma-Hydroxybutyrate (GHB)
PHARMACOLOGY
GHB is a structural analogue and metabolite of GABA (a neurotransmitter with neuroinhibitory effects). GHB is often used as a performance-enhancing drug, because it causes release of growth hormone.
· Route: Oral
· Onset: Within 15 min.
· Duration: Wake up abruptly within 4–6 h

PSYCHOACTIVE EFFECTS
GHB has sedative effects similar to those of alcohol and other sedatives. Disinhibition and euphoria characterize mild intoxication. At higher doses, patients may become somnolent, waking up abruptly after several hours. Alcohol and other sedatives potentiate its effects. GHB has a narrow margin of safety; doubling the euphoric dose can cause coma. GHB is also used as a "date-rape" drug, leading to potentially fatal overdoses.
· Lower doses: Sedation and short-term amnesia
· Higher doses: Coma, myoclonus, bradycardia

SCREENING

Refer to MDMA (see pages 132–133). GHB present in urine drug screen for < 12 h (by chromotography). *Warn patients not to mix GHB with alcohol.*

DEPENDENCE

Case reports suggest that GHB can cause psychological dependence.

WITHDRAWAL

GHB can cause a withdrawal syndrome similar to sedative withdrawal. Withdrawal has been described among people who have used doses of 40–150 g/day for more than 6 weeks.

· Onset: 1–6 hours after last dose
· Duration: 5–15 days

CLINICAL FEATURES OF GHB WITHDRAWAL
· Autonomic instability: Tremor, diaphoresis, hypertension, tachycardia
· Seizures
· Auditory and visual hallucinations
· Agitation, confusion, delirium

MANAGEMENT OF GHB WITHDRAWAL
Barbiturates (phenobarbital, pentobarbital) or benzodiazepines (lorazepam, diazepam). Barbiturates may be more effective than benzodiazepines. High doses may be necessary. Titrate to control symptoms; taper over 1–2 weeks. Antipsychotics may also be required.

ACUTE MEDICAL COMPLICATIONS

General
· Hypothermia

Cardiovascular
· Bradycardia (usually asymptomatic)
· Atrial fibrillation (rare)
· Hypotension if alcohol co-ingested

Respiratory
· Respiratory depression, particularly if alcohol co-ingested
· Airway obstruction due to loss of gag reflex, flaccid tongue, vomitus

Neurological
· Somnolence leading to coma within 30 min
· Hypotonia, dilated pupils
· Myoclonus, sometimes mistakenly attributed to seizure activity
· Seizures (not common)

GI
Salivation, nausea, vomiting

Psychiatric
Emergence from coma may be associated with delirium (confusion, combative-ness), vomiting and myoclonic jerking.

🅿 ACUTE MANAGEMENT OF GHB USE
· May require airway support, oxygen
· iv access
· Cardiac monitoring
· Admit if still symptomatic after 6 h
· If known ingestion of large amount (e.g., suicide attempt), nasogastric activated charcoal (protect airway if gag reflex absent)

Emergence delirium
Usually brief, resolving without intervention. Avoid benzodiazepines if possible as it may make it difficult to assess level of consciousness.

Flunitrazepam (Rohypnol®)
Flunitrazepam (not legally available in Canada) is a potent benzodiazepine. It has been used as a "date rape drug," although alcohol remains the most common drug associated with sexual assault.

PHARMACOLOGY
Duration of action: Recovery within 12 h

CLINICAL EFFECTS
Retrograde amnesia, decreased inhibition, sedation

OVERDOSE MANAGEMENT
Similar to that of benzodiazepines

Dextromethorphan

PHARMACOLOGY

Lower doses can cause euphoria and mild sensory disturbances. Higher doses (above 7.5 mg/kg) can cause misperceptions, hallucinations and other psychotic symptoms. Effects are similar to those of dissociative anaesthetics such as ketamine and phencyclidine.

· Duration: 4–6 hours
· Route: Oral usually. If powder obtained from manufacturer, can be taken by parenteral route.
· Drug interactions: Severe serotonergic syndrome (fever, hypertension, dysrhythmias) when combined with MAOI. Ingestion of large amounts of dextromethorphan may cause toxicity from other ingredients such as decongestants and acetaminophen.

P EMERGENCY TREATMENT FOR DEXTROMETHORPHAN USE
Effects may be partially reversible with naloxone.

24

INTOXICATION AND OVERDOSE: ALCOHOL, OPIOIDS, BENZODIAZEPINES, COCAINE, METHANOL, ETHYLENE GLYCOL

Approach to suspected overdose

Key principles

· "ABCs" to ensure cardiovascular and respiratory stability. *THEN look for clues* to the depressed level of consciousness.
· *Do not assume that alcohol or drugs are the sole cause of a patient's coma.*
· Consider trauma, metabolic abnormalities, other drug use, infections, cardiovascular events, seizures, hypoxemia or hypercapnea.
· Address substance use once overdose is cleared:
  – Treat withdrawal.
  – Screen for depression and suicidal ideation.
  – Recommend treatment options for psychiatric problems and/or problem substance use.

ABCs for the comatose patient

AIRWAY

· Ensure the airway is unobstructed and well protected. If oral airway tolerated, leave it in.
· Intubate if the airway is compromised.
· Do not hyperextend the neck until C-spine fracture has been ruled out.

BREATHING
· Check for adequacy of air entry, cyanosis, adventitial breath sounds, deviated trachea, stridor, symmetry of chest movement, evidence of chest wall trauma.

CIRCULATION/CARDIAC
· Check blood pressure, BP asymmetry (aortic dissection), HR, JVR, heart sounds/murmurs, perfusion of extremities.
· IV NS or Ringer's if hypotensive or dehydrated. Blood products for blood loss; may require volume expansion e.g., pentastarch (Pentaspan®).
· Do not infuse large amounts of glucose-containing solutions such as D5W until thiamine has been given (unless coma NYD could be caused by hypoglycemia).

P PROTOCOL FOR TREATING THE COMATOSE PATIENT
· Fingerprick for capillary glucose level
· Give 50 cc D50W iv push
· Naloxone 2 mg iv (lower dose if suspect opioid dependence, see pages 146–147)
· Thiamine 50–100 mg im
· Arterial blood gases
· Send blood for CBC, electrolytes, urea, creatinine, glucose, troponin/cardiac enzymes, liver transaminases, INR, bilirubin, albumin, calcium, phosphorus, magnesium, TSH, serum osmolality, culture
· Blood drug screen (alcohol, acetaminophen, ASA levels, methanol, ethylene glycol)
· ECG
· UDS
· CK if suspect seizure or lying on ground for indeterminate length of time
· Chest X-ray
· C-spine X-ray if concerned about C-spine integrity

P GENERAL SURVEY AFTER STABILIZATION
· Temperature
· GI (check for peritoneal signs)
· Neurotrauma screen (substance use places patient at risk for falls, fights):
  – Maintain C-spine stability until fracture ruled out
  – Check for contusions on head, body
  – Pupils; extraocular movements if possible

– Battle sign
– Discharge from nose and/or ears
– Focal neurological deficits or signs
· Check skin for clues: abscesses, track marks, bleeding, petechiae, jaundice
· Other clues: Medic Alert® bracelet, medications in pockets or purses, wallet for medication lists and physicians' cards
· If available, obtain collateral history from family and friends.
· Chart the Glasgow Coma Scale score.
· If coma persists, do CT scan to rule out subdural hematoma, even if no signs of trauma or localizing neurological deficits. CT scan also useful to diagnose subarachnoid hemorrhage, meningitis or encephalitis.

❸ AFTER THE PATIENT HAS REGAINED CONSCIOUSNESS
· Ask about depression, suicidal ideation. Consult psychiatry if indicated.
· Explain the risk of death from overdose.
· Mention treatment options:
– Outpatient, inpatient counselling programs
– Mutual aid groups such as NA
– Methadone treatment for opioid dependence
· Recommend follow-up with family physician or addiction medicine specialist.
· Have plan for treating withdrawal.
· Once medically stable, send to withdrawal management centre if patient does not have a supportive home environment.

The patient who is drowsy and alcohol-intoxicated

KEY PRINCIPLE

If drowsiness is out of keeping with reported alcohol intake and BAC, look for other causes. For interpretation of BAC see page 21.

CAUSES OF DROWSINESS IN THE PATIENT WHO IS INTOXICATED
· Trauma: Head injury (e.g., subdural hematoma)
· Intoxications: Alcohol, methanol, ethylene glycol, sedatives, opioids, ASA, acetaminophen
· Withdrawal: Delirium tremens (but usually agitated)
· Encephalopathy: Hepatic, Wernicke's

· Cardiorespiratory: Hypoxia, dysrhythmia, MI
· Neurological: Seizure (postictal), subarachnoid hemorrhage, CVA
· Infections: Meningitis, brain abscess, endocarditis, sepsis
· Metabolic: Severe dehydration, hyper- or hypoglycemia, acidosis, other electrolyte abnormalities, hypercalcemia
· Other: Anemia because of blood loss, hypothermia

HISTORY
· Recent head trauma
· Alcohol consumption including methanol, ethylene glycol
· Other drugs (esp. opioids, benzodiazepines)
· Medications and compliance
· Past health

Note: Collateral history is very important.

PHYSICAL EXAMINATION
· Vital signs
· Hydration status
· Look for signs of head trauma
· Neurological examination:
  - Orientation, level of consciousness
  - Pupil size and reactivity, fundi, extra-ocular movements
  - Tone, power, reflexes
  - Gait, asterixis

LABORATORY INVESTIGATIONS
· Blood toxicology screen for alcohol, acetaminophen, ASA, methanol, ethylene glycol
· CBC, electrolytes, creatinine, glucose, calcium, magnesium, serum osmolality, AST, ALT, bilirubin, albumin, amylase, INR; +/– cardiac enzymes, TSH
· ABG, ECG, +/– CXR
· Urine drug screen

MONITORING IN THE ER
Drowsiness because of alcohol resolves quickly as the BAC declines. If preliminary work-up is negative and the patient is stable, yet doubt remains about the cause of drowsiness:

· Observe for several hours.
· Do vital signs and neurological vitals every hour: BP, HR, pupils, best verbal and motor response

CT SCANNING FOR HEAD TRAUMA
CT scanning should be considered in patients who present with alcohol or other drug intoxication and minor head trauma (brief loss of consciousness following trauma, but normal neurological exam and Glasgow Coma Scale score of ≥ 15). One recent study found that 13% of such patients had a positive CT scan (e.g., cerebral contusion, subdural hematoma). [41]

Opioid overdose
FACTORS CONTRIBUTING TO OVERDOSE
· Dose and potency of opioid
· Parenteral administration
· Lack of tolerance to opioids (tolerance can decline significantly within 3 days of last use)
· Taken shortly before onset of sleep
· Lack of pain
· Other sedative and psychoactive drug use
· Age, illness (esp. cardiorespiratory)

CLINICAL FEATURES OF OPIOID OVERDOSE
Opioid overdose presents with a clinical triad of respiratory depression, CNS depression and miosis.
· Drowsiness, "nodding off"
· Slurred, drawling speech
· Pinpoint pupils
· Ataxia, emotional lability
· Respiratory rate < 12/min
· Bradycardia, hypotension
· May progress to coma (slowly with methadone; rapidly with parenteral opioids)
· May be complicated by non-cardiogenic pulmonary edema

ⓟ PROTOCOL FOR MANAGEMENT OF OPIOID OVERDOSE

Naloxone dosing

· If the patient has respiratory depression, give 2 mg naloxone iv.
· If no respiratory depression and suspect opioid dependence (e.g., track marks), give naloxone 0.01 mg/kg body weight to avoid precipitating severe withdrawal.
· If no response after initial dose, repeat naloxone 2–4 mg every 2–3 min.
· If no response after 10–20 mg naloxone, search for other causes of the coma.
· If patient responds to naloxone, infuse at 2/3 the effective dose per hour.
· To prevent a drop in naloxone levels, give a bolus of 1/2 the effective dose 15–20 min after starting the infusion.
· Titrate dose up or down to avoid severe withdrawal while maintaining respiratory status.
· Infuse for 12–24 h (longer with methadone overdose—see page 147).
· Discontinue infusion after 12–24 h, if the patient has adequate spontaneous respirations and is alert.
· Once infusion is discontinued, observe in ICU for several hours (longer with methadone overdose).
· Continue observation for up to 12 h on the medical ward (longer with methadone overdose).
· If patient shows signs of renarcotization, resume the infusion. This suggests the patient may have taken a long-acting opioid such as methadone.
· Watch for and treat withdrawal.

Intubation

· Intubation can be an alternative to naloxone. Intubation avoids risks associated with naloxone while protecting the airway.
· Intubation is necessary if:
  –Respirations are inadequate (RR < 12; hypercapnea; persistent desaturation despite supplemental oxygen).
  –Patient fails to respond to naloxone within 2 min.

NALOXONE: PRECAUTIONS

· The duration of action of naloxone is much shorter than that of opioid agonists. Its peak effect is 5–15 min and duration of action is only 60 min. Patients who respond to naloxone must not be discharged until opioid effects have completely worn off.

· There have been case reports of ventricular dysrhythmias and cardiac arrest in patients with naloxone-induced opioid withdrawal, although some of these patients may also have been withdrawing from alcohol and other substances.
· Naloxone-induced withdrawal may cause the patient to become agitated and leave against medical advice.
· Be prepared for withdrawal-induced emesis.
· If no vascular access, naloxone may be given through other routes: sc, im or endotracheal.

Note: sc and im routes have erratic absorption.

Methadone overdose

Because of its long half-life, methadone overdose has a more gradual onset of coma (the patient may appear somewhat drowsy, and drift off into sleep). Deaths have been reported 72 h or longer after a methadone overdose.

P MANAGEMENT OF METHADONE OVERDOSE
· Continue intubation and/or naloxone infusion for up to 48–72 h.
· Closely observe respirations and level of consciousness for another 12 h in the ICU and 12 h on the general medical floor after last dose of antagonist is given.

Meperidine toxicity

Repeated parenteral doses of meperidine can lead to accumulation of normeperidine, which can cause seizures and delirium. Naloxone blocks normeperidine and should be administered when meperidine toxicity is suspected.

Benzodiazepine intoxication and overdose

Clinical features of benzodiazepine intoxication and overdose

Intoxication	· Resembles alcohol intoxication: Sedation, slurred speech, drowsiness, agitation, disinhibition and rage
Overdose	· Sedation
	· Can cause respiratory, cardiac arrest if given rapidly iv (> 5 mg/min)
	· Respiratory depression, possible death if: –Combined with alcohol or other CNS depressants or –Severe cardiorespiratory disease

TREATMENT WITH FLUMAZENIL

Flumazenil is a specific antidote to benzodiazepine overdose.

Note: The use of flumazenil should be restricted to reversal of iatrogenic benzodiazepine overdose (e.g., when a nurse or physician administers an excess benzodiazepine dose to a hospitalized patient) because:

· Flumazenil can trigger severe withdrawal, including seizures and dysrhythmias, in patients physically dependent on benzodiazepines.

· It is usually impossible to tell if an overdose patient is physically dependent.

· Benzodiazepine overdose is rarely fatal unless combined with other drugs.

· Deaths have been reported when flumazenil has been administered to patients who have taken an overdose of tricyclic antidepressants.

PROTOCOL FOR FLUMAZENIL

· 0.3 mg iv over 30 s

· Repeat at 60 s intervals until effect achieved or a total of 2.0 mg has been given.

· If no effect, drowsiness probably has other causes.

· If improvement, maintain iv infusion 0.1–0.4 mg/h (titrate to level of arousal).

Cocaine intoxication and overdose

CLINICAL FEATURES

See "Acute Medical Complications" of amphetamines, page 131.

🅟 GENERAL PROTOCOL FOR COCAINE INTOXICATION AND OVERDOSE

Provide basic life support and close monitoring of vital signs and neurological status.

Seizures
· Diazepam iv is treatment of choice.
· Add pentobarbital or phenytoin if seizures continue.
· For intractable seizures, use general anaesthesia and paralysis to facilitate ventilation (but this does not stop seizure activity).

Hypertension
· Should be treated only if severe
· Propanolol 1 mg iv q 2 min to a total of 8 mg (note that β-blockers may result in a paradoxical rise in BP because of unopposed α-adrenergic activity)
· Labetalol may be superior (works as both an α- and β-blocker)
· Other options: Phentolamine (α-adrenergic blocker); nifedipine, nitroglycerin; sodium nitroprusside drip if very severe

Tachyarrhythmias
· Atrial: Observation (often resolve spontaneously); propanolol; verapamil
· Ventricular: Propanolol; lidocaine (but lowers seizure threshold), other antidysrhythmics. Refer to ACLS protocols.

Chest pain
· Order serial ECGs and cardiac enzymes
· If fever and myalgias, order urine myoglobulin to rule out rhabdomyolysis
· Observe for 24 h

Note: CK/CKMB can be elevated because of motor activity and tachycardia. Often non-specific baseline ECG abnormalities make ECG interpretation difficult.

Cocaine-induced MI
· Thrombolytics are controversial. There have been case reports of intracerebral hemorrhage, and the prognosis is generally good in cocaine-induced MI, so clear evidence of benefit is lacking.
· β-blockers should be avoided because they cause unopposed α-activity.
· Use of labetalol, a combined α- and β-blocker (5:1 β to α) is controversial.
· Usual treatments (ASA, NTG, α-blockers and calcium channel blockers) may be used.

Agitation

Reassurance, sl lorazepam

Psychosis, delirium

Antipsychotic medication

Hyperthermia

· Control agitation, seizures.
· Initiate rapid cooling (cooling blanket, cbi); monitor vital signs closely.

Acute tubular necrosis

· Forced alkaline diuresis
· Fluid and electrolyte treatment
· May require dialysis

Body packing and body stuffing

A body packer smuggles drugs by concealing packages in vagina, rectum or stomach, in sealed packages (e.g., triple-wrapped condom balloons).

A body stuffer quickly swallows a package to avoid charges of possession.

COMPLICATIONS

· Mechanical obstruction at gastric outlet or splenic flexure
· Overdose due to leakage or rupture of package. Body stuffers are at greater risk for leakage than body packers.

INVESTIGATION

· Abdominal films may show obstruction, or multiple radiographic defects

🅐 MANAGEMENT OF BODY PACKING

· Search for packages in body cavities.
· Usually patients are placed in a "dry" cell (i.e., holding area with no toilet) until package excreted.
· If patient shows signs of drug toxicity: nasogastric lavage, activated charcoal. Surgical removal sometimes necessary.
· If mechanical obstruction: surgery.

Methanol, ethylene glycol overdose

Methanol and ethylene glycol are found in antifreeze, window-washer fluid and other products. They may be mistaken for alcohol if placed in non-labelled containers. Disadvantaged populations may drink them if alcohol is not available.

CLINICAL FEATURES OF INTOXICATION
Clinically indistinguishable from alcohol intoxication, until complications occur (blindness, renal failure)

LABORATORY DETECTION
Serum methanol, ethylene glycol levels are the most accurate and reliable methods of detection.

Osmolar gap
· Ethanol, methanol and ethylene glycol create an osmolar gap, therefore this test is not helpful in distinguishing among the 3.
· Osmolar gap may be normal if tested within minutes of ingestion, or after complete metabolism hours later.

Calculation of osmolar gap
Serum osmolarity = 2Na + BUN + glucose (mmol/L)

Osmolar gap = (measured − calculated) serum osmolarity. Range of normal gap: −10 to +10 mOsm/L

METABOLIC ACIDOSIS
Alcohol does not cause metabolic acidosis because it is quickly and completely metabolized to carbon dioxide and water. Therefore metabolic acidosis in an intoxicated patient requires urgent investigation.

Methanol and ethylene glycol do not cause metabolic acidosis until hours after ingestion, esp. if alcohol has been consumed in addition to these agents (alcohol slows their metabolism).

IDENTIFICATION
Order serum methanol and ethylene glycol levels if:
· Intoxicated patient has a metabolic acidosis
· Patient is not certain of the source of his or her alcohol (beer, wine or spirits)
· Patient is comatose and unable to give a history.

🅿 PROTOCOL FOR METHANOL AND ETHYLENE GLYCOL OVERDOSE

· If strong suspicion of methanol or ethylene glycol use, begin ethanol loading treatment even if levels are not available.
· Ethanol loading to maintain BAC ≥ 23 mmol/L. To block metabolism, BAC must be at least 10% of methanol or glycol concentration. Loading dose: 10 cc 10%. ethanol/kg iv bolus. Maintain 10% alcohol infusion at 1.5–2.0 cc/kg per h (heavy daily drinker), or 1 cc/kg per h (light drinker). Several days of infusion may be needed (methanol has an elimination half-life of 30 h).
· Bicarbonate if severe acidosis.
· Folic acid 50 mg iv q 4 h (methanol).
· Thiamine 100 mg iv q 6 h, pyridoxine 50 mg iv q 6 h (ethylene glycol).

Indications for hemodialysis
· Methanol level ≥ 16 mmol/L, ethylene glycol level ≥ 8 mmol/L
· Metabolic acidosis
· End-organ damage (visual impairment, renal failure, crystalluria)
· Ingestion of potentially lethal amounts. Lethal amount of methanol 100%: 0.5 cc/kg; ethylene glycol 100%: 1.0–1.5 cc/kg.
· If levels are not available, begin hemodialysis if patient *may* have ingested a lethal amount.

Acetaminophen and ASA overdose

Acetaminophen and ASA overdose should always be considered when patients present with suspected alcohol or other drug overdose. Acetaminophen-opioid and ASA-opioid combinations are common drugs of abuse.

RISK
People who drink heavily, and those who use barbiturates, have a greater risk of acetaminophen toxicity because of enzyme induction.

DETECTION
Serum acetaminophen and ASA levels.

TREATMENT
· Use standard protocols.
· N-acetylcysteine is a specific antidote for acetaminophen toxicity.
· ASA overdose is treated with urine alkalinization and hemodialysis.

25

INJECTION DRUG USE AND INFECTIOUS DISEASE

Hepatitis C [42, 43]

EPIDEMIOLOGY

In most large Canadian cities, 50–80% of people who use injection drugs have been exposed to hepatitis C.

TRANSMISSION
- Injection drug use, blood transfusions (before screening).
- Long-term sexual partners of carriers have a low risk of infection (1–4%).
- Infection rate is 5% for infants born to mothers with hepatitis C virus (HCV) RNA +ve serum, regardless of vaginal or caesarian delivery. [44]
- No evidence of transmission through breast milk.

SEROLOGY
- HCV antibody does not distinguish between acute, chronic or resolved infection.
- Seroconversion usually occurs within 15 weeks of exposure.
- HCV RNA can be used to confirm active infection if antibody present but ALT consistently normal.
- HCV antibody transferred from mother to infant can last up to 12 months and does not indicate neonatal infection. If infection has occurred, RNA can be detected at 1–2 months of age.

NATURAL HISTORY
Risk of becoming a carrier
80% of infected patients become chronic carriers.

Risk of cirrhosis

10–20% develop cirrhosis. Risk factors: Age > 40 years at time of infection; males; alcohol use > 10 g/day (1 standard drink: 13.6 g); certain genotypes.

Risk of complications in patients with compensated cirrhosis

· 1–4% per year will develop hepatocellular carcinoma.
· 25% will develop liver failure over 10 years.
· 50% of those with liver failure will die after 5 years.

Screening for hepatitis C

PATIENT CATEGORY	SCREENING
All patients < 60 years	Ask about a current or past history of injection drug use.
History of injection use	Hepatitis A Ab, hepatitis BsAg and Ab, hepatitis C Ab, HIV Ab.
Younger people who use substances and who deny injection use	As above (patients often unwilling to disclose needle use).
Infants of HCV-positive mothers	Hepatitis C Ab at 12 months of age, or HCV RNA at 2 months of age.

Hepatitis C: Baseline investigations

INVESTIGATION	COMMENT
AST, ALT, GGT	Elevated GGT could indicate alcohol abuse.
Bilirubin, albumin, INR	Abnormalities indicate cirrhosis.
Ultrasound	Splenomegaly indicates possible cirrhosis.
CBC	Low platelet count suggests possible cirrhosis with splenomegaly and portal hypertension.
ANA, TSH, glucose, urine for cryoglobulins	Hepatitis C is associated with autoimmune disorders and other medical complications (including thyroiditis, porphyria cutanea tarda, rheumatoid arthritis, diabetes, cryoglobulinemia, lymphoma).

LONG-TERM MONITORING

Disease activity is monitored with ALT.

· If ALT normal on 3–4 tests in 1 year, monitor ALT every 6–12 months thereafter.

· If ALT increased, recheck in 3 months.

REFERRAL FOR TREATMENT

Refer to a hepatologist if the patient meets any of the following criteria:

· ALT elevated 1.5–2 times above upper limit of normal on at least 2 occasions over 3–6 months

· Clinical or laboratory evidence of cirrhosis (splenomegaly on ultrasound, high bilirubin, high INR, low albumin)

· Combined HBV and HCV, or combined HCV and HIV.

MONITORING PATIENTS WITH CIRRHOSIS

· Endoscopy recommended to detect esophageal varices (bleeding can be prevented by nadolol +/– nitrates and banding).

· Screening for hepatoma (with yearly ultrasound and alpha fetoprotein) does not appear to decrease mortality.

ANTIVIRAL THERAPY

Indications

Persistently elevated ALT, positive HCV RNA and inflammation, fibrosis or necrosis on liver biopsy.

Not indicated if

Normal ALT, advanced cirrhosis (can cause liver failure and infections), pregnancy, problem alcohol use or ongoing injection drug use.

Effectiveness

· Interferon–ribavarin combination has sustained response of 40–50%.

· Interferon alone has sustained response of 15–20%.

· Patients with cirrhosis are less likely to respond to treatment.

· Interferon administered during acute phase of illness may prevent chronicity.

Contraindications

Interferon is contraindicated in hepatic decompensation, major depression and autoimmune disorders.

LIVER TRANSPLANTATION
· Increases short-term survival in patients with end-stage liver disease.
· Reinfection with HCV always occurs—interferon–ribavarin may be effective.
· Accelerated progression of disease (liver failure may occur within 10 years).

PREVENTION OF TRANSMISSION: ADVICE FOR PATIENTS
Advice about needle-sharing
· It is not safe, even with people you know.
· Always use new needles from a pharmacy or needle exchange.
· Use clean water.
· Do not share filters, straws or spoons.
· Bleach may not be completely effective for cleaning syringes. If bleach is used, a longer time is required to kill HCV than HIV. Strict bleaching guidelines should be followed.
· Best approach is abstinence and participation in treatment.

Advice about sexual and household practices
· Avoid high-risk sexual practices.
· If in a monogamous relationship, the patient should inform the partner.
· Avoid sexual contact during menstruation.
· If in a short-term relationship, use barrier contraception.
· Limit exposure to blood. Do not share razors or toothbrushes and cover open wounds.

LIMITING DISEASE PROGRESSION
· Vaccinate against hepatitis A and B.
· Even moderate drinking (< 14 drinks/week) may accelerate progression to liver failure. Recommend abstinence or less than 2 standard drinks/week.
· Avoid regular use of acetaminophen.
· Avoid other hepatotoxic medications.

Hepatitis B
NATURAL HISTORY
Only 5% of infected persons become chronic HBV carriers.

TRANSMISSION

Compared with HCV, HBV is a hardier virus and is more easily transmitted through sexual and household contacts.

See also above: Screening for hepatitis C; Prevention of transmission; Advice for patients; and Limiting disease progression.

IMMUNIZATION

· Immunize all patients who use injection drugs and are susceptible (HBsAg and anti-HB Ab negative) with the recombinant vaccine series (0, 1 and 6 months). An accelerated schedule can also be used (0, 1, 2 and 12 months).
· Immunize household and sexual contacts with hepatitis B immune globulin followed by the vaccine.
· Give hepatitis B immune globulin and vaccine to neonates of infected mothers within 12 h of birth, followed by vaccine doses at 1 and 6 months to complete primary series. Check immunity at 1 year of age.
· Immunocompetent patients generally do not need boosters.
· Alcohol-dependent patients and patients with liver disease have a lower immune response to vaccination. A high dose, accelerated series is recommended (0, 1, 2 and 12 months using 40 μg doses). [45] This schedule is similar to that used for hemodialysis patients. Anti-HBs titres are recommended after completion of the primary series and every few years thereafter. Booster doses should be given for low titres. [46]

MONITORING

ALT (as with HCV).

REFERRAL FOR TREATMENT

Refer to a hepatologist if ALT > 2 x N over 4–6 month period, and/or evidence of liver dysfunction (↑ bilirubin and INR, ↓ albumin, hepatomegaly on exam or ultrasound).

TREATMENT

Interferon is treatment of choice. Response rate 40–50% in HBeAg +ve patients.

Hepatitis A

Immunization recommended for:
· Injection drug users (drugs and paraphenilia may be contaminated)
· Patients with chronic liver disease (Hepatitis A may cause further liver damage)
Immunization: Hepatitis A inactivated vaccine may be given alone, with a booster
at 1 year, or in a combined Hepatitis A/B vaccine, with a primary series at 0, 1
and 6 months.

Human immunodeficiency virus

HIV rates among people who use injection drugs in Canada vary from 4–25%. Rates
have risen dramatically in certain cities in the past few years (e.g., Vancouver,
Ottawa).

🔊 SCREENING
· Ask all patients < 60 about past or present use of injection drugs.
· Screen all current or past users and their sexual partners.
· Consider screening all patients who report substance use even if they deny ever
  using injection drugs (they may have forgotten their injection use, or do not wish
  to disclose it; or they may be engaging in high-risk sexual behaviour).
· Repeat testing every 6 months for patients with ongoing injection drug use or
  other risk factors.
· Offer screening to all pregnant women early in pregnancy; for high-risk women,
  repeat testing in the third trimester.

PREVENTION
· Advise patients about the risks of needle-sharing (see page 156, Prevention of
  transmission: Advice for patients) and needle exchanges in your area.
· Advise about safe sex.
· Refer patients for drug treatment.
· Refer patients with opioid dependence for methadone treatment (this has been
  shown to markedly reduce HIV transmission rates in people who use injection
  opioids).

COMPLICATIONS OF HIV AND DRUG USE

Suicide

Common cause of death (e.g., when patients are first informed they are HIV-positive). Psychosocial supports must be in place.

Infections

Infections associated with drug use are more common and more malignant in HIV-positive patients including STDs, TB, endocarditis, viral hepatitis and pneumonia.

APPROACH TO MANAGEMENT

· Compliance is increased when HIV treatment is combined with substance use treatment at the same site.
· Use benzodiazepines and opioids with caution. While people with HIV who use injection drugs often have legitimate sources of pain, many are also either opioid-dependent or at high risk for opioid dependence.
· Be aware of drug interactions (e.g., rifampin and phenytoin increase the metabolism of methadone).

STDs

Unsafe sexual practices are common in this population.
· Advise patients about safe sex.
· Routinely screen for chlamydia and GC.
· Ensure that women who use substances receive regular Pap smears.

Tuberculosis [47]

People who use injection drugs, patients who are HIV positive and patients living in shelters for the homeless are at high risk for tuberculosis. Because it is difficult to determine if alcohol dependence is an independent risk factor, it is not currently listed as a medical condition requiring screening and prophylaxis.
· Mantoux testing is recommended for all patients who use injection drugs, are HIV positive or are homeless.
· High-risk patients and alcohol-dependent patients who present with a cough, weight loss or fever should receive Mantoux testing and chest X-ray.
· Consider INH prophylaxis if tuberculin positive on Mantoux screening with no evidence of active TB.

P PROTOCOL FOR INH PROPHYLAXIS
- INH should be administered with pyridoxine, especially if the patient is at risk for peripheral neuropathy (alcohol-dependent or HIV positive).
- If alcohol-dependent, liver disease or Hepatitis C positive: Order AST, ALT and bilirubin at baseline and follow-up. Monthly clinical monitoring is recommended.
- INH is contraindicated in active hepatitis and end-stage liver disease, but may be given to most patients with underlying liver disease. Patient education and careful clinical and laboratory monitoring is essential.
- INH should be given for 6 months if HIV negative, and 9 months if positive. It may be given in a dose of 300 mg daily, or 900 mg twice per week. The latter regime should be administered under direct observation.

Sepsis, endocarditis
- Right-sided endocarditis is more common than left-sided in people who use injection drugs, therefore classic signs of endocarditis are often absent. Fever may be the only presentation.
- Blood cultures should be taken in all people who use injection drugs and present with a fever with no obvious source. If temperature is above 38.5 °C, they should be hospitalized pending results. Consider 2D echocardiogram, esp. if blood culture is positive.

26

PREGNANCY AND SUBSTANCE USE

Fetal effects
It is difficult to separate the direct toxic effects of a substance from other frequently associated factors such as poor nutrition, poor prenatal care and concurrent use of tobacco and other drugs.

Alcohol
Fetal alcohol syndrome is the most common preventable cause of mental retardation.

FETAL ALCOHOL SYNDROME (FAS)
Mechanism
Caused by the direct effect of alcohol, or metabolites such as acetaldehyde or formic acid.

Prevalence
Population rate: 1 in 1,000 live births. Rate among women who drink heavily: 4–5% of live births.

Features of FAS
· Growth retardation
· Characteristic facial anomalies (e.g., microcephaly, micrognathia, short palpebral fissures, flat philtrum)
· CNS neurodevelopmental abnormalities (developmental delay, brain malformations, intellectual impairment, behavioural problems).

FETAL ALCOHOL EFFECTS (FAE)
Prevalence
More common than FAS: 1 in 100 live births

Clinical features
FAE is a milder form of FAS with any 1 of the above 3 features. It is difficult to diagnose; it may present primarily with developmental delay, attention deficit, impulsivity and behavioural problems.

OTHER COMPLICATIONS OF ALCOHOL USE
Fetal loss is approximately 17% with chronic alcohol use.
· Spontaneous abortion
· Fetal distress
· Third-trimester hypertension with abruptio placentae and other complications

SAFE DRINKING LEVELS
There is no known safe level of alcohol consumption in pregnancy, and pregnant women are best advised to abstain from alcohol. However, there is no evidence of harm from the occasional drink consumed before the patient became aware she was pregnant.

Tobacco smoke
Mechanism
Effects are mediated through thiocyanates, carbon monoxide and nicotine.

Complications
· Intrauterine growth retardation
· Preterm birth
· Spontaneous abortion, ectopic pregnancy, placenta previa, abruptio placentae
· Sudden Infant Death Syndrome (SIDS)
· Increased risk of learning disabilities, behavioural problems, conduct disorder, ADHD

Cocaine
Mechanism
Cocaine causes fetal damage primarily through hypertension and vasospasm of the uteroplacental vessels, leading to acute and chronic hypoxia and malnutrition.

Complications
· Spontaneous abortion
· Preterm birth
· Intrauterine growth retardation
· Abruptio placentae
· Intrauterine cerebrovascular accident
· Possible genitourinary malformations
· Possible learning disabilities

Heroin

Mechanism
Heroin withdrawal causes uterine irritability and fetal distress. Heroin may also have a direct effect on fetal growth.

Complications
· Spontaneous abortion (withdrawal)
· Preterm labour (withdrawal)
· Fetal death (withdrawal)
· Intrauterine growth retardation
· Placenta previa, abruptio placentae
· Microcephaly
· Neonatal withdrawal
· SIDS

🔊 SCREENING FOR SUBSTANCE USE DURING PREGNANCY
· Record substance use history for all patients.
· Ask about number of standard drinks per day and per week, and max. consumption on any 1 day since pregnancy began.
· Ask about the use of street drugs, benzodiazepines, prescription opioids and OTC preparations including "herbal" medications.
· If alcohol use is suspected, order GGT and MCV, and use the T-ACE questionnaire. (The T-ACE is more sensitive than the CAGE in detecting at-risk drinking in pregnant women; see below.)
· If injection drug use is suspected, order HIV, hepatitis B and C serology and ALT.
· Look for "red flags" suggesting possible substance use (see next page).

T-ACE Test†

T	How many drinks does it take to make you feel high? (**T**OLERANCE).	Record # of drinks	
A	Have people **A**NNOYED you by criticizing your drinking?	Y	N
C	Have you felt you ought to **C**UT DOWN on your drinking?	Y	N
E	Have you ever had a drink first thing in the morning to steady your nerves or get rid of a hangover? (**E**YE-OPENER).	Y	N

Scoring the **T-ACE**:
T: 2 points if it takes 3 or more drinks to make her feel high
A,C,E: 1 point for each yes
A total of 2 or more points indicates that the patient is likely to have an alcohol problem.

†Reprinted with permission from R.J. Sokol, S.S. Martier & J.W. Ager. (1989). The T-ACE questions: Practical prenatal detection of risk-drinking. *American Journal of Obstetrics & Gynecology 160*, 863–870. Copyright 1989.

Red flags indicating possible substance use

· Repeated injuries, ER visits
· Partner who is abusive or uses substances
· Lack of prenatal care, missed appointments, non-compliance
· Intoxication or drowsiness during office visit
· Requests for opioids or benzodiazepines
· Previous child with FAS
· STDs, HIV/AIDS, HBV and HCV
· Family history of substance use problems
· Previous preterm delivery, fetal demise or abruptio placentae
· Chaotic lifestyle
· Psychiatric disorders

Assessment

Once a substance use problem is suspected, a comprehensive assessment is required (see Chapters 3, 4 and 5). The assessment should include:
· Alcohol and other drug history

· Consequences of use (physical, social, occupational, legal, financial)
· Social situation, including:
  – Abuse by partner
  – Safety of children living at home
  – Sex trade work
· Psychiatric history:
  – Depression, anxiety, psychosis
  – Post-traumatic stress disorder stemming from childhood physical or sexual abuse.

Investigations

· Urine drug screen: Cocaine, opioids including MAM (mono-acetylmorphine, a metabolite of heroin), cannabis, benzodiazepines, barbiturates. If there is a concern that the patient may tamper with her urine, arrange for a supervised sample and order creatinine and urine pH (see also pages 28–29).
· GGT, AST, ALT, MCV, hepatitis B and C, HIV, VDRL
· Collateral history from family members and previous care providers if possible

Note: Sometimes patients discontinue drug use suddenly upon discovering pregnancy. Patients should be warned that sudden cessation of opioids and sedatives should be done only under medical supervision.

Prenatal care of women who use substances
Involvement of other care providers

· A case manager should co-ordinate care if possible.
· Consultation should be considered with an obstetrician, neonatologist, psychiatrist and social worker.
· Contact an addiction medicine specialist with expertise in pregnancy.
· Involve other services such as social assistance, food bank, clothing exchange and housing.
· Arrange substance use treatment for the patient and for significant others if indicated. Some treatment programs will accept urgent inpatient admissions for pregnant patients.
· Refer for methadone treatment if opioid-dependent.
· Report to child protection agency if the patient is actively using substances during pregnancy.

Approach to prenatal visits

· Establish good rapport. Expect some minimization of the problem in the first few visits.
· Negotiate the frequency of visits. A once-weekly visit establishes a routine and provides time to deal with multiple issues.
· Since patients may miss appointments, try to get as much done as possible on each visit (i.e., provide opportunistic prenatal care, investigations and interventions).
· Avoid prescribing opioids or benzodiazepines.
· Monitor with urine drug screening.

Working with pregnant women who use substances: Dos and don'ts

· Do not pass judgment.
· Do not increase her guilt.
· Be clear about dangers, but provide hope.
· If possible, introduce the patient to women with success stories.
· Be flexible—give opportunistic care.
· Follow up on missed appointments.
· Communicate care plans to other providers.
· Be patient! Eventually many women become engaged in treatment (for some patients, change comes after baby is born).
· Reinforce positive changes.

Schedule of visits and tests

MANOEUVRE	FREQUENCY
Prenatal visits	Weekly if possible
Pap	Baseline
STD screen	Baseline and 3rd trimester
HBV, HCV, HIV, VDRL, Mantoux	Baseline. Repeat every 3 months if negative and at continued risk.
Ultrasound	Baseline for dates (if needed) 18 and 32 weeks (for internal growth), then as needed

| Biophysical profile | 32 and 35 weeks, then weekly |
| Non-stress test | 35 weeks, then weekly alternating with BPPs (3–4 days apart) |

Biophysical profile
· Instruct women not to smoke for at least ½ h before the test.
· Drugs (particularly opioids) affect fetal beat-to-beat variability on the non-stress test.
· Absent fetal breathing is a common finding among patients taking opioids. If all other parameters are normal, patient can be sent home. To minimize opioid effects, do BPP before or 6–8 h after patient takes her methadone dose.
· Low amniotic fluid volume indicates probable fetal compromise.

Drug screening
URINE DRUG SCREENING (UDS)
UDS is useful for monitoring treatment progress and enhancing patient motivation. However, it can have both false-positive and false-negative results. Even 1 positive UDS can affect decisions regarding child custody, therefore:
· Consider UDS at each visit. Weekly UDS should be considered, particularly if child protection agency is involved.
· Order full screens, specifically requesting cocaine, cocaine metabolite, benzodiazepines, cannabis, methadone and its metabolite, and the different types of opioids including the heroin metabolite mono-acetylmorphine (MAM).
· Samples should be supervised and carefully labelled.
· The sample should not be discarded until the results are obtained.
· Positive results should be flagged for prompt attention.
· An unexpected positive result requires confirmatory testing on the saved sample, using a different laboratory technique (i.e., chromatography; see Chapter 6, Laboratory Detection of Alcohol and Other Drug Use).

NEONATAL UDS
A positive neonatal UDS indicates recent illicit drug use by the mother, or opioids, benzodiazepines or barbiturates administered in labour.

MATERNAL AND NEONATAL HAIR SAMPLING

Hair sampling may provide confirmation of UDS results. Hair growth is affected by many factors, including nutrition, hair dye, sweat, washing and other genetic factors such as race. For this reason it is not yet a component of standard care.

A positive maternal hair sample indicates substance use within the past several months, up to 1 year. A positive hair sample in a newborn indicates in utero drug exposure after 24 weeks gestation.

CONSENT FOR DRUG TESTING

· The mother should be asked to give consent before her urine or hair samples are tested.
· The mother should be informed of neonatal urine or hair testing. If drug use is suspected, consent for neonatal testing is not required (check with your jurisdiction), but is recommended so as not to jeopardize the physician/patient relationship.

Reporting to the child protection agency

If the physician has concerns or suspicions that a pregnant patient is currently dependent on or abusing alcohol or other drugs, she should be reported to the child protection agency. Although physicians are not legally obligated to report until the baby is born (check with your jurisdiction), early reporting may allow for better risk assessment and discharge planning.

COUNSELLING THE PATIENT

· Inform the patient of your legal obligation to report concerns about child safety.
· Promote hope and optimism. Many patients do well with appropriate treatment and support. Review ways that she may be able to prevent relapse and retain custody of her infant: abstinence, monitoring with supervised UDS, involvement in treatment, ongoing counselling, supports in the home. Emphasize that the child protection agency can provide valuable support and useful services.
· Encourage the patient to consider self-reporting to the child protection agency prior to delivery.

Apprehension of the infant

If the protection agency apprehends the infant:

· Admit the neonate to a protected area.
· Arrange for a quiet area to discuss the issue with the patient.
· Ensure your own safety and that of staff.
· Arrange for appropriate grief counselling if necessary.
· Discuss interventions to prevent relapse.

Prevention of maternal-fetal transmission of hepatitis and HIV

MOTHER	NEONATE
HBV surface antigen positive	Immunoglobulin + vaccine within 12 h of birth. Vaccine at 1 and 6 months.
HCV positive	No prevention. Test for antibody in infant at 1 year, or RNA at 2 months
HIV positive: Oral AZT from after 14 weeks until labour. Dose: 100 mg 5 times per day. iv AZT during labour and delivery until clamping of cord. Dose: 2 mg/kg iv AZT over 1 h, then continuous iv infusion at 1 mg/kg/h.	Oral AZT to infant within 12 h of birth, to 6 weeks. Dose: 2 mg/kg po q 6 h. If unable to take orally: iv 1.5 mg/kg over 30 minutes, q 6 h.

Safety of breastfeeding in substance-using mothers*

DRUG	RISK OF TOXICITY	RECOMMENDATION
Cocaine	Enters breast milk and can cause toxicity.	Advise women not to breastfeed if they are currently using cocaine regularly.
Alcohol	Enters breast milk; may affect psychomotor development (dose-response relationship). May affect let-down reflex and suppress lactation.	Advise women not to breastfeed if they are currently drinking heavily (0.5g/kg per day, or 3 drinks/day in a 70 kg woman). Exposure can be limited if breastfeeding withheld for 2–3 h after each drink. [48]
Cannabis	May cause lethargy and poor feeding in infant. May affect development.	Probably best to avoid breastfeeding if daily use is heavy (i.e., ≥ 1 "joint"/day).

continued on next page

Safety of breastfeeding, continued

Opioids	Therapeutic doses of prescription opioids enter breast milk in minimal amounts. There is no evidence of harm.	Breastfeeding not contraindicated if moderately using opioids. [48]
Methadone	Enters breast milk in very small amounts. There is no evidence of harm.	Breastfeeding not contraindicated, although caution is advised if on very high dose (i.e., > 120 mg/day). [49]
HCV	No evidence of transmission, [50] but cannot guarantee.	Individual decision by patient.
HBV	No evidence of transmission but cannot guarantee.	Individual decision by patient.
HIV	Enters breast milk.	Breastfeeding contraindicated.

*When advising about breastfeeding to women who use substances, remember that breastfeeding promotes bonding between mother and infant and may have important health benefits.

Management of withdrawal during pregnancy

Alcohol and other drug withdrawal can cause miscarriage, fetal distress or demise, and preterm labour.

Nicotine withdrawal

(see also Chapter 13, Nicotine and Smoking Cessation)

For those women not able to quit smoking with behavioural interventions, consider using nicotine replacement therapy (NRT). NRT appears to be safe in pregnancy (although evidence is limited), and the benefits of cessation likely outweigh the risks. NRT may not be effective after the first trimester due to increased metabolism. The safety of bupropion in pregnancy has not been established.

If NRT is prescribed:
· Use for a short duration only.
· Choose the lowest effective dose.

· Consider removing the patch at night or prescribing the 18-h patch.
· Consider discontinuing after the first trimester.

Alcohol withdrawal

· Admit to hospital.
· Monitor for fetal distress.
· Treat with diazepam loading protocol or symptom-triggered lorazepam (see pages 44–45).

ALCOHOL WITHDRAWAL DURING LABOUR

· Notify neonatology (large amounts of benzodiazepines can cause "floppy baby syndrome").
· Use lorazepam rather than diazepam (diazepam may have a prolonged duration of action in the neonate).

Benzodiazepine withdrawal

Management is similar to that of non-pregnant adults (see pages 105–109). Use lorazepam during labour.

Barbiturate withdrawal

Management is similar to that of non-pregnant adults (see pages 109–112).

Phenobarbital should be used in the lowest safe dose and for as brief a time as possible because it has been identified as a possible teratogen.

Cocaine withdrawal

No specific pharmacotherapy is indicated; provide supportive therapy.

Cannabis withdrawal

No specific pharmacotherapy is indicated.

Opioid withdrawal

See next page.

Safety in pregnancy of drugs used in the treatment of substance use disorders

DRUG	SAFETY IN PREGNANCY
Disulfiram	Teratogenic; contraindicated in pregnancy.
Naltrexone	Safety of naltrexone in pregnancy is not known. Prescribe naltrexone for alcohol dependence only if behavioural interventions fail.
Bupropion	Evidence is limited regarding safety in pregnancy; not recommended at this time.
Nicotine patch	Prescribe only if behavioural interventions fail. Use lowest effective dose for short period.
Methadone	May cause neonatal withdrawal, but treatment of choice for opioid dependence (see below).

Opioid use during pregnancy and childbirth
Complications of maternal opioid withdrawal
(see page 90 for clinical features of opioid withdrawal)

Severe withdrawal can cause uterine irritability and fetal distress. Complications include:
· Spontaneous abortion
· Preterm labour
· Fetal demise.

Moderate prescription opioid use during pregnancy
For patients using moderate, therapeutic doses of oral opioids (e.g., Tylenol #3® 3–4 tablets/day), who are not psychologically or physically dependent:
· Taper the medication by about 10% per week under close supervision.
· Taper during the second trimester (14–32 weeks) to reduce the risk of miscarriage or preterm labour.
· If tapering is difficult, maintain on the lowest effective dose. Consider switching to equivalent dose of sustained-release opioid (e.g., Codeine Contin®).
· Consider consultation with pain expert and addiction medicine specialist.

Methadone maintenance during pregnancy

Note: This section is not intended for methadone prescribers, but for physicians who occasionally provide care to pregnant patients on methadone. Methadone should only be prescribed by physicians experienced in its use during pregnancy (see also Chapter 17, Pharmacotherapy for Opioid Dependence).

Women who are opioid-dependent have a high infant mortality rate, primarily because of complications of prematurity and low birthweight. Methadone maintenance treatment (MMT) dramatically reduces the infant mortality rate in these women with marked improvements in birthweight and gestational age. MMT also decreases maternal opioid use and lowers the risk of HIV and HCV, while improving maternal health status and compliance with prenatal care.

Methadone is not teratogenic, and does not appear to cause significant long-term developmental problems, although published studies are small and poorly controlled. Infants born to women on methadone are slightly smaller than infants born to mothers who have not used opioids; this difference disappears by 1–2 years. Neonates born to women on methadone are at high risk of undergoing withdrawal (see pages 175–182).

INDICATIONS
Pregnant women who are physically and psychologically dependent on opioids (see page 93).

DURATION OF THERAPY
Most require maintenance during pregnancy and at least 6 months postpartum.

P PROTOCOL FOR METHADONE DOSING DURING PREGNANCY
Initiation of methadone
· Admit to hospital; consult with obstetrician.
· Administer 10–15 mg methadone po with the onset of withdrawal symptoms.
· Provide doses of 5–10 mg of methadone po q 4 h prn for withdrawal symptoms, to a 24 h max of 35 mg on day 1.
· The following day, give the previous day's total dose as a single morning dose, followed by 5 mg tid prn (to a max. of 45 mg).
· Do not increase the dose beyond 45 mg on days 3–5, because of the risk of bioaccumulation and potential overdose.

· If the patient becomes drowsy, hold the methadone and monitor closely (see "Prescribing precautions," page 94).
· By day 3 to 5 the patient is usually able to take 1 daily dose and can be discharged. Advise the patient to take her dose at the same time every day.

Follow-up outpatient methadone dosage adjustment
· Titration: Adjust the dose upward by 5–10 mg every 5–7 days if the woman complains of withdrawal.
· Maximum dose: There is little information on the safety of methadone doses > 80 mg/day during pregnancy. However, higher doses are sometimes necessary to prevent ongoing drug use or to relieve difficult withdrawal symptoms.
· Split dose: Patients on doses of 100 mg or above should receive a bid dose (split 60:40 or 50:50).
· Third trimester: The rate of metabolism of methadone increases in the third trimester, causing withdrawal symptoms and craving in some women. If this occurs, the dose should be increased by 10–15 mg od.

Methadone tapering
Pregnant women who taper off methadone have a high rate of relapse, so tapering is generally not indicated. Tapering should only be attempted between 14 and 32 weeks of gestation, to reduce the risk of spontaneous abortion or preterm labour. The methadone dose should be tapered by no more than 5 mg every 2 weeks.

Labour and postpartum
The patient should receive her regular methadone dose during labour. If she received a 3rd trimester dose increase, she may require a dose reduction of 10–20 mg in the first few days postpartum.

Breastfeeding
Methadone appears to be safe when breastfeeding; very small amounts are present in breast milk. [49] Women can limit infant exposure by not breastfeeding for 4 h or more after their dose, although this is often not practical. It is sometimes recommended that babies be weaned at 3–4 months, by which time they are ingesting large volumes of breast milk and larger methadone doses.

Labour and women who use opioids

ANALGESIA DURING LABOUR

Many women with substance use disorders choose to have epidural anaesthesia during labour. If opioids are indicated, women who are dependent on opioids may require larger and/or more frequent doses, because of tolerance. Adequate analgesia will not worsen the addiction.

OTHER ISSUES DURING LABOUR

Patients may have poor venous access from injection drug use. Planned iv access is recommended in case of emergency. Avoid the placement of a fetal scalp clip if possible, to minimize the risk of transmission of HBV, HCV and HIV.

Postpartum care

Prescribe adequate analgesia, including opioids if necessary. Do not discharge with more than a few days' supply of opioids.

Weekly follow-up of mother and infant is recommended. Assess the discharged neonate for neglect, failure to thrive and the emergence of delayed withdrawal from opioids. Delayed withdrawal from opioids can occur up to 2 weeks after birth.

Neonatal abstinence syndrome

Neonatal withdrawal occurs in 40–60% of infants born to women on opioids such as heroin, and up to 85% of infants born to women on methadone.[51] There may be a direct (but weak) correlation between the maternal methadone dose and the risk of neonatal withdrawal.

ONSET [52]

· Methadone: 2–7 days after birth. For most affected infants, withdrawal will begin within 3–4 days. For 5–10% of affected infants, withdrawal will begin at 7 days or later.
· Other opioids: usually within first 24 h (e.g., heroin), but can be 1–3 days after birth.
· Late presentations may occur at up to 2–4 weeks.
· Presentation of withdrawal depends on timing of mother's last dose of opioid before delivery.

DURATION [52]
· Several weeks. Sub-acute presentations can last as long as 4–6 months.

SYMPTOMS AND SIGNS
· Irritability, crying
· Increased tone, tremors, myoclonus
· Poor feeding, vomiting, regurgitation
· Sweating, hyperthermia, mottled skin
· Metabolic disturbances (e.g., hypoglycemia)

Note: Presentation similar to neonatal sepsis, hypoglycemia, hypocalcemia, intracranial hemorrhage.

COMPLICATIONS
Neonatal withdrawal can result in seizures and neonatal death if untreated. There is no evidence of any long-term sequelae.

TREATMENT
· Admit all neonates born to women on methadone to neonatal intensive care for 4–5 days. Discharge only if the infant shows no signs of withdrawal.
· Monitor for signs of withdrawal, using Neonatal Abstinence Scoring Scale (see below). [36]
· Give oral morphine according to body weight and score (see below).

Neonatal Abstinence Scoring (NAS) Scale for opioid withdrawal

The neonatal abstinence scoring system is a 21-item scale designed to titrate the dose of oral morphine according to the severity of neonatal withdrawal symptoms. Variations of the NAS scale have been derived from the original 32-item scale. [53, 54]

Note: Nurses and paediatricians ideally should receive some training in the use of the NAS Scale. If marked discrepancies in scoring are noted between care-givers, try to reach a consensus on the most appropriate score. If your hospital rarely treats neonatal withdrawal, consider referring the infant to a centre with more experience or consult with a neonatologist familiar with withdrawal management.

NAS INITIATION
· Initiate scoring within 2 h of admission to nursery.
· Score for 4–5 days, or as long as morphine treatment and weaning is necessary.

SCORING INTERVAL
· Continue scoring q 4 h for 4–5 days; if score ≥ 8, score q 2 h when possible.
· An item is scored if it occurs at any time within the 4 h interval.
· Infants should not be awakened to obtain score.

Neonatal abstinence score sheet†

SIGNS AND SYMPTOMS	SCORE	AM					PM					COMMENTS
DATE:				DAILY WEIGHT:								
Excessive high-pitched (or other) cry	2											
Continuous high-pitched (or other) cry	3											
Sleeps < 1 hour after feeding	3											
Sleeps < 2 hours after feeding	2											
Sleeps < 3 hours after feeding	1											
Hyperactive Moro reflex	2											
Marked hyperactive Moro reflex	3											
Mild tremors disturbed	1											
Moderate-severe tremors disturbed	2											
Mild tremors undisturbed	3											
Moderate-severe tremors undisturbed	4											
Increased muscle tone	2											
Excoriation (specific areas)	1											
Myoclonic jerks	3											
Generalized convulsions	5											
Sweating	1											
Fever < 101 (99–100.8°F/37.2–38.2°C)	1											
Fever > 101 (38.4°C and higher)	2											
Frequent yawning (> 3–4 times/interval)	1											
Mottling	1											
Nasal stuffiness	1											
Sneezing (> 3–4 times/interval)	1											
Nasal flaring	2											
Respiratory rate > 60 min.	1											
Respiratory rate > 60 min. with retractions	2											
Excessive sucking	1											
Poor feeding	2											
Regurgitation	2											
Projectile vomiting	3											
Loose stools	2											
Watery stools	3											
TOTAL SCORE												
INITIAL OF SCORER												

† Reprinted with permission from: Hoekelman, et al.: *Primary Pediatric Care,* page 1372. Copyright 1992, St. Louis: Mosby.

Definitions of NAS scoring items†

ITEM (SCORE)	DEFINITION	CLINICAL MANEUVER
Crying: Excessive high-pitched (2)	Unable to decrease crying within 15 s using self-consoling measures *or* cries intermittently or continuously for up to 5 min despite caregiver interventions. Crying may not be high-pitched.	Observe
Crying: Continuous high-pitched (3)	Unable to decrease crying within 15 s using self-consoling measures *and* cries intermittently or continuously for > 5 min despite caregiver interventions	Observe
Hyperactive Moro reflex (2)	*Pronounced* jitteriness (tremulousness) of hands (slight jitteriness is normal)	Calm infant if crying or irritable. Lift infant slightly off crib by arms; allow infant to fall back onto mattress
Markedly hyperactive Moro reflex (3)	Jitteriness *and* clonus of hands or arms	To elicit clonus: abruptly dorsiflex wrist or ankle, using short brisk movement
Mild tremors: Disturbed (1)	Observable tremors of *hands* or *feet* when handled. State of baby does not matter (asleep, drowsy, awake). (Note: A few jerking movements while asleep are normal and should not be scored)	Observe when handling
Moderate-severe tremors: Disturbed (2)	Tremors of *arms* (one or both) or *legs* (one or both) when handled	Observe when handling
Mild tremors: Undisturbed (3)	Tremors of hands or feet when not handled	Observe for at least two 1 min periods prior to temperature-taking or diaper changing

continued on next page

NAS definitions, continued

Moderate-severe tremors: Undisturbed (4)	Tremors of arms (one or both) or legs (one or both) when not handled	Observe as above
Increased muscle tone (2)	No head lag, body rigid	With infant supine, grasp hands and pull upright to sitting position
Excoriation (1)	Excoriation on chin, knees, cheeks, elbows, toes, nose (not diaper area)	Observe
Myoclonic jerks (1)	Twitching or jerking movements of face, arms or legs	Observe
Generalized seizure (5)	Generalized jitteriness stops when limbs touched or flexed; seizures are not stopped by touching or flexing. Seizures may be accompanied by eye staring, rapid eye movements, chewing, rowing or bicycling motions, back arching, fist clenching.	Observe. Touch or flex involved limbs.
Sweating (1)	Sweating not due to overheating or swaddling	Observe
Fever (1,2)		Rectal or axillary temperature, taken over 3 min
Nasal stuffiness (1)	Noisy respirations due to nasal exudates, +/− runny nose	Observe
Respiratory rate > 60/min (1) with retractions (2)		Quiet infant. Count for 1 full min.
Excessive sucking (1)	More than 3 times during interval: Rooting, attempting to suck on hands or pacifier	Observe

Poor feeding (2)	Normal feeding is co-ordinated sequence of sucking, swallowing, breathing. Poor feeding: sucks infrequently, difficulty sucking and swallowing, continuously gulps while eating, stopping frequently to breathe.	Observe
Regurgitation (2)	2 or more times, not associated with burping	Observe
Projectile vomiting (3)	Projectile vomiting during or immediately after feeding	Observe
Loose stools (2)	Curdy, liquidy but no water ring on diaper	Check diaper
Watery stools (3)	Water ring on diaper	Check diaper

†Reprinted with permission from: D'Apolito, K. *A Scoring System for Assessing Neonatal Abstinence Syndrome: Instructional Manual.* Copyright 1994, University of Washington.

Initiation of morphine

· Morphine is administered as a scheduled, fixed dose. The initial dose is determined by body weight and NAS scores (see table below). Morphine administration is not meant to be given on a sliding scale (like hyperglycemia and regular insulin), nor is it meant to be given on a prn basis.

· Morphine is not indicated if consecutive total abstinence scores, or the average of any 3 consecutive scores, continue to be 7 or less.

· An average score of ≥ 8 for 3 consecutive readings indicates the need for oral morphine. Administer according to the table below.

· If score ≥ 12 for 2 consecutive intervals, or average of any 2 scores is 12, start treatment at the appropriate dosage for that score before more than 2–4 h elapse.

Maintenance dose

The neonate should continue on the dose of morphine that keeps the scores < 8 for 24–48 h before weaning commences.[53]

Dosage schedule according to abstinence score†

SCORE	MORPHINE DAILY DOSE (ADMINISTER IN 4 DIVIDED DOSES)	MORPHINE SINGLE DOSE
8–10	0.32 mg/kg/day	0.08 mg/kg
11–13	0.48 mg/kg/day	0.12 mg/kg
14–16	0.64 mg/kg/day	0.16 mg/kg
17 +	0.8 mg/kg/day	0.2 mg/kg

†Reprinted with permission from: Hoekelman et al.: *Primary Pediatric Care*, page 1375. Copyright 1992, St Louis: Mosby.

Weaning morphine
· Weaning of morphine can ensue as long as scores remain below 8.
· Weaning is usually by 0.05 mg/kg *of daily dose*, every 2–4 days. [53, 55]
· Discontinuation of morphine can occur when the neonate is stable for 2–4 days on a dose as low as 0.05–0.1 mg/kg per day.
· Duration of weaning is usually for 2–8 weeks. [55]
· Most infants started on morphine only require 0.32 mg/kg per day and are weaned within 2–3 weeks. Others require higher doses and up to 8 weeks of weaning.

Discharge from hospital
· Keep all neonates whose mothers took methadone in pregnancy in hospital for at least 4–5 days. Discharge only if the infant shows no signs of withdrawal.
· If morphine treatment is initiated, the infant must remain in the hospital until fully weaned off morphine and is no longer in withdrawal.
· On discharge, carefully instruct the mother to look for signs of withdrawal and to call immediately if they occur.
· Assess the infant within 1–2 days of discharge.

27

SUBSTANCE USE AND MENTAL ILLNESS

Substance-induced disorders

Substance-induced disorders can mimic virtually any primary psychiatric disorder. Identification of substance-induced disorders is essential to avoid inappropriate and delayed treatment.

DSM-IV DIAGNOSTIC CRITERIA FOR SUBSTANCE-INDUCED DISORDERS

The following are criteria for Substance-Induced Disorders, adapted from the DSM-IV:

· Symptoms developed during, or within a month of, substance intoxication or withdrawal.
· Substance is known to cause symptoms of anxiety, depression or psychosis.
· Symptoms cannot be better explained by a disorder that is not substance-induced.

These disorders include: Substance-Induced Psychotic Disorder (predominant hallucinations or delusions), Substance-Induced Mood Disorder (predominant depressed mood, or euphoric/irritable mood) and Substance-Induced Anxiety Disorder (predominant anxiety, panic attacks or obsessions and compulsions).

All the major drugs of abuse can cause Substance-Induced Disorders, particularly Mood and Anxiety Disorders.

Common Substance-Induced Disorders

DISORDER	ASSOCIATED SUBSTANCE
Psychotic Disorder	Cocaine, amphetamines and other stimulants, cannabis, hallucinogens
Mood Disorder	Alcohol, cocaine, amphetamines and other stimulants, benzodiazepines and other sedatives, opioids, hallucinogens
Anxiety Disorder	Alcohol, cocaine, amphetamines and other stimulants, caffeine, cannabis, benzodiazepines and other sedatives

PRIMARY VERSUS SUBSTANCE-INDUCED DISORDERS

Often it is difficult to distinguish primary and Substance-Induced Disorders until the patient has had at least several weeks of abstinence or reduced use.

Primary versus Substance-Induced Disorders

CLINICAL FEATURES	PRIMARY	SUBSTANCE-INDUCED
Onset of symptoms precedes substance use	Sometimes	No
Use heavy or often enough to explain symptoms	Often not	Yes
Resolution with abstinence	No	Yes, within 1–3 months
Use of substance for symptom control	Often	Sometimes

Clinical example: Alcohol, depression and anxiety

· Heavy alcohol use can induce organic depression that is clinically indistinguishable from major depression. The depression usually resolves within a few weeks of abstinence.

· Patients with primary depression may use alcohol as a form of self-medication. Heavy alcohol use may worsen the depression. The depression will improve but not resolve with abstinence.

· Alcohol is a potent anxiolytic and patients with Anxiety Disorders are at greater risk for developing alcohol problems. Tolerance rapidly develops with daily use, often causing alcohol use to escalate. Eventually the patient's anxiety increases due to alcohol-induced withdrawal, insomnia, fatigue and social difficulties. Although abstinence will improve the anxiety, it will not resolve completely if the patient has a primary Anxiety Disorder.

Screening and assessment

All patients presenting with a Mood, Anxiety or Psychotic Disorder should be screened for substance use (see Chapters 3, 4 and 5). Similarly, all patients with a Substance Use Disorder should have a mental status examination to identify depression, anxiety and psychosis.

Pharmacotherapy of Substance-Induced Disorders

· Benzodiazepines and opioids should be avoided, if possible, except in treating acute withdrawal.
· Patients with milder mood or anxiety disorders who are able to achieve abstinence should be monitored for 4–12 weeks. If the mood/anxiety disorder persists or worsens over this time period, pharmacotherapy should be considered (treat with antidepressants or anxiolytics such as buspirone). However, the psychiatric diagnosis may remain unclear until the patient has achieved 3–6 months of recovery.
· Consider initiating pharmacotherapy earlier than 4–12 weeks if symptoms are severe or if there is strong suspicion that the patient has a primary psychiatric disorder.
· If the patient cannot achieve abstinence, consider pharmacotherapy if a primary psychiatric disorder is suspected.
· In patients who continue to use alcohol heavily, use caution when prescribing sedating drugs, drugs that can be fatal in an overdose, or drugs that can be arrythmogenic (e.g., tricyclic antidepressants).

Risk of suicide

Patients with Substance-Induced Disorders are at high risk for suicide, particularly during intoxication and withdrawal. Such patients should be observed and admitted. Often their mental state improves in 24–48 h.

Concurrent disorders

Patients with both a Substance Use Disorder and a primary psychiatric disorder are said to have concurrent disorders.

· All the substances that cause Substance-Induced Disorders can also exacerbate primary psychiatric disorders. For example, cannabis can precipitate psychosis, and can exacerbate symptoms in patients with pre-existing Schizophrenia.
· Patients with primary psychiatric disorders can also develop Substance-Induced Disorders. For example, a patient with an Anxiety Disorder can develop Alcohol-Induced Depression.
· Substance use can interfere with treatment of the primary disorder by causing non-compliance, behavioural problems and interpersonal difficulties.

Management

Abstinence is the preferred option for most patients with concurrent disorders. Patients with concurrent disorders need comprehensive case management, and an integrated treatment approach that involves both addiction and mental health treatment.

PHASE 1: GETTING STARTED
Goals include: medical withdrawal management, comprehensive assessment and stabilization of mental illness. The physician should focus on engagement and motivation.

PHASE 2: ADDICTION TREATMENT
Addiction treatment consists of counselling, education, group therapy, mutual aid (e.g., AA), family counselling, life skills and behavioural treatments.

PHASE 3: RELAPSE PREVENTION
Mutual aid, addiction after-care and concurrent mental health case management provide long-term follow-up and support.

28

SURGERY AND SUBSTANCE USE

All patients presenting with a substance-induced surgical or medical illness should have their substance use addressed while in hospital. Evidence suggests that a substantial proportion of patients receiving such advice will attend treatment and reduce their substance use, leading to improved health outcomes and fewer hospital readmissions.

Alcohol use

Compared with matched controls, people who drink heavily and undergo elective surgery have:[56]
· 2–3 times the morbidity rate
· 50% longer hospital stay (3–9 days depending on type of operation)
· Poorer outcomes after 3 months
· Significantly more secondary surgery.

PERIOPERATIVE COMPLICATIONS
Patients who are dependent on alcohol are at risk for a number of perioperative complications. Mechanisms include impaired T-cell immunity, impaired wound healing, cardiomyopathy, reduced platelet count and function, and exaggerated surgical stress response. Common complications are listed on the next page.

Alcohol use and surgery: Common complications

COMPLICATION	COMMENT
Alcohol withdrawal syndrome	Alcohol withdrawal plus the stress of surgery increases risk of severe withdrawal and delirium tremens
Infection	Pneumonia (aspiration and other), abscesses, sepsis and wound infection (heavy alcohol use is a strong predictor of wound infection)
Bleeding	Hematoma and wound rupture are most common
Dysrhythmias	Caused by withdrawal, cardiomyopathy
Congestive heart failure	Cardiomyopathy
Sedative, opioid withdrawal	Caused by polysubstance dependence

A PREOPERATIVE SCREENING AND ASSESSMENT
· Ask all patients about daily and weekly alcohol consumption.
· Use the CAGE, GGT, MCV.
· Ask patients who drink heavily about withdrawal symptoms—morning/afternoon tremor relieved with drinking; seizures.
· Inquire about other drug use, esp. benzodiazepines and opioids.
· Assess for medical complications (e.g., cardiomyopathy).
· Assess for alcoholic liver disease. Order CBC, electrolytes, creatine, glucose, AST, ALT, GGT, bilirubin, INR, albumin, Mg, phosphorus, HBV and HCV.

Alcohol withdrawal

Postoperative alcohol withdrawal is common. Evidence suggests that preoperative treatment of withdrawal and several weeks of abstinence reduces surgical morbidity and length of stay in people who drink heavily who are undergoing elective surgery. [56]

P PROTOCOL FOR ELECTIVE SURGERY
If history of withdrawal or drinking > 40 drinks/week:
· Book for a "planned withdrawal" at least 1 week prior to surgery (see pages 44–45).
· Advise patient to have last drink the night before clinic appointment.

· Use CIWA-A to monitor withdrawal.
· Use diazepam or lorazepam as per protocol (see Chapter 9, Alcohol Withdrawal).
· Have plan for maintaining abstinence until surgery (e.g., disulfiram, outpatient counselling, mutual aid).
· Discontinue naltrexone at least 3 days prior to surgery.

P PROTOCOL FOR URGENT SURGERY
If history of withdrawal or drinking > 40 drinks/week:
· Observe closely for signs of withdrawal using CIWA-A.
· Use diazepam or lorazepam as per protocol (see Chapter 9, Alcohol Withdrawal).
· If possible, postpone surgery until treatment completed.

P PROTOCOL FOR EMERGENCY SURGERY
· As above for urgent surgery
· Observe closely for postsurgical withdrawal and delirium tremens if surgery must be performed while patient is intoxicated or before withdrawal can be treated

Liver dysfunction and surgical risk

Patients with liver dysfunction (elevated INR, low albumin) or liver failure (ascites, encephalopathy) are at significant surgical risk. Try to correct problems preoperatively. Operate only if no alternative.

Surgical management of alcoholic liver disease

SURGICAL RISK	MANAGEMENT
Massive ascites	· Aspiration risk. Postpone surgery until ascites reduced.
Acute, severe alcoholic hepatitis	· Postpone surgery if possible. Re-evaluate after 2–3 weeks of abstinence. Operate if: – Patient asymptomatic – AST, ALT < 3 x normal – INR, albumin close to normal
Thrombocytopenia	· Correct severe thrombocytopenia. Surgical hemostasis is achieved with platelet counts of 50,000 (higher for cardiac surgery).
Coagulation defect	· Correct high INR with vitamin K (phytonadione 15 mg im/sc/day) or plasma transfusion.

continued on next page

Surgical management, continued

Encephalopathy	· Watch for triggers (e.g., sedatives, diuretics, infections, GI bleeding; see Chapter 11, Alcoholic Liver Disease).
	· Monitor level of consciousness, ammonia levels.
	· If possible, postpone surgery until encephalopathy resolves.
Withdrawal	· Use lorazepam; diazepam has prolonged duration of action in cirrhosis.

Alcohol consumption and trauma

Approximately 50% of patients admitted to a trauma centre are under the influence of alcohol. Most of these patients are problem drinkers. Brief counselling interventions for problem drinkers have been shown to reduce alcohol consumption, and to reduce the risk of injury recurrence by up to 40%. A recent life-threatening injury may increase the patient's receptivity towards alcohol counselling (see Chapter 31, Counselling and Motivational Interviewing).

ADVICE TO THE TRAUMA PATIENT
· Inform the patient of his or her level of intoxication at admission.
· Emphasize that alcohol greatly increases the risk of injury.
· Review the negative social and physical consequences of alcohol when present.
· Show the patient abnormal laboratory values.
· Give the patient a list of treatment resources and self-help groups in the community.
· For alcohol dependency, suggest naltrexone (unless on or about to receive opioids).
· Advise the patient to follow up with his or her family physician.

Other drug use
Nicotine dependence

Hospitalization on a medical/surgical ward is an ideal time to stop smoking. Patients hospitalized for smoking-related illnesses may be very receptive to smoking-cessation interventions.

Bupropion is not effective until 1–2 weeks after initiation so may not help the hospitalized person in acute nicotine withdrawal. Nicotine replacement therapy (NRT) is effective immediately. NRT may also improve the patient's comfort and compliance (see also Chapter 13, Nicotine and Smoking Cessation).

Benzodiazepine and barbiturate dependence

Sudden withdrawal from benzodiazepines and barbiturates can cause complications similar to alcohol withdrawal, including seizures, dysrhythmias and delirium. If possible, arrange a medically supervised taper prior to surgery (see Chapter 19, Benzodiazepine and Barbiturate Dependence and Withdrawal).

Opioid dependence

See also Chapters 15, 16 and 17.

WITHDRAWAL

If possible, complete managed withdrawal prior to surgery (see Chapters 15 and 16) using clonidine, tapering doses of opioids or methadone.

Note: Clonidine can cause symptomatic hypotension and conduction abnormalities such as prolonged Q-T interval. Avoid giving clonidine to patients with unstable cardiorespiratory status.

PAIN MANAGEMENT IN THE PATIENT DEPENDENT ON OPIOIDS

Undertreatment of pain may be as great a risk for relapse as overtreatment.
· If effective non-opioid analgesics are available, use them as first line.
· If opioids are used, the amount and duration of opioid use should be comparable to that of patients undergoing similar surgery.
· Minimize concurrent use of benzodiazepines and other sedatives.
· Safety and good pain control are the most important priorities. Where possible, however, choose the type, route and dose of opioid that will lower the risk of dependence and abuse.

Dependence liability of opioids

VARIABLE	LOWER RISK OF DEPENDENCE	HIGHER RISK OF DEPENDENCE
Route	Oral route	Parenteral
Duration	Long-acting	Shorter-acting
Administration	Scheduled	PRN
Specific medications	Codeine, morphine	Oxycodone, meperidine, hydromorphone

DISCHARGE
- Consider consultation and referral for methadone treatment.
- Prolonged postsurgical use of benzodiazepines or opioids is a risk for relapse. Do not prescribe for longer than would normally be required by patients undergoing similar surgery.

Management of drug use on the ward

- Warn people who use street drugs not to use drugs on the ward. Urine drug screening is recommended if patients go on a pass. Cancel passes for patients who return intoxicated; hold benzodiazepines and other sedatives until intoxication resolves.
- Manage drug-seeking using principles outlined in Chapter 29.
- If possible, avoid central lines that give venous access to patients who use injection drugs.

29

DRUG-SEEKING

Clinical features of drug-seekers

· Tend to gravitate towards services with high volume of new patients (walk-in clinics, ER)
· Seek out physicians known to prescribe opioids or benzodiazepines
· Make false claims of pain or distress
· Present with medical conditions that lack objective signs (e.g., migraine headache, renal colic, back pain)
· Ask for their drug of choice by name
· Refuse all other therapeutic options (unless accompanied by drug of choice)
· Make it difficult to confirm their story (e.g., come in late Friday afternoon when it is hard to reach other physicians)
· Create a sense of urgency (e.g., will not tolerate deferral of prescription pending tests or review of previous records)
· Become angry, threatening, or tearful when refused

P MANAGEMENT
· Use general policy statements ("We don't prescribe opioids to new patients.").
· Only give opioids if you honestly believe that the patient is "on the level."
· Do not make decisions based on stereotypes (e.g., age, social class).
· Try to confirm the patient's story. Contact the physician or pharmacist.
· Ask patients if they have received a prescription for opioids within the past 30 days. It is a criminal offence for patients to receive narcotics without telling the prescribing physician about opioid prescriptions received within 30 days.
· Ask whether the patient has a problem with the drug he or she is requesting.

("This drug is a powerful narcotic and sometimes patients can become addicted to it. Do you feel you may have a problem with this drug?")
· Always offer some form of treatment even if the patient rejects it.
· Tamper-proof prescriptions (see page 81).
· Do not attempt an outpatient opioid taper. Outpatient tapering should be reserved for patients at minimal risk for double-doctoring (i.e., the stable chronic pain patient). Use clonidine instead for treating withdrawal.
· Opioid drugs other than methadone should not be used in the treatment of opioid dependence. Do not prescribe opioids while waiting for the patient to enter treatment.
· Offer referral to treatment programs.
· It is your right to say no. Physicians are no more obliged to prescribe opioids than to prescribe digoxin if they do not feel it is indicated.

Clinical uncertainty (see pages 82–83)

If uncertain whether the patient is genuine or is drug-seeking:
· Take a thorough alcohol and other drug history.
· Get information from the spouse, previous physician or pharmacist.
· Order UDS, GGT, MCV.
· Look for evidence of injection drug use: track marks, positive HBV or HCV serology, elevated ALT.
· Implement strict treatment agreement (see page 80).
· Dispense small amounts for short periods.
· Avoid parenteral opioids and short-acting opioids with high dependence liability.
· Consult addiction medicine specialist.

30

PSYCHOSOCIAL TREATMENT FOR SUBSTANCE USE

Withdrawal management centres

Withdrawal management centres ("detox centres") are intended for patients who do not require medical attention but do need a safe, supervised environment to recover from intoxication or withdrawal. The non-medical staff provides counselling, support and referral to formal treatment programs and social agencies. Patients are referred to the local ER if they require medical management for withdrawal. Depending on local policy, staff may not be allowed to dispense benzodiazepines or opioids, even if prescribed by a physician. The usual length of stay is 3–5 days.

Formal treatment programs

Formal outpatient, day or inpatient rehabilitation programs use a combination of group therapy and individual counselling. Specific programs are available for women, adolescents and the elderly, and patients with coexisting psychiatric disorders. Programs are also organized by substance (e.g., cocaine, heroin, problem drinking, smoking). After formal treatment is completed, most programs provide regular follow-up group sessions for up to 2 years.

COMPONENTS OF FORMAL TREATMENT PROGRAMS
· Comprehensive assessment
· Health education and lifestyle modification
· Group support and acceptance
· Enhancement of motivation and commitment
· Cognitive-behavioural approaches (e.g., identifying triggers to substance use, and practising strategies to cope with urges to use)

OUTPATIENT, DAY PROGRAMS

These programs are probably as effective as inpatient programs for socially stable patients with less severe psychosocial or substance use problems. Outpatient programs usually meet once or twice per week in a group setting, for several months. Day programs last 2–8 h per weekday for several weeks.

INPATIENT PROGRAMS

Indicated for patients who:
· Have failed at outpatient treatment
· Are at high risk for severe withdrawal and require medically supervised withdrawal management
· Are medically or psychiatrically unstable
· Live in an unsupportive or dangerous home environment, e.g., with an abusive or substance-using partner, or alone with no social supports

HALFWAY HOUSES

Patients who have completed a treatment program can live in a halfway house for 6 months or longer, enabling them to find work and permanent accommodation. Abstinence is usually required.

Formal treatment for specific populations

Older adults, women and adolescents often face specific barriers that discourage their participation in treatment. Physicians should know how to access specific programs for these populations.

OLDER ADULTS

Older adults tend to have fewer social supports and can be intimidated by younger patients, group therapy and travel requirements.

Treatment options include: Home-visitation programs, individual counselling, group programs for older adults.

WOMEN

Women may find it difficult to attend formal treatment for a number of reasons:
· Fear of consequences (e.g., loss of children to child protection agency)
· Child care responsibilities
· Lack of support from family/partner
· Most treatment participants are male, making personal disclosure difficult.

Treatment options include: Women-specific treatment programs, programs that provide child care, proactive involvement of child protection agency (see Chapter 26, Pregnancy and Substance Use).

ADOLESCENTS
Adolescents must attend school, and should remain in contact with important family supports. Participation in adult treatment programs would expose adolescents to adults with substance use problems.

Treatment options include: Programs specific for adolescents, combining academics with therapy and support.

Mutual aid groups

Mutual aid groups include groups such as Alcoholics Anonymous (AA), Narcotics Anonymous (NA), Methadone Anonymous (MA), Cocaine Anonymous (CA), Al-Anon (for relatives of alcohol-dependent individuals) and Alateen (for adolescent relatives).

Most mutual aid groups are based on the 12 Steps, a set of principles that emphasize personal responsibility and honesty. For example, Step 1 of AA states, "We admitted we were powerless over alcohol—that our lives had become unmanageable."

MEETINGS
Open meetings are open to the general public; closed meetings are attended only by group members. At closed meetings, members review the 12 Steps, and discuss personal issues in confidence.

SPONSORS
A group member is encouraged to choose a more senior group member as a sponsor. The role of the sponsor is to provide advice and support and to assist in relapse prevention.

Advantages of mutual aid groups

PERSONAL GROWTH
The 12-Step program offers many people a deeply meaningful approach to recovery. "Working the program" promotes emotional and spiritual growth.

PRACTICAL ADVICE

Members in AA provide advice on how to avoid relapse and maintain a healthy lifestyle, e.g., members are advised to avoid HALT states (hungry, angry, lonely, tired), common triggers for relapse.

ACCEPTANCE

By admitting they have an alcohol problem to others in the group, the burden of shame and guilt is lifted and members can develop a more positive approach to recovery.

SOCIAL SUPPORT

A close bond often develops between group members. This helps them overcome the social isolation and loneliness that puts them at risk for relapse.

MENTORING

The sponsor often plays a crucial role in the person's recovery, providing support, advice and assistance.

LONG-TERM COMMUNITY FOLLOW-UP

Because members can attend AA indefinitely, AA has an important role in relapse prevention.

NO COST

AA is supported by members' voluntary donations.

Role of the physician in mutual aid groups

· Explain to your patients the importance of attending AA. Encourage them to call the central AA number for meeting times and locations.
· Tell patients the only requirement for membership is a desire to quit drinking. They do not have to believe in God.
· Have an AA contact (e.g., a patient in your office) who will, with mutual consent, accompany patients new to AA to their first meeting.
· Encourage patients to try several AA groups until they find one they feel comfortable attending on an ongoing basis.

31

COUNSELLING AND MOTIVATIONAL INTERVIEWING

Physicians and nurses have an essential role in motivating patients to modify their substance use and enter treatment.

General approach to counselling

· Establish a trusting relationship.
· Do not use negative labels (e.g., "alcoholic," "drug addict"); use terms such as "alcohol dependence."
· Tell patients they are suffering from an illness, not a moral weakness. Tell them that their illness is treatable and that you can help.
· Try to get them to acknowledge that their troubles are caused by substance use and not the other way around (but do not argue).
· Involve the family. They can be powerful motivators for change.

Basic components of counselling

The following basic counselling approach can be used even by the busy clinician (see Chapter 7, Problem Drinking).

· Explain the health effects of substance use, linking them to the patient's current health problems.
· Mention non-specific effects common to most substances, e.g., fatigue, insomnia, low mood.
· Discuss the effects of substance use (if any) on family and work. Ask if the spouse has expressed any concerns about substance use.
· Review treatment options, e.g., treatment programs, mutual aid groups, pharmacotherapy. Ask the patient which options he or she would prefer to try.

· Arrange referrals to treatment programs and a follow-up visit with the family physician and an addiction specialist.
· Monitor substance use with appropriate laboratory measurements (urine drug screen or GGT for alcohol use).
· Provide motivational counselling as needed.

Common mistakes in counselling

COMMON MISTAKES	PATIENT REACTION
Labelling	Patient feels shame or guilt.
Lecturing	Thinks of reasons not to change.
Providing unwanted advice	Avoids discussing substance use.
Pushing patient to enter treatment before he or she is ready to change	Thinks of excuses to avoid treatment.
Not addressing the substance use problem, or minimizing it ("I will talk about it when the patient is ready")	Patient feels you are not concerned about his or her substance use or that it is not important medically.

Stages of change model

The stages of change model provides a simple yet effective counselling approach. The model describes 6 stages of readiness to change: precontemplation, contemplation, preparation, action, maintenance and relapse. Patients may pass through each stage several times before maintaining a permanent change in behaviour.

Physicians should match their intervention to the patient's stage, while recognizing that readiness to change can shift dramatically with changing circumstances. Physicians should be alert to opportunities for promoting change, e.g., an acute substance-related illness or personal crisis.

Overview of Stages of Change†

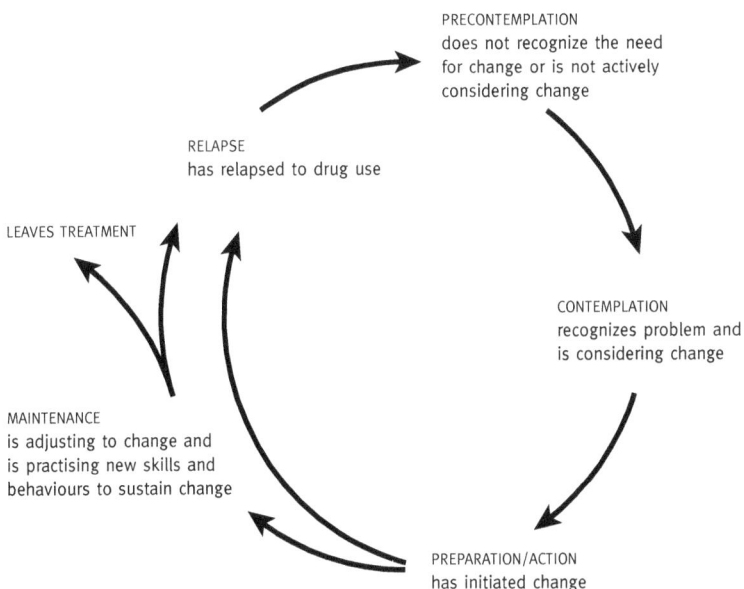

PRECONTEMPLATION
does not recognize the need
for change or is not actively
considering change

RELAPSE
has relapsed to drug use

LEAVES TREATMENT

CONTEMPLATION
recognizes problem and
is considering change

MAINTENANCE
is adjusting to change and
is practising new skills and
behaviours to sustain change

PREPARATION/ACTION
has initiated change

†Adapted from: Prochaska, J.O., and DiClemente, C.C. (1982). Transtheoretical therapy: Toward a
more integrative model of change. *Psychotherapy: Theory, Research and Practice*, 19 (3), 276-288.

ASSESSING PATIENT'S READINESS TO CHANGE: SAMPLE QUESTIONS
· "What concerns do you have about your use of _____? What benefits does
it give you?"
· "How ready are you to change your use of _____?" (Can put this on a scale
of 1 to 10.)
· "Would you be willing to change your use of _____ in the next 6 months?
In the next month?"

Precontemplation

Patients in precontemplation do not view their substance use as a problem.

STRATEGIES

· Provide health information (e.g., low-risk drinking guidelines); link substance use to patients' symptoms and/or condition.

· Encourage patients to discuss the role the substance plays in their life.

🔊 PRECONTEMPLATION: SAMPLE QUESTIONS

· "How do you feel about your use of _____?"

· "Tell me about a typical day. Where does your use of _____ fit in?"

· "How does your use of _____ affect your health?"

· "Would you be interested in knowing more about the effect of _____ on _____?"

Contemplation

Most people who use substances are in this phase. They are ambivalent; the substance use causes problems but also has perceived benefits. Patients are weighing pros and cons of changing versus staying the same.

STRATEGIES

Encourage patients to elaborate on the benefits and risks of continuing substance use, and the benefits and risks of abstinence or cutting down. Explore in detail their concerns about drinking and their reasons for considering abstinence or cutting down. This helps patients persuade themselves of the need for change.

🔊 CONTEMPLATION: SAMPLE QUESTIONS

· "What are some of the good things about your use of _____?"

· "What are some of the less good things about your use of _____?"

· "How does your use of _____ affect you at the moment?"

· "How would you like things to be different in the future?"

· "What concerns do you have about your use of _____?"

· "What concerns do you have about changing your use of _____?"

· "Where does this leave you now?" (This question can lead patients to consider options for change.)

DECISIONAL BALANCE TABLE

A decisional balance table is useful for patients in the contemplation phase.

Draw the following chart on a piece of paper and ask your patients to complete the 4 cells. Review each cell with your patients, reinforcing the cons of continuing their current behaviour and the pros of changing their behaviour.

Decisional balance table

	PROS	CONS
Current behaviour		
Change in behaviour		

Preparation/action

Patients become committed to changing their substance use.

STRATEGIES
· Describe treatment options, and elicit patients' preferences.
· Provide support and referral. Act promptly before patients return to the contemplation stage.

PREPARATION: SAMPLE STATEMENT
· "There are many treatment options. You are the best judge of what will work for you."

Maintenance

Patients have completed a treatment program and have reached their treatment goals for 6 months.

STRATEGIES
· Emphasize need to attend aftercare program.
· Encourage frequent attendance at mutual aid meetings and frequent contact with their sponsors.
· Monitor response to pharmacotherapy.
· Do not prescribe sedatives.

· Prescribe opioids with caution.
· Acknowledge dry-dates and recovery anniversaries.
· Discuss management of cravings and urges.
· Increase counselling and support during times of stress.

Relapse
The physician should be alert to clues for potential relapse.

CLUES TO RELAPSE
· Irritability, isolation
· Unwillingness to talk about recovery program
· Request for mood-altering medications
· Missed appointments
· Decreased attendance at mutual aid meetings and/or formal therapy

MANAGEMENT OF RELAPSE
Most people with substance use problems have at least 1 or 2 periods of relapse during their recovery. The health provider's role is to recognize relapse and work with the patient to resolve it as quickly as possible.
· Do not worsen patients' guilt and self-blame.
· Help the patients to view relapse as a learning experience.
· Develop new strategies for dealing with cravings and triggers to substance use.
· Have a plan for treating withdrawal.
· Intensify the treatment program (more frequent attendance at AA and/or formal therapy, pharmacotherapy).
· Provide more frequent follow-ups.

Counselling the spouse/family of a person with a substance use problem
The spouse often tries hard to control the partner's substance use, maintain the family's finances and reputation and compensate for the partner's neglect of family responsibilities. These tasks can lead to exhaustion and despair. The physician can help by providing ongoing support.
· If there are concerns about violence, meet with the spouse separately or refer to another physician.

· Ask about abuse, neglect and safety of the children. Provide assistance and referral if necessary.
· Assess the spouse for anxiety, depression and substance use.
· Explain the nature of substance dependence, including withdrawal and its risks. Review treatment approaches.
· Encourage the spouse to attend Al-Anon or investigate other programs designed for spouses/family. Often formal treatment programs offer adjunct programs for family members.
· Advise the person to avoid helping the partner to acquire the substance (e.g., buying liquor).
· Emphasize that the spouse did not cause and cannot control the partner's substance use; the partner has to take responsibility for his or her own behaviour.
· Encourage the spouse to maintain his or her own interests and friendships.
· Help the spouse to develop strategies to maintain the family's finances and health. This may include asking the partner who is using substances to leave the house. Caregivers should not argue for (or against) this option, but should support the spouse's right to protect him- or herself and the family. While this may anger the partner, it may also act as a catalyst for change.

32

PHYSICIAN AND NURSE IMPAIRMENT

Most of us would find it very difficult to approach a medical or nursing colleague whom we suspect has an alcohol or other drug problem. However, we have a collegial responsibility for our colleague's well-being, and a professional responsibility to our colleague's patients.

Timely intervention by a colleague may prevent an impaired nurse or physician from getting into serious trouble. If the warning signs of problem substance use are ignored, the problem may get progressively more serious, eventually leading to loss of career and family, or death from an overdose, accident or suicide.

Epidemiology
· Lifetime risk of substance dependence among physicians: 6–10%; [57] among nurses: 5–20% [58]
· Current heavy drinking among physicians: 6% (equivalent to the general population) [57]

General risk factors
· Denial of basic needs: Sleep deprivation, meal skipping, no family time or leisure activities
· Medical personality traits: Perfectionism, intellectualization, guilt, sacrifice of personal needs
· Professional demands: Patient care responsibilities, conflict between professional and personal life roles
· Access to mood-altering substances

· Poor medical care: Self-diagnosis and treatment, no personal family physician, corridor consultation, resistance to the patient role
· Environment of denial: Friends, colleagues and co-workers often reluctant to address obvious signs of impairment

Predisposing factors
· Family history of substance dependence
· Family history of depression
· History of physical, sexual or emotional abuse
· History of psychiatric illness

Warning signs of use
· Recent changes in personality
· Change in work habits (cancelling clinics, doing late rounds, etc.)
· Increased sick days
· Sloppy work habits
· Heavy or unusual wastage of drugs
· Withdrawal from collegial activities such as meetings, conferences, rounds
· Significant family problems (addiction causes difficulties in the home long before problems appear at work)
· Unusual patient or staff complaints
· Inappropriate prescribing

Physical changes
· Appears fatigued
· Frequent generalized complaints of backache, flu-like symptoms
· Decline in hygiene and personal care
· Smell of alcohol or frequent use of breath mints / mouthwash
· Tremulous or sweaty
· Runny nose, watery eyes, flushed face
· Weight loss or weight gain

Behaviours of nurses and physicians who are dependent on opioids

PHYSICIANS	NURSES
. Offers to "help the nurse" by administering narcotics to inpatients or ER patients	· Offers to take over the care of patients requiring opioids
· In the clinic or hospital at late or unusual hours, or when not on duty	· Offers to administer other patients' analgesia
· Asks patients to return "leftover" opioid medications	· Frequently seeks overtime and double shifts
· Increased narcotic prescribing "for the office"	· Frequent narcotic count discrepancies
· Writes scripts for home-bound patients or family members; picks up medication from pharmacy	· Frequent narcotic wastage, spillage
· Steals from narcotics cupboard	· Patient complains of inadequate pain management only on that nurse's shift

Approaching a medical or nursing colleague: What to do and say

· Arrange a meeting with the colleague.
· Express concern about the alcohol/drug use ("I'm really worried about you," "You seem to be going through a difficult time").
· Mention specific examples (e.g., alcohol on the breath, unsteadiness last night).
· Avoid negative terms and labels ("You were drunk yesterday").
· Ask for your colleague's version of events.
· Ask your colleague to agree to a consultation by an addiction medicine specialist.
· Suggest practical options for accessing treatment (gather this information before the meeting). See below.
· Express a willingness to provide support and help.

Options if the colleague refuses treatment

· Organize a more formal meeting of your colleagues to confront the person about his or her substance use.
· For physicians—contact a confidential physician advisory service, if one exists in your jurisdiction.
· If the colleague exhibits signs of ongoing substance use and continues to refuse

treatment, physicians should consider contacting their chief of staff or departmental chief, and nurses should contact the patient care manager or nursing director. Ultimately the college of physicians or the college of nurses may need to be contacted.

Physician Health Program

In Ontario, the OMA Physician Health Program is an arm's length, confidential service that provides advice to impaired physicians and their colleagues and family members. The program facilitates treatment and monitoring, and (if necessary) advocates for the physician with the licensing authorities.

Role of licensing authorities

Physicians

Physicians whose substance use has been brought to the attention of the licencing authority (College of Physicians) may be asked to appear before a board of inquiry. The board reviews the physician's substance use and may ask for further assessments from an addiction medicine specialist or psychiatrist.

The College may ask the physician to agree to attend treatment and provide ongoing monitoring of the drug use. Physicians who have been misusing opioids may have their narcotic-prescribing privileges suspended for a period of time. Although jurisdictions vary, physicians' licences are usually not suspended unless they continue their drug use and refuse to attend treatment, or they have repeated relapses.

Nurses

Nurses go through a somewhat similar process with the College of Nurses, culminating in a terms of work agreement (if the nurse agrees to attend treatment and undergo ongoing monitoring) or suspension of registration (if the nurse refuses treatment or continues to relapse).

Treatment programs

Physicians and nurses attending treatment generally have a very good prognosis. The optimal treatment is an intensive program, followed by a structured follow-up program over several years. Some programs have special streams for health care workers and can accept them into treatment within days.

COMPONENTS OF TREATMENT

These treatment components are often spelled out in an "advocacy contract" between the patient and the addiction medicine specialist. This includes such items as:

· Assessment to identify drug problem(s) and concurrent psychiatric and medical disorders
· Intensive inpatient or outpatient treatment program
· Mutual aid groups such as AA (including regular contact with AA sponsor)
· Health care professionals' support group, facilitated by an addiction medicine specialist
· Program of ongoing monitoring (e.g., urine drug screens)
· Regular contact with family physician and addiction medicine specialist
· Agreement not to self-medicate
· Focus on family and spiritual life (time with family, journaling, meditation)
· Gradual return to work with agreement of health care professionals' support group and addiction medicine specialist. Return to work may have conditions (e.g., no unsupervised access to narcotic medications).

ISSUES IN RECOVERY

Physicians and nurses in recovery are encouraged to work on developing a balanced lifestyle: Exercise, sleep, regular meals, family, and avoidance of overwork.

Physician's self-prescribing and prescribing to colleagues

Sometimes physicians inadvertently contribute to addiction by prescribing psychoactive medications for themselves or for their colleagues.

· Physicians should never prescribe psychoactive medication for themselves. All physicians should have a personal family doctor.
· Physicians should only prescribe for medical and nursing colleagues within the context of a formal physician-patient relationship (no corridor prescriptions).

APPENDIX

Substance use resources in Ontario

Addiction Clinical Consultation Service	1-888-720-2227
Drug and Alcohol Registry of Treatment (DART)	1-800-565-8603
Metro Addiction Assessment Referral Service (MAARS)*	416-599-1448
Centre for Addiction and Mental Health	1-416-535-8501
OMA Physician Health Program	1-800-268-7215 x 2972
MotheRisk Alcohol and Substance Abuse Helpline	1-877-327-4636
Ontario Problem Gambling Helpline	1-888-230-3505
Canadian Society of Addiction Medicine	1-613-541-3951

Note: Metro Toronto only.

REFERENCES

1. Single, E., Robson, L., Rehm, J. & Xi, X. (1999). Morbidity and mortality attributable to alcohol, tobacco, and illicit drug use in Canada. *Am J Public Health, 89*(3), 385–390.

2. Single, E., Robson, L., Xie, X. & Rehm, J. (1998). The economic costs of alcohol, tobacco and illicit drugs in Canada, 1992. *Addiction, 93*(7), 991–1006.

3. Kahan, M., Wilson, L. & Becker, L. (1995). Effectiveness of physician-based interventions with problem drinkers: A review. *CMAJ, 152*(6), 851–859.

4. Fleming, M.F., Barry, K.L., Manwell, L.B., Johnson, K. & London, R. (1997). Brief physician advice for problem alcohol drinkers. A randomized controlled trial in community-based primary care practices. *JAMA, 277*(13), 1039–1045.

5. Spies, C.D. & Rommelspacher, H. (1999). Alcohol withdrawal in the surgical patient: Prevention and treatment. *Anesth Analg, 88*(4), 946–954.

6. Tonnesen, H., Rosenberg, J., Nielsen, H.J., Rasmussen, V., Hauge, C., Pedersen, I.K. & Kehlet, H. (1999). Effect of preoperative abstinence on poor postoperative outcome in alcohol misusers: Randomised controlled trial. *BMJ, 318*(7194), 1311–1316.

7. Tonnesen, H. (1999). The alcohol patient and surgery. *Alcohol and Alcoholism, 34*(2), 148–152.

8. New York State Office of Alcoholism and Substance Abuse Services (1993). *Health Care Intervention Services: Third Formative Report 1993*. Albany: New York State Office of Alcoholism and Substance Abuse Services.

9. O'Brien, C.P. & McLellan, A.T. (1996). Myths about the treatment of addiction. *Lancet, 347*(8996), 237–240.

10. Holder, H.D. & Blose, J.O. (1992). The reduction of health care costs associated with alcoholism treatment: A 14-year longitudinal study. *J Stud Alcohol,* *53*(4), 293–302.

11. Fleming, M., Mundt, M.P., French, M.T., Manwell, L.B. & Stauffacher, E.A. (2000). Benefit-cost analysis of brief physician advice with problem drinkers in primary care settings. *Med Care, 38*(1), 7–18.

12. Cherpitel, C.J., Soghikian, K. & Hurley, L.B. (1996). Alcohol-related health services use and identification of patients in the emergency department. *Ann Emerg Med, 28*(4), 418–423.

13. Mayfield, D., McLeod, G. & Hall, P. (1974). The CAGE questionnaire: Validation of a new alcoholism screening instrument. *Am J Psychiatry, 131*(10), 1121–1123.

14. Bradley, K.A., Boyd-Wickizer, J., Powell, S.H. & Burman, M.L. (1998). Alcohol screening questionnaires in women: A critical review. *JAMA, 280*(2), 166–171.

15. Smith-Warner, S.A., Spiegelman, D., Yaun, S.S., van den Brandt, P.A., Folsom, A.R., Goldbohm, R.A., Graham, S., Holmberg, L., Howe, G.R., Marshall, J.R., Miller, A.B., Potter, J.D., Speizer, F.E., Willett, W.C., Wolk, A. & Hunter, D.J. (1998). Alcohol and breast cancer in women: A pooled analysis of cohort studies. *JAMA, 279*(7), 535–540.

16. Volpicelli, J.R., Alterman, A.I., Hayashida, M. & O'Brien, C.P. (1992). Naltrexone in the treatment of alcohol dependence. *Arch Gen Psychiatry, 49*(11), 875–880.

17. O'Malley, S.S., Jaffe, A.J., Chang, G., Schottenfeld, R.S., Meyer, R.E. & Rounsaville, B. (1992). Naltrexone and coping skills therapy for alcohol dependence. A controlled study. *Arch Gen Psychiatry, 49*(11), 881–887.

18. Sass, H., Soyka, M. & Zieglgansberger, W. (1996). Relapse prevention by acamprosate. Results from a placebo-controlled study on alcohol dependence. *Arch Gen Psychiatry, 53*(8): 673–680.

19. Johnson, B.A., Roache, J.D. Javors, M.A., DiClemente, C.C., Cloninger., C.R., Prihoda, T.J., Bordnick, P.S., Ait-Doaud, N. & Hensler, J. (2000). Ondansetron for reduction of drinking among biologically predisposed alcoholic patients: A randomized controlled trial. *JAMA, 284*(8), 963–971.

20. Ramond, M.J., Poynard, T., Rueff, B., Mathurin, P., Theodore, C., Chaput, J.C. & Benhamou, J.P. (1992). A randomized trial of prednisolone in patients with severe alcoholic hepatitis. *N Engl J Med, 326*(8), 507–512.

21. Orrego, H., Blake, J.E., Blendis, L.M., Compton, K.V. & Israel, Y. (1987). Long-term treatment of alcoholic liver disease with propylthiouracil. *N Engl J Med, 317*(23), 1421–1427.

22. Maldonado, J.R. & Keeffe, E.B. (1997). Liver transplantation for alcoholic liver disease: Selection and outcome. *Clinics in Liver Disease*, 1997. 1(2).

23. Bosch, J. (1998). Medical treatment of portal hypertension. *Digestion, 59*(5), 547–555.

24. Villanueva, C., Balanzo, J., Novella, M.T., Soriano, G., Sainz, S., Torras, X., Cusso, X., Guarner, C. & Vilardell, F. (1996). Nadolol plus isosorbide mononitrate compared with sclerotherapy for the prevention of variceal rebleeding. *N Engl J Med, 334*(25), 1624–1629.

25. Blei, A.T. & Cordoba, J. (2001). Hepatic encephalopathy. *Am J Gastroenterol, 96*(7), 1968–1976.

26. Fiore, M.C., Bailey, W.C. Cohen, S.J. et al. (2000). *Treating Tobacco Use and Dependence. Clinical Practice Guidelines*. Rockville, MD: U.S. Department of Health and Human Services. Public Health Service.

27. Prochazka, A.V., Weaver, M.J., Keller, R.T., Fryer, G.E., Licari, P.A. & Lofaso, D. (1998). A randomized trial of nortriptyline for smoking cessation. *Arch Intern Med, 158*(18), 2035–2039.

28. Hall, S.M., Reus, V.I., Munoz, R.F., Sees, K.L. Humfleet, G., Hartz, D.T., Frederick, S. & Triffleman, E. (1998). Nortriptyline and cognitive-behavioral therapy in the treatment of cigarette smoking. *Arch Gen Psychiatry, 55*(8), 683–690.

29. Arkinstall, W., Sandler, A., Goughnour, B., Babnul, N., Harsanyi, Z. & Darke, A.C. (1995). Efficacy of controlled-release codeine in chronic non-malignant pain: A randomized, placebo-controlled clinical trial. *Pain, 62*(2), 169–178.

30. Moulin, D.E., Iezzi, A., Amireh, R., Sharpe, W.K., Boyd, D & Merskey, H. (1996). Randomised trial of oral morphine for chronic non-cancer pain. *Lancet, 347*(8995), 143–147.

31. Watson, C.P. & Babul, N. (1998). Efficacy of oxycodone in neuropathic pain: A randomized trial in postherpetic neuralgia. *Neurology, 50*(6), 1837–1841.

32. Gearing, F.R. & Schweitzer, M.D. (1974). An epidemiologic evaluation of long-term methadone maintenance treatment for heroin addiction. *Am J Epidemiol, 100*(2), 101–112.

33. Ball, J. C. & Ross, A. (1991). *The Effectiveness of Methadone Maintenance Treatment: Patients, Programs, Services, and Outcome.* New York: Springer-Verlag.

34. Uehlinger, C., Deglon, J., Livoti, S., Petitjean, S., Waldvogel, D. & Ladewig, D. (1998). Comparison of buprenorphine and methadone in the treatment of opioid dependence. Swiss multicentre study. *Eur Addict Res, 4*(Suppl 1), 13–18.

35. Eder, H., Fischer, G., Gombas, W., Jagsch, R., Stuhlinger, G. & Kasper, S. (1998). Comparison of buprenorphine and methadone maintenance in opiate addicts. *Eur Addict Res, 4*(Suppl 1), 3–7.

36. Fischer, G., Gombas, W., Eder, H., Jagsch, R., Peternell, A., Stuhlinger, G., Pezawas, L., Aschauer, H.N. & Kasper, S. (1999). Buprenorphine versus methadone maintenance for the treatment of opioid dependence. *Addiction, 94*(9), 1337–1347.

37. McLean, W. (2000). New guidelines for barbiturate-containing analgesics: Don't start, and help stop!. *CMAJ, 163*(4), 414–415.

38. Sellers, E.M. (1988). Alcohol, barbiturate and benzodiazepine withdrawal syndromes: Clinical management. *CMAJ, 139*(2), 113–120.

39. Hambrecht, M. & Hafner, H. (2000). Cannabis, vulnerability, and the onset of schizophrenia: An epidemiological perspective. *Aust N Z J Psychiatry, 34*(3), 468–475.

40. Bolla, K.I., McCann, U.D. & Ricaurte, G.A. (1998). Memory impairment in abstinent MDMA ("Ecstasy") users. *Neurology, 51*(6), 1532–1537.

41. Haydel, M.J., Preston, C.A., Mills, T.J., Luber, S., Blaudeau, E. & DeBlieux, P.M. (2000). Indications for computed tomography in patients with minor head injury. *N Engl J Med, 343*(2), 100–105.

42. Centers for Disease Control and Prevention. (1998). Recommendations for prevention and control of hepatitis C virus (HCV) infection and HCV-related chronic disease. *Morb Mortal Wkly Rep, 47*(RR-19), 1–39.

43. Canadian Liver Foundation & Health Canada, (2000). *Hepatitis C: Medical Information Update*. Toronto: Canadian Liver Foundation.

44. Zanetti, A.R., Tanzi, E. & Newell, M.L. (1999). Mother-to-infant transmission of hepatitis C virus. *J Hepatol, 31* (Suppl 1), 96–100.

45. Rosman, A.S., Basu, P. Galvin, K. & Lieber, C.S. (1997). Efficacy of a high and accelerated dose of hepatitis B vaccine in alcoholic patients: A randomized clinical trial. *Am J Med, 103*(3), 217–222.

46. Nalpas, B.V., Thepot, V., Driss, F., Pol, S., Courouce, A.M., Saliou, P. & Berthelot, P. (1993). Secondary immune response to hepatitis B virus vaccine in alcoholics. *Alcohol Clin Exp Res, 17*(2), 295–298.

47. Committee on Latent Tuberculosis Infection. (2000). Targeted tuberculin testing and treatment of latent tuberculosis infection. *MMWR, 49*(6).

48. Moretti, M.E., Lee, A. & Ito, S. (2000). Which drugs are contraindicated during breastfeeding? Practice guidelines. *Can Fam Physician, 46*, 1753–1757.

49. Wojnar-Horton, R.E., Kristensen, J.H., Yapp, P., Ilett, K.F., Dusci, L.J. & Hackett, L.J. (1997). Methadone distribution and excretion into breast milk of clients in a methadone maintenance programme. *Br J Clin Pharmacol, 44*(6), 543–547.

50. Polywka, S., Schroter, M., Feucht, H.H., Zollner, B.& Laufs, R. (1999). Low risk of vertical transmission of hepatitis C virus by breast milk. *Clin Infect Dis, 29*(5), 1327–1329.

51. Bell, G.L. & Lau K. (1995). Perinatal and neonatal issues of substance abuse. *Pediatr Clin North Am, 42*(2), 261–281.

52. American Academy of Pediatrics Committee on Drugs. (1998). Neonatal drug withdrawal. *Pediatrics, 101*(6), 1079–1088.

53. Finnegan, L.P. (1975). A scoring system for evaluation and treatment of the neonatal abstinence syndrome: A new clinical and research tool. In P.L. Moselli, S. Garattini & F. Sereni (Eds.), *Basic and Therapeutic Aspects of Perinatal Pharmacology*. Raven Press: New York.

54. Zahorodny, W., Rom, C., Whitney, W., Giddens, S., Samuel, M., Maichuk, G. & Marshall R. (1998). The neonatal withdrawal inventory: A simplified score of newborn withdrawal. *Dev Behav Pediatr, 19*(2), 89–93.

55. Osborn, D. (2001). *Neonatal Abstinence Syndrome. Department of Neonatal Medicine Protocol Book* [on-line]. New South Wales: Royal Prince Alfred Hospital. Available: www.cs.nsw.gov.au/rpa/neonatal/default/htm

56. Tonnesen, H., Rosenberg, J., Nielsen, H.J., Rasmussen, V., Hauge, C., Pedersen, I.K. & Kehlet, H. (1999). Effect of preoperative abstinence on poor postoperative outcome in alcohol misusers: Randomised controlled trial. *BMJ, 318*(7194), 1311–1316.

57. Brewster, J.M. (1992). *Drug Use among Canadian Professionals*. Ottawa: Health and Welfare Canada.

58. Griffith, J. (1999). Substance abuse disorders in nurses. *Nurs Forum. 34*(4), 19–28.

INDEX

A

AA. *See* Alcoholics Anonymous; mutual aid groups

ABCs, 58, 129, 134, 141-142

Abdominal cramps, opioid withdrawal and, 90

Abruptio placentae, 121, 162, 163, 164

Acetaminophen, 14, 57, 76, 78, 81, 82, 86, 95, 125, 140, 142, 143, 144, 152, 156

Acidosis. *See* metabolic acidosis

Acne: anabolic steroids and, 126, 127; disulfiram and, 52

ADHD, 134, 162

Adolescents: anabolic steroids and, 127; cannabis and, 123; inhalants and, 128-129; MDMA and, 132; methylphenidate and, 134; substance use screening for, 17, 18, 19; treatment options for, 195, 196, 197. *See also* young adults

Al-Anon, 197, 205. *See also* mutual aid groups

Alateen, 197. *See also* mutual aid groups

Alcohol consumption history, 9, 11

Alcohol dependence: consumption rates indicating, 12; effectiveness of treatment for, 7; pharmacotherapy for, 38, 44, 48, 50-53; versus problem drinking, 32-33

Alcohol problems: anxiety and, 10, 12, 34, 38, 39, 40, 41, 43, 44; assessment of, 9-12, 35, 143-144; ataxia and, 10, 13, 35, 40, 47; CAGE and, 11, 18, 79, 163, 188; cardiomyopathy and, 10, 13, 30, 38, 63, 64, 187, 188; cerebellar disease and, 10, 35, 40, 62; depression and, 10, 12, 40, 53, 184-185, 186; detection of, 10, 13, 17, 19; hepatitis and, 10, 23, 30, 45, 54, 55, 56, 57, 64; hypertension and, 10, 13, 30, 32, 64; infertility and, 10, 65; insomnia and, 10, 32, 33, 185; laboratory investigations for, 11, 13, 40, 144; low birthweight and, 10; magnesium and 13, 40, 66, 142, 144; other drugs and, 12; peripheral neuropathy and, 10, 62; physical examination for, 13; polysubstance use and, 12, 188; pregnancy and (*See* pregnancy); psychosis and, 10, 12, 15, 39; suicide and, 12, 40; T-ACE and, 11, 18, 163, 164; trauma and, 190; treatment programs for, 32-33, 38-49; violence and, 10, 31

Alcohol use: anemia and, 64, 144; blackouts and, 62; breastfeeding and, 169; cardiovascular complications of, 63-64; cirrhosis and, 10, 13, 30, 32, 45, 54, 55, 56-58; delirium and, 15, 38, 39, 43, 48, 114, 143, 188, 189; drowsiness and, 21, 143-144; dysrhythmias and, 7, 10, 15, 30, 38, 39, 40, 46, 47, 48, 52, 63-64, 144, 188; endocrine and metabolic complications of, 65-66; fetal alcohol effects and, 65, 161, 162; fetal alcohol syndrome and, 65, 161-162; GGT and, 23, 188; GHB and, 27, 138; GI complications of, 63, 64, 65; hematological complications of, 64; infections and, 66; insomnia and, 10, 32, 33, 185; laboratory detection of, 20-23; liver disease and (*See* alcoholic liver disease); malignancies and, 65; MCV and, 23, 188; neurological problems and, 10, 62; opioids and, 30, 39, 79, 143-145; overdose from, 143-145; pregnancy and, 30, 161-162, 170, 171; relapse to, 6, 32, 52, 57, 72; reproductive complications of, 65; respiratory complications of, 64; seizures and, 15, 30; substance-induced disorders and, 184; surgery and, 7, 66, 187-190; sweating and, 15; vomiting and, 63; thrombocytopenia and, 23, 55, 64, 189; urine drug screen for, 13, 23-25, 27, 36, 144; women and, 9, 11, 12, 13, 35

Alcohol withdrawal: assessment of, 39-44; benzodiazepines and, 41, 43, 44, 49, 115; blood alcohol concentration and, 45; compared with other drug withdrawal, 114; complicated, 38, 45-46, 71-72, 109 (*See also* polysubstance use; withdrawal); diazepam loading for, 20, 39, 41, 44-49, 63, 114, 115, 116, 171; headache and, 38, 40, 43; hypertension and, 38, 39; insomnia and, 38, 44; lorazepam for, 44-45, 108, 109, 116, 137, 138, 189; management of, 44-45; in older adults, 38; physical examination for, 39-40; pregnancy and, 171 (*See also* fetal alcohol effects; fetal alcohol syndrome); seizures and, 35, 38, 39, 40, 44, 46, 47, 48, 49, 52, 71, 73, 114, 188; surgery and, 188, 190; sweating and, 13, 38, 40, 41, 42, 44; symptoms, 15, 38-39, 114; tachycardia and, 15, 38, 19; thiamine and, 44, 48; treatment programs for, 38-49; tremor and, 12, 13, 15, 38, 39, 40, 41, 42, 44, 188; vomiting and, 15, 38, 39, 40, 41

Alcoholic liver disease: alcoholic hepatitis, 54, 55, 56, 57; cardiomyopathy and,

63; cirrhosis, 10, 13, 30, 32, 45, 54, 55, 58; clinical features of, 54; fatty liver, 10, 32, 54, 55; liver transplant, 57; lorazepam for, 59, 190; peritonitis, 61; surgery and, 189-190. *See also* hepatitis; ascites; cirrhosis

Alcoholics Anonymous, 32, 72, 186, 197-198, 204, 210. *See also* mutual aid groups

Alprazolam, 4, 103, 105, 106, 108, 109

Amenorrhea, 65. *See also* menstrual cycle

Amnesia: flunitrazepam and, 139; GHB and, 137; ketamine and, 135

Amobarbital, 111

Amphetamine, 4, 19, 25, 26, 28, 130-132, 184

Anabolic steroids, 4, 19, 73, 125-127, 128

Anaesthesia: 58, 135, 136, 149, 175; naltrexone and, 50

Analgesics, 50, 76, 78, 85, 86, 87, 88, 91, 97, 109, 191. *See also* acetaminophen; ASA; opioids

Androstenedione, 127

Anemia, 58, 64, 144

"Angel dust." *See* PCP

Anhedonia, 119

Antabuse®. *See* disulfiram

Antidepressants, 73, 101, 102, 103, 119, 128, 185. *See also* bupropion; monoamine oxidase inhibitors; SSRIs; tricyclic antidepressants

Antifreeze, 151. *See also* methanol; ethylene glycol

Antihistamines, 78, 102, 125

Anxiety: alcohol and, 10, 12, 34, 38, 39, 40, 41, 43, 44; anabolic steroids and, 126; assessment of, 100, 185; barbiturates and, 15, 105; benzodiazepines and, 15, 99-101, 103, 105, 106, 107, 108; buspirone for, 100; cannabis and, 123; causes of, 99; chronic pain and, 79; cocaine and, 117; dimenhydrinate and, 125; drug withdrawal and, 15; MDMA and, 133; non-medical management of, 100; opioid dependence and, 86; opioid withdrawal and, 83, 90, 91; selective serotonin reuptake inhibitors for, 101; smoking and, 71; substance use and, 14, 16, 18, 19, 79, 86, 113, 165, 183, 184, 185, 186, 205. *See also* insomnia

Anxiolytics. *See* sedatives

Apnea. *See* obstructive sleep apnea

Arthritis, rheumatoid, 154

ASA, 81, 86, 109, 125, 142, 143, 144, 149, 152

Ascites, 54, 55, 59, 60-61, 189

Assessment: of alcohol problems, 9-12, 35, 143-144; of alcohol withdrawal, 39-44; of anabolic steroid use, 127; of anxiety, 100; of chronic pain, 79; CIWA-A, 41-43; of concurrent disorders, 185, 186; defined, 4; of drug use, 14-16, 23; in formal treatment programs, 195; of hallucinogen use, 130; of inhalant use, 129; of insomnia, 101-102; of intoxication, 35; of nurse impairment, 210; nurses role in, 5; of opioid dependence, 86, 87; of physician impairment, 209, 210; of polysubstance use, 113; preoperative, 188; of pseudoaddiction, 86; of substance use during pregnancy, 164-165, 168. *See also* screening

AST, 13, 23, 40, 55, 127, 144, 160, 165, 188

Asterixis, 59, 60, 144

At-risk drinking, defined, 3. *See also* alcohol use

Ataxia, 10, 13, 35, 40, 47, 62, 145

Athletes, anabolic steroid use by, 125, 127

Ativan®. *See* lorazepam

Autonomic hyperactivity: alcohol withdrawal and, 38-39, 47; barbiturates and, 110; benzodiazepines and, 15, 106

AZT, 169

B

BAC. *See* blood alcohol concentration

Barbiturates: acetaminophen and, 152; alcohol and, 13, 44, 113, 115; benzodiazepines and, 103, 113, 116; effects of, 15, 110; equivalence table for, 111; examples of, 4; for GHB withdrawal, 138; neonates and, 167; opioids and, 116; pregnancy and, 165, 171; smoking and, 73; surgery and, 191; tapering, 111, 112, 191; urine drug screen for, 25, 27, 28, 29; withdrawal from, 15, 109-110, 113, 114, 115, 116, 171, 191. *See also* amobarbital, butabarbital, butalbital, fiorinal, pentobarbital, phenobarbital, secobarbital

Benzodiazepines: 5, 139, 185, 195; adverse effects of, 104; alcohol and, 12, 13, 30, 39, 144; alcohol withdrawal and, 41, 43, 44, 49, 115; alternatives to, 104; anxiety and, 99-101, 108, 184; assessment for, 14, 15; barbiturates and, 115; bupropion and, 73; for chronic pain, 79, 89; cocaine and, 117, 118, 119; dependence on, 105; effects of, 15, 103, 104, 148; equivalence table for, 109;

examples of, 4; for GHB use, 138, 139; half-lives of, 103; hepatic encephalopathy and, 58-59, 60; HIV and, 159; for inhalant complications, 129; for insomnia, 102-104; intoxication on, 148; ketamine and, 135; neonates and, 167; older adults and, 17; opioids and, 78, 79, 80, 89, 91, 94, 95, 116; overdose of, 148; for PCP use, 137, 138, 139; for polysubstance withdrawal, 113, 114; pregnancy and, 163, 164, 165, 166, 167, 171; prescribing, 103; screening for, 14, 15; substance-induced disorders and, 184, 185; surgery and, 188, 191, 192; tapering, 106-109, 111, 114, 191; urine drug screen for, 25, 27, 167; withdrawal from, 15, 105-106, 113, 114, 115, 116, 171, 191; women and, 18. *See also* alprazolam, bromazepam, chlordiazepoxide, clonazepam, clorazepate, diazepam, flunitrazepam, flurazepam, lorazepam, midazolam, nitrazepam, oxazepam, temazepam, triazolam

Benzoylecgonine, 27, 118

Binge drinking, defined, 3. *See also* alcohol problems; alcohol use; problem drinking

Birthweight. *See* low birthweight

Blackouts, 62

Blindness, 151

Blood alcohol concentration: 20, 143; alcohol withdrawal and, 45; clinical interpretation of, 21; decline of, 21, 144; drinking and driving and, 35, 37; for ethylene glycol overdose, 152; factors influencing, 20; for methanol overdose, 152; per drink table, 22; tolerance correlation and, 21; women and, 31

Blood drug screen, 81, 86, 142, 144, 160

Blood transfusions: 58, 142; and hepatitis, 153

Body packing, 121, 150

Body stuffing, 150

Bowel: motility, 63; irritable, 77, 87; ischemia, 121; opioids and, 78

Bradycardia, 137, 138, 145

Breast cancer, 7, 31, 65

Breastfeeding, 30, 153, 169-170, 174

Breathalyser, 20

Bromazepam, 27, 109

Bruxisms, MDMA and, 133

B12 deficiency, 23

Buprenorphine, 84, 92, 95, 96-97, 98
Bupropion, 70-71, 72-73, 75, 134, 170, 172, 190
Buspirone, 100-101, 185
Butabarbital, 111
Butalbital. *See* Fiorinal®
Butorphanol, 95

C
CA. *See* Cocaine Anonymous; mutual aid groups
Caffeine, 184
CAGE, 11, 18, 79, 163, 188
Cannabis: 122-124, 129; adolescents and, 123; alcohol and, 12, 13; anxiety and,
    123; assessment of use, 14, 15, 19; breastfeeding and, 169; cocaine and, 117;
    depression and, 14, 123; dysrhythmias and, 64; effects of, 122; examples of,
    4; medical complications of, 124; medical uses of, 122; mood disorders and,
    123; pregnancy and, 165, 167, 171; psychosis and, 186; schizophrenia and,
    123, 186; screening for, 123; substance-induced disorders and, 184, 186; UDS
    for, 24, 25, 80, 123, 165, 167; withdrawal from, 123, 171
Cardiomyopathy: alcohol problems and, 10, 13, 30, 38, 46, 63, 64, 187, 188;
    inhalants and, 129
Cardioprotection, alcohol and, 30
Catecholamine, 39, 66, 128, 136
Cellulitis, 14, 120
Cerebellar degeneration, 62, 129
Cerebellar disease, alcohol problems and, 10, 35, 40, 62
Cerebellar dysfunction, alcohol and, 13
Chest pain: cocaine and, 121, 149; disulfiram and, 52; MDMA and, 133
Child protection agency, 23, 24, 165, 167, 168-169, 196, 197
Chlamydia, 159
Chloral hydrate, 111
Chlordiazepoxide, 4, 103, 104, 105, 109
Chromatography, 24, 25, 26, 27, 80, 167. *See also* urine drug screen
Chronic pain: assessment of patient for, 79; benzodiazepines and, 79, 89; insom-
    nia and, 101; meperidine for, 81; methadone for, 87; neuropathic, 77; opioids

for (*See* opioids for chronic pain); somatic, 76; visceral, 77. *See also* acetaminophen; NSAIDs

Cirrhosis: alcohol and, 10, 13, 30, 32, 45, 54, 55, 56-58; antiviral therapy and, 155; cardiomyopathy and, 46; diazepam and, 190; disulfiram and, 53; hepatitis and, 54; hepatitis C and, 154, 155; interferon and, 155; naltrexone and, 51; surgery and, 190

CIWA-A, 40, 41-43, 48; management based on score, 44, 45, 46, 116; surgery and, 189

Clinical Institute Withdrawal Assessment for Alcohol. *See* CIWA-A

Clonazepam: 103; equivalence to diazepam, 109; risk of dependence on, 105; tapering, 107, 108, 114; urine drug screen for, 24, 27

Clonidine: contraindications for, 94, 96, 191; opioid withdrawal and, 87, 89, 91, 94, 114, 191, 194; polysubstance withdrawal and, 114, 115, 116; smoking cessation and, 75; surgery and, 191

Clorazepate, 103, 109

Cocaine: 2, 117-121, 130, 131, 134; alcohol and, 12, 13, 19, 64; assessment for, 14, 15, 118; breastfeeding and, 169; bupropion and, 73; cardiovascular complications of, 120, 121, 149; classification of, 4; clinical presentation of, 14, 118; cravings for, 119; delirium and, 120; depression and, 118, 119; diazepam and, 113; dysrhythmias and, 64; fetal effects of, 162-163; hallucinations and, 119; hepatitis and, 118, 120; HIV and, 118; infertility and, 121; insomnia and, 118; intoxication from, 148-150; laboratory detection of, 118; mechanism of action of, 117; medical complications of, 120, 121; MI induced by, 120, 149; neurological complications and, 120; opioids and, 80; overdose, 148-150; pattern of use of, 117-118; pharmacology of, 117; pharmacotherapy for, 119; pregnancy and, 121, 162-163, 165, 167, 171; psychoactive effects of, 117; psychosis and, 120, 184; psychosocial treatments for use, 195, 197; risk of infections from, 120; seizures and, 73, 120, 149, 150; substance-induced disorders and, 119-120, 184; treatment outcome for use, 8; urine drug screen for, 24, 25, 27, 118, 165, 167; withdrawal from, 15, 119, 120, 171. *See also* body packing; body stuffing

Cocaine Anonymous, 197. *See also* mutual aid groups

Codeine: 2, 81; with acetaminophen, 14, 78, 82, 95, 125; with ASA, 125; barbiturates and, 109; for chronic pain, 82; classification of, 4; dependence liability of, 191; for headache, 78, 109; hydrocodone and, 25; methadone and, 95; morphine as metabolite of, 25, 26; other opioids and, 89; over-the-counter, 14, 125; pregnancy and, 172; screening for, 14; tapering, 88-89, 172; titration, 82, 88; UDS and, 25, 26, 81

College: of Nurses, 209; of Physicians, 209

Coma: ABCs for, 141-142; alcohol intoxication and, 145; amphetamines and, 131; ethylene glycol overdose and, 151; GHB and, 137, 139; hepatic encephalopathy and, 59, 60; methadone and, 94, 147; methanol overdose and, 151; naloxone and, 146; opioids and, 77, 145, 146; PCP and, 136; suspected overdose and, 141, 142, 143

Comatose patient, treating, 142

Complicated alcohol withdrawal, 38, 45-48, 71-72, 109. See also polysubstance use; withdrawal

Concurrent disorders, 71, 105, 186, 210. See also anxiety; depression; psychosis; schizophrenia; substance-induced disorders

Contraceptive use: anabolic steroids and, 127; hepatitis C and, 156. See also safer sex

Counselling: 199-205; after overdose, 143; alcohol and, 32, 33, 36, 50, 190; anabolic steroids and 128; anxiety and, 99, 100; benzodiazepines and, 106; child protection authorities and, 168, 169; chronic pain and, 79; cocaine and, 119; common mistakes in, 200; for concurrent disorders, 186; family members and, 204-205; for insomnia, 102; opioids and, 88, 89, 92, 93, 96; psychosocial treatment and, 195-198; for smoking cessation, 7, 67, 68-69, 70, 71, 72, 74; stages of change model for, 200-204; surgery and, 189

Cramps. See abdominal cramps

Creatinine: in blood, 13, 40, 121, 142, 144; in urine drug screen, 28, 29, 165

Crohn's disease, chronic pain and, 77

Cryoglobulinemia, hepatitis C and, 154

Crystal methamphetamine. See amphetamine

D

Dalmane®. See flurazepam

"Date-rape" drug. See flunitrazepam; GHB

Daypro®. See oxaprosin

Death: from alcohol, 6, 12, 21, 31, 63, 186, 188; from alcohol and disulfiram, 52; from benzodiazepine overdose, 148; from cirrhosis, 154; from drinking and driving, 37; fetal, 163; from flumazenil, 148; from GHB overdose, 137; from MDMA, 133; neonatal, 91, 176; from opioid overdose, 96, 147; from overdose, 143, 206; from PCP overdose, 136; from smoking, 6, 7. *See also* sudden infant death syndrome; suicide

Dehydration: alcohol withdrawal and, 39, 40, 47, 48; hepatic encephalopathy and, 58, 59; MDMA and, 133, 134; suspected overdose and, 142, 144

Delirium: alcohol and, 15, 38, 39, 43, 48, 114, 143, 188, 189; barbiturates and, 15, 110, 191; benzodiazepines and, 15, 106, 191; cocaine and, 120, 150; complicated withdrawal and, 47; GHB and, 138, 139; hallucinogens and, 130; ketamine and, 135; MDMA and, 133; opioids and, 77, 147

Delusions, 120, 127, 128, 130, 131, 136, 183

Dementia, 10, 13, 17, 62, 99, 104

Depression: 16, 113, 183, 205, 207; adolescents and, 19; alcohol problems and, 10, 12, 40, 53, 184-185, 186; amphetamines and, 131; anabolic steroids and, 126, 127, 128; anxiety and, 99, 184-185, 186; benzodiazepines and, 103, 104, 106, 107, 108; cannabis and, 14, 15, 123; cocaine and, 2, 14, 15, 118, 119; disulfiram and, 52; hallucinogens and, 14; interferon and, 155; MDMA and, 133; older adults and, 17; opioids and, 15, 78; overdose and, 141, 143; PCP and, 136; pregnancy and, 165; smoking and, 69, 71, 75; SSRIs and, 105; stimulants and, 131

Detox centres. *See* withdrawal management centres

Dextromethorphan, 137, 140

Diabetes, 23, 65, 73, 77, 154

Diaphoresis: alcohol withdrawal and, 39, 40; GHB and, 138; MDMA and, 133

Diarrhea, 10, 63, 90

Diazepam: anxiety and, 100; benzodiazepine tapering and, 39, 106, 107, 108, 114, 115, 116; classification of, 4, 103; for cocaine overdose, 149; equivalence to other drugs, 109; GHB withdrawal and, 138; insomnia and, 103, 104; loading, for alcohol withdrawal, 20, 39, 41, 44-49, 63, 114, 115, 116, 171; lorazepam as alternative to, 44-45, 59, 108, 109, 116, 137, 138, 171, 190; for PCP use, 137, 138; polysubstance withdrawal and, 113; pregnancy and, 171; risk of dependence on, 105; surgery and, 189; tapering, 39, 114, 115, 116;

urine drug screen for, 27; withdrawal, 15

Dimenhydrinate, 14, 91, 125

Diphenhydramine, 137

Disulfiram, 7, 32, 51-53, 172, 189

Doctors. *See* physicians

Dopamine, 53, 67, 72, 117, 130, 132, 136

Drinking: at-risk/high risk, 3, 12, 33, 34, 38, 163; binge, 3; low-risk, 3, 30-31, 33, 36, 55, 56, 64, 79, 202; problem, 3, 30-34, 190. *See also* alcohol dependence; alcohol problems; alcohol use

Drinking and driving, 12, 21, 35-37

Drowsiness: alcohol and, 21, 143-144; barbiturates and, 110; benzodiazepines and, 108, 148; ketamine and, 135; inhalants and, 129; neonatal, 179; opioids and, 82, 85, 91, 94, 95, 96, 147, 174, 145; pregnancy and, 164, 174

Drug overdose. *See* overdose

Drug-seeking, 5, 10, 86-87, 118, 192, 193-194

DSM-IV criteria: abbreviated, for cocaine withdrawal, 119; for substance abuse, 3; for substance dependence, 1-2; for substance-induced disorders, 183

Dyspepsia, 10, 63

Dysperceptions, 15, 106

Dysphoria, 15, 67, 78, 83, 86, 90, 91, 119, 133

Dysrhythmias: alcohol and, 7, 10, 15, 30, 38, 39, 40, 46, 47, 48, 52, 63-64, 144, 188; amphetamines and, 131; barbiturate withdrawal and, 110, 191; benzodiazepine withdrawal and, 106, 148, 191; cannabis and, 122, 124; cocaine and, 149; dextromethorphan and, 140; inhalants and, 128, 129; ketamine and, 135; MDMA and, 133; naloxone-induced opioid withdrawal and, 147; nicotine replacement therapy and, 74; opioids and, 77

E

Economic costs of substance use, 6

Ecstasy. *See* MDMA

Ectopic pregnancy, 162. *See also* pregnancy

EDDP, 25-26

Effexor®. *See* venlafaxine

EIA. *See* enzyme immunoassay

Emesis. *See* vomiting

Encephalitis, 143

Encephalopathy: alcoholic hepatitis and, 54, 56; hepatic, 58-60, 143; inhalants and, 129; SBP and, 61; surgery and, 189, 190; Wernicke's, 47-48, 154

Endocarditis, 120, 144, 159, 160

ENT, 65, 120

Enzyme immunoassay, 25, 26, 27, 118. *See also* urine drug screen

Epinephrine, 132

Equagesic®. *See* meprobamate

Equianalgesic opioid doses, 88, 89

Erectile dysfunction, 52, 65, 68, 78

Esophagitis, 55, 63

Ethanol loading, 152

Ethchlorvynol, 111

Ethylene glycol, 142, 143, 144, 151-152

Euphoria: amphetamines and, 131; cocaine and, 117; dextromethorphan and, 140; GHB and, 137; inhalants and, 128; MDMA and, 132; opioids and, 3, 85, 88, 92

Excoriation, 178, 180

F

FAE. *See* fetal alcohol effects

Fanconi-like syndrome, 129

FAS. *See* fetal alcohol syndrome

Fatigue: alcohol and, 10, 17, 32, 33; anabolic steroid withdrawal and, 126; anxiety and, 185; cocaine withdrawal and, 119; disulfiram and, 52; hepatic encephalopathy and, 59; hepatitis and, 54; inhalants and, 126; nicotine and, 67, opioid use and, 78; opioid withdrawal and, 90 126, 128, 185, 199, 207

Fatty liver, 10, 32, 54, 55

Fetal alcohol effects (FAE), 65, 161, 162

Fetal alcohol syndrome (FAS), 65, 161-162

Fetal effects: of alcohol, 161-162; of cocaine, 162-163; of heroin, 163; of opioids, 167, 172 (*See also* Neonatal Abstinence Scoring Scale); of tobacco smoke, 162. *See also* breastfeeding; infants; neonates; pregnancy

Fever: alcohol withdrawal and, 39; alcoholic hepatitis and, 54; cocaine and, 121,

149; dextromethorphan and, 140; endocarditis and, 160; MDMA and, 133; NAS and, 178, 180; PCP and, 136; SBP and, 61; tuberculosis and, 159
Fibromyalgia, 77
"Fingerprinting," 29
Fiorinal®, 4, 109, 110, 111, 112, 116
Flashbacks, 130
"Floppy baby syndrome," 104, 171. *See also* neonates
Flumazenil, 60, 148
Flunitrazepam, 27, 139
Fluoxetine, 101
Flurazepam, 103, 104, 109

G
GABA, 136, 137
Gait, alcohol and, 40, 62, 144
Galactorrhea: cannabis and, 124; cocaine and, 121
Gamma glutamyl transferase. *See* GGT
Gamma-hydroxybutyrate. *See* GHB
Gasoline. *See* inhalants
Gastritis, 10, 30, 55, 63
GGT, 13, 16, 23, 29, 33, 36, 40, 55, 127, 154, 163, 165, 188, 194, 200
GHB, 19, 27, 137-139
GI complications: 19; of alcohol use, 63, 64, 65; of cocaine use, 121; of disulfiram use, 53; of encephalopathy, 58, 190; of GHB use, 139; of inhalant use, 128; of opioid withdrawal, 90; of prednisolone use, 56
Glasgow Coma Scale, 143, 145. *See also* coma
Glue. *See* inhalants
Gravol®. *See* dimenhydrinate
Growth retardation: cocaine and, 163; FAS and, 161; heroin and, 163; tobacco and, 162
Gynecomastia, 54, 126, 127

H
Hair sampling, 168

Halcion®. *See* triazolam

Halfway houses, 196

Hallucinations: alcohol withdrawal and, 39, 40, 42, 43, 47; amphetamines and, 131; cocaine and, 119, 120; dextromethorphan and, 140; dimenhydrinate and, 125; GHB withdrawal and, 138; hallucinogens and, 129-130; inhalants and, 128; ketamine and, 135; MDMA and, 133; methylphenidate and, 135; opioids and, 77; PCP and, 136; substance-induced psychotic disorders and, 183. *See also* hallucinogens

Hallucinogens, 4, 14, 129-130, 132, 184. *See also* cannabis; LSD; MDMA; PCP; psilocybin

Haloperidol, 47, 137

HBV, 120, 126, 155, 156-157, 164, 166, 169-170, 175, 188, 194. *See also* hepatitis; hepatitis B

HCV, 120, 126, 153-157, 164, 166, 169-170, 175, 188, 194. *See also* hepatitis; hepatitis C

Head trauma, 77, 143-145. *See also* subdural hematoma

Headache: and alcohol withdrawal, 38, 40, 43; and bupropion, 72; and buspirone, 101; and disulfiram, 52; and inhalants, 128; medication-induced, 78; and nicotine withdrawal, 67; and opioids, 77, 78, 87. *See also* migraine

HEADSS, 18

Hematoma, 188. *See also* subdural hematoma

Hemodialysis: ethylene glycol intoxication and, 152; hepatitis and, 157; methanol intoxication and, 152

Hepatic encephalopathy, 56, 58-60, 143

Hepatitis: alcohol and, 10, 23, 30, 45, 54, 55, 56, 57, 64; anabolic steroids and, 126; bupropion and, 73; with cirrhosis, 54, 56, 57, 154, 155; cocaine and, 118, 119; diazepam and, 45; disulfiram and, 52, 53; hepatitis A, 57, 156, 158; hepatitis B, 13, 16, 55, 57, 86, 156-157, 163, 165; hepatitis C, 13, 14, 16, 29, 54, 55, 57, 73, 86, 153-156, 157, 160, 163, 165; with HIV, 159; injection drugs and, 14, 16, 29, 118, 120, 153, 154, 157, 158, 163, 194; interferon and, 155, 156, 157; naltrexone and, 51; neonatal transmission of, 170; opioids and, 86; pregnancy and, 163, 165, 169; surgery and, 189. *See also* HBV; HCV

Hepatocellular carcinoma, 126, 154

Hepatoma, 55, 65, 155

Heroin: 14, 19; buprenorphine treatment and, 96-97; chromatography and, 25, 26; classification of, 4; cocaine and, 117; methadone treatment for, 93, 94-96; naltrexone treatment for, 97-98; neonates and, 175; pregnancy and, 163, 165, 167; treatment programs, 195. *See also* opioids; injection drug use

High-risk situations, drinking, 33, 34

Hirsutism, anabolic steroids and, 126, 127

HIV: 13, 164, 166; anabolic steroids and, 126; breastfeeding and, 170; cocaine and, 118, 120; injection drugs and, 16, 118, 120, 126, 154, 155, 156, 158-159; pregnancy and, 158, 163, 164, 165, 166, 169, 173, 175; sexual practices and, 158; suicide and, 159; tuberculosis and, 159-160

Human immunodeficiency virus. *See* HIV

Hydrocodone, 4, 25, 26

Hydromorphone, 4, 26, 81, 88, 89, 93, 96, 191

Hyperactivity, 131

Hypercalcemia, 144

Hypercapnea, 141, 146

Hyperglycemia, 144, 181

Hyperpyrexia. *See* fever

Hypersplenism, alcohol and, 64

Hypertension: alcohol use and, 10, 13, 30, 32, 64; alcohol withdrawal and, 38, 39; amphetamines and, 131; barbiturate withdrawal and, 110; benzodiazepine withdrawal and, 106; cocaine and, 120, 149; dextromethorphan and, 140; disulfiram and, 53; GHB withdrawal and, 138; MDMA and, 133; opioid use and, 77; opioid withdrawal and, 90, 91; PCP and, 136, 137; portal, 23, 55, 58, 154; pregnancy, alcohol and, 162; pregnancy, cocaine and, 162

Hyperthermia: NAS and, 176; PCP and, 137; stimulants and, 131, 133, 134, 150

Hyperuricemia, 65

Hypoglycemia: alcohol and, 66; bupropion and, 73; hepatic encephalopathy and, 58; intoxication and overdose and, 142, 144; NAS and, 176; PCP and, 136, 137

Hypogonadism, 78

Hypokalemia: alcohol withdrawal and, 38, 39, 40, 47; hepatic encephalopathy and, 58

Hypomagnesemia, 38, 40

Hypomania, 126

Hyponatremia, 133

Hypotension: clonidine and, 91, 191; disulfiram and, 52, 53; GHB and, 138; intoxication and overdose and, 142, 145; opioids and, 77, 91, 145, 191

Hypothermia, 138, 144

Hypothyroidism, 23, 57, 58

Hypotonia, 139

Hypoxia, 57, 58, 144, 162

Hypoxemia, 141

I

IBS. *See* irritable bowel syndrome

"Ice." *See* amphetamine

Immunization: hepatitis A, 57, 157, 158; hepatitis B, 57, 157

Infants: apprehension of, 168; cannabis and, 169; hepatitis B and, 157; hepatitis C and, 152, 153, 154, 169; HIV and, 169; methadone and, 173, 174, 175; mortality, 173; opioids and, 175, 176, 182. *See also* neonates

Infertility: alcohol and, 10, 65; cocaine and, 121

INH prophylaxis, for tuberculosis, 159-160

Inhalants, 4, 19, 128-129

Injection drug use: 12, 13, 14, 16, 82, 153-160, 192, 194; cocaine and, 117, 118, 120; detecting in urine drug screen, 29, 118; endocarditis and, 120, 160; hepatitis A and, 158; hepatitis B and, 16, 120, 157, 163; hepatitis C and, 14, 16, 29, 118, 120, 153-156, 163; HIV and, 13, 16, 118, 120, 126, 156, 158-159, 163; immunization and, 157; labour and, 175; methadone and, 93, 94, 158; needle-sharing and, 16, 126, 156; pregnancy and, 163; sepsis and, 160; tuberculosis and, 159-160; young adults and, 154. *See also* opioids; HIV

Insomnia: alcohol problems and, 10, 32, 33, 185; alcohol withdrawal and, 38, 44; amphetamines and, 131; assessment of, 101-102; barbiturate withdrawal and, 15; benzodiazepines for, 101-104; benzodiazepine withdrawal and, 15, 106; cannabis withdrawal and, 123; causes of, 101; cocaine use and, 118; cocaine withdrawal and, 15, 119; drug use and, 14, 19, 189; nicotine withdrawal and, 67, 72; non-medical management of, 102; opioid withdrawal and, 15, 90, 91; rebound, 103, 104. *See also* anxiety

Interferon, 155, 156, 157

Intoxication: alcohol (*See* alcohol); benzodiazepine, 148; cocaine, 148-150; pregnancy and, 164

Intrauterine growth retardation, 162, 163. *See also* fetal effects; pregnancy

Irritable bowel syndrome, 77, 87

J

Jaw-clenching. *See* bruxisms

K

Ketamine, 19, 135, 140

Ketoacidosis, 66

Korsakoff's syndrome, 10, 47

L

Labetalol, 149

Laboratory detection: of alcohol, 20-23; of anabolic steroids, 127; of cocaine, 118; of drug use, 23-29; of ethylene glycol, 151; of methanol, 151. *See also* urine drug screen

Laboratory investigations: for alcohol problems, 11, 13, 40, 144; for drug problems, 16, 144; for hepatic encephalopathy, 59; for opioid dependence, 86; for substance use during pregnancy, 165

Labour, 104, 167, 169, 171, 174, 175. *See also* premature labour

Lacrimation, 15, 90

Lectopam®. *See* bromazepam

Libido, 14, 118, 121, 127

Librium®. *See* chlordiazepoxide

Lidocaine, 149

Liver disease. *See* alcoholic liver disease

Liver transplant, 57, 60, 156

Lorazepam: as alternative to diazepam for alcohol withdrawal, 44-45, 108, 109, 116, 137, 138, 189; and alcoholic liver disease, 59, 190; for benzodiazepine tapering, 108; classification of, 4, 103; for cocaine overdose, 150; equivalence to other benzodiazepines, 109; risk of dependence on, 105; tapering, 116; urine drug screen for, 27; use during labour, 171

Low birthweight, 10, 121, 173. *See also* neonates

Low-risk drinking, 3, 30-31, 33, 36, 55, 56, 79. *See also* alcohol use

LSD, 4, 19, 129-130

Lymphoma, 154

Lysergic acid diethylamide. *See* LSD

M

MA. *See* Methadone Anonymous; mutual aid groups

Magnesium, alcohol problems and, 13, 40, 66, 142, 144. *See also* hypomagnesemia

Mallory-Weiss tear, 63

MAM, 25, 26, 165, 167

Mantoux testing, 159, 166

MAOIs. *See* monoamine oxidase inhibitors

Marijuana. *See* cannabis

MCV, 16, 23, 29, 33, 36, 55, 163, 165, 188, 194

MDA. *See* amphetamine

MDMA (ecstasy): 19, 26, 129, 132-134; classification of, 4

Mean cell volume. *See* MCV

Memory impairment: amphetamines and, 131; Korsakoff's syndrome and, 47; MDMA and, 132; PCP and, 136

Meningitis, 143, 144

Menstrual cycle, 10, 14, 78, 121, 124, 126, 127, 156

Mental illness, substance-induced, 183-184. *See also* concurrent disorders; substance-induced disorders

Mental retardation, fetal alcohol syndrome and, 161

Meperidine: chromatography and, 25; for chronic pain, 81; classification of, 4; dependence liability of, 191; enzyme immunoassay and, 25; migraine and, 77; overdose, 147; tapering, 89; toxicity, 77, 147; UDS detection period for, 26

Meprobamate, 111

Mescaline: 129; classification of, 4

Metabolic acidosis, 66, 144, 151, 152

Methadone: acute pain and, 95; benzodiazepines and, 95; breastfeeding and, 170, 174; chronic pain and, 84; drug interactions with, 159; for heroin dependence, 93; missed doses, 94; neonatal withdrawal from, 173, 175, 176, 182; for opioid dependence, 87-88, 92-96, 143, 158, 165, 191, 192, 194; for opioid withdrawal, 96, 114; overdose, 94, 145, 146, 147; pregnancy and, 94, 165, 167, 172-174; protocol for dosing, 94; tapering, 174, 191; urine drug screen for, 25-26, 28, 88, 94, 167; versus buprenorphine, 96-97; versus naltrexone, 97-98

Methadone Anonymous, 197. *See also* mutual aid groups

Methamphetamine. *See* amphetamine

Methanol, 142, 143, 144, 151-152

Methylenedioxyamphetamine. *See* amphetamine

Methylphenidate, 134

MI. *See* myocardial infarction

Midazolam, 103, 137

Migraine: barbiturates and, 109; drug-seeking and, 193; opioids and, 77, 78

Miosis: opioid overdose and, 145; PCP and, 136

Miscarriage: cocaine and, 163, 121; drug withdrawal and, 15, 91, 163, 170, 172. *See also* pregnancy; premature labour

Mogadon®. *See* nitrazepam

Mono-acetylmorphine. *See* MAM

Monoamine oxidase inhibitors, 73, 77, 133, 140

Moro reflex, 179

Morphine: acute pain and, 95; chromatography and, 25; for chronic pain, 76, 82; classification of, 4; complications of use, 78; dependence liability of, 191; diversion, 80, 81; for neonatal opioid withdrawal, 176-177, 181-182; tapering, 88, 89; urine drug screen for, 25, 26, 80, 81

Motivational interviewing, 33, 199-205. *See also* Stages of Change

Mushrooms. *See* psilocybin

Mutual aid groups, 32, 48, 87, 143, 186, 189, 197-198, 199, 203, 204, 210

Myalgias: cocaine and, 121, 149; opioid withdrawal and, 15, 83, 90, 91

Mydriasis, MDMA and, 133

Myocardial infarction: alcohol and, 7; amphetamines and, 131; cocaine-induced, 149; nicotine replacement therapy and, 74

Myocarditis: cocaine and, 120; neonates and, 176

Myoclonus: GHB and, 137, 139; ketamine and, 135; MDMA and, 133

Myoglobinuria, cocaine and, 121
Myopathy, 10

N

NA. *See* Narcotics Anonymous; mutual aid groups
Naloxone: 97, 140, 142, 146-147; challenge test, 98
Naltrexone: 32, 189; for alcohol use, 50-51, 190; for opioid use, 97-98; pregnancy and, 172
Narcotic bowel syndrome, 78
Narcotics Anonymous, 197. *See also* mutual aid groups
NAS Scale. *See* Neonatal Abstinence Scoring Scale
Nausea, 15, 41, 78, 83, 90, 101, 122, 125, 139
Needle-sharing, 126, 128 156. *See also* injection drug use
Nefazodone, 101
Neomycin, 60
Neonatal Abstinence Scoring Scale (NAS Scale), 176-181
Neonates: abstinence syndrome, 175-177; apprehension of, 168-169; alcohol withdrawal and, 171; cocaine and, 121; hair sampling and, 168; hepatitis transmission and, 153, 157, 169, 170; HIV transmission and, 169; NAS Scale and, 176-181; opioid withdrawal and, 90, 91, 163, 175-176; urine drug screen and, 167; withdrawal by, 91, 172-173, 175-182. *See also* breastfeeding; infants; pregnancy
Neuropathy. *See* peripheral neuropathy
Nicotine: 67-75; classification of, 4; pharmacotherapy for, 67, 70-75; pregnancy and, 162, 170-171, 172; replacement therapy, 7, 45, 71, 72, 73-75, 170, 172, 190; treatment outcome, 8. *See also* tobacco
Nicotine withdrawal: alcohol withdrawal and, 45, 71; clinical features of, 67; pregnancy and, 170-171; surgery and, 190. *See also* smoking cessation
Nifedipine, 149
Nitrazepam, 103, 109
Nitroglycerin, 149
Nitroprusside, 137, 149
Nonsteroidal anti-inflammatory drugs. *See* NSAIDs
Norepinephrine: amphetamines and, 130; bupropion and, 72; cocaine and, 117;

MDMA and, 132; nicotine and, 67, 72

Normeperidine, 77, 147. *See also* meperidine

Nortryptiline, 75

Norvir®. *See* ritonavir

NSAIDs, 61, 76, 77, 78, 91. *See also* analgesics

Nurses: impairment and, 206-210; intervention by, 6; motivating patients, 199; NAS Scale and, 176; responsibilities of, 5

Nystagmus: barbiturates and, 110; PCP and, 136; Wernicke's encephalopathy and, 47

O

Obstructive sleep apnea, 64, 78, 101

Olanzapine, 47

Older adults: alcohol withdrawal and, 38; barbiturates and, 110, 111; benzodiazepines and, 104, 108; blood alcohol content in, 20; identification of substance use problems in, 9; insomnia in, 101; methadone and, 94; psychosocial treatment for, 196

OMA Physician Health Program, 209

Ondansetron, 53

Ophthalmoplegia, Wernicke's encephalopathy and, 47

Opioids: acetaminophen and, 152; alcohol and, 30, 39, 79, 143-145; ASA and, 152; assessment/screening for, 12, 14, 18 (*See also* UDS for); benzodiazepines and, 103, 104, 118; breastfeeding and, 170; chronic pain and, 76-84, 159; classification of, 4; clinical uncertainty, 82-83, 194; cocaine and, 118; complications of prescription use, 77-78; counselling and, 204; dependence liability, 191; drug-seeking and, 193-194; effectiveness of, 76-77; equianalgesic comparisons, 89; fetal effects of, 167; hepatic encephalopathy and, 58; indications for prescribing, 76-77; intoxication, 16, 143; ketamine and, 135; neonates and, 167; overdose, 15, 81, 94, 145-147; pregnancy and, 163, 164, 165, 166, 167; substance-induced disorders and, 184, 185; surgery and, 188, 190, 191-192; sustained-release, 81-82, 87; tapering, 83, 84, 88, 172, 191; titrating, 79, 80, 82; tolerance to, 2, 83, 88, 145; treatment agreement for, 80; treatment outcomes, 8; UDS for 13, 23, 24-25, 80-81, 85, 98, 165, 167. *See also* buprenorphine; butorphanol; clonidine; codeine; heroin; hydrocodone;

hydromorphone; meperidine; methadone; morphine; naloxone; naltrexone; oxycodone; pentazocine

Opioids for chronic pain: acute complications of, 77-78; analgesics and, 89, 191; assessing patient for, 79-80; chronic adverse effects of, 78; clinical uncertainty regarding, 82-83; conditions where not recommended, 77; dependence on, 85-89; effectiveness of, 76-77; pregnancy and, 172; surgery and, 191-192; tapering, 88-89; titration, 80-82; withdrawal-mediated, 83-84 (*See also* opioids, withdrawal from). *See also* codeine; hydromorphone; meperidine; morphine; oxycodone

Opioid dependence: assessment of, 86; chronic pain and, 76, 81, 83, 85-89, 191; clinical features of, 87; HIV and, 158; indications for pharmacotherapy for, 93, 98; labour and, 175; management of, with chronic pain, 87, 95; neonates and, 173, 175-182; nurses and, 208; overdose and, 15, 90, 91, 93, 94, 96, 97, 98, 145-147, 174; pharmacotherapy for, 23, 92-98, 143, 173-174, 194; physicians and, 208; pregnancy and, 88, 90, 94, 163, 164, 165, 172-175; pseudoaddiction and, 86-87; suicide and, 90, 91; tapering, 87, 88-89, 96, 97, 114, 172, 174, 191, 194; tolerance, 15, 85, 90, 91, 92, 94, 95, 175; withdrawal and, 15, 90-91, 96, 98, 114, 115-116, 172, 175, 176, 188, 191-192; withdrawal with naloxone and, 142, 146-147; withdrawal with naltrexone and, 50; withdrawal-mediated pain and, 83-84, 88. *See also* buprenorphine; methadone; naloxone; naltrexone

Osmolar gap, 151

OTC drugs: pregnancy and, 163; screening for, 12, 14, 19, 80, 124, 125. *See also* acetaminophen; antihistamines; ASA; codeine; dextromethorphan; dimenhydrinate

Overdose: 141-152, 206; ABCs for, 141-142; acetaminophen, 152; alcohol, 143-145; amphetamine, 131; ASA, 152; benzodiazepine, 148; body packing/stuffing and, 150; cocaine, 148-150; ethylene glycol, 152; flumazenil for benzodiazepine, 148; flunitrazepam, 139; GHB, 137; MDMA, 134; meperidine, 147; methadone, 94, 145, 146, 147; methanol, 143, 144, 152; naloxone for opioid, 146-147; opioid, 15, 81, 90, 91, 93, 94, 96, 97, 98, 145-147, 174; polysubstance, 185; treating, 141-143. *See also* death

Over-the-counter drugs. *See* OTC drugs

Oxaprosin, 27

Oxazepam, 4, 103, 105, 109
Oxycodone, 4, 25, 26, 80, 81, 88, 89, 191

P

Pain. *See* chronic pain
Pancreatitis: alcohol and, 10, 30, 32, 39, 63, 65; chronic pain and, 77
Panic, 43, 106, 122, 130, 133, 183
Panic disorder, 99, 101, 103
Pap smears, 159, 166
Paranoia, 117, 120, 131, 133, 136
Parkinsonian symptoms. *See* pseudo-Parkinsonism
Paroxetine, 101
Paxil®. *See* paroxetine
PCP, 4, 26, 136-139
Pentastarch (Pentaspan®), 142
Pentazocine, 95
Pentobarbital, 111, 138, 149
Perioperative complications. *See* surgery
Peripheral neuropathy: alcohol problems and, 10, 62; disulfiram and, 52; inhalants and, 129; INH prophylaxis and, 160
Peritonitis, 54, 58, 59, 61, 66
Pharmacotherapy: for alcohol dependence, 38, 44, 48, 50-53; for cocaine withdrawal, 119, 171; counselling and, 199, 203, 204; for nicotine dependence, 67, 70, 72-75; for opioid dependence, 92-98; for substance-induced disorders, 185. *See also* buprenorphine; bupropion; clonidine; diazepam; disulfiram; lorazepam; methadone; naltrexone; nicotine
Phencyclidine. *See* PCP
Phenobarbital: equivalence table, 111; for GHB withdrawal, 138; loading, 110, 114, 115, 116; for polysubstance withdrawal, 114; pregnancy and, 171; tapering, 111-112, 115, 116; urine drug screen for, 27
Phenothiazines, 137
Phentolamine, 137, 149
Phenytoin, 23, 26, 149, 159
Physical dependence on substances: defined, 2; when to review risk of, 80

Physician Health Program, 209

Physicians: clinical uncertainty, 82; counselling by, 199-205; impairment and, 206-210; responsibilities of, 5-6, 35, 168, 194, 196, 199; role in screening and assessment, 9, 14, 16, 18, 39

Piloerection, opioid withdrawal and, 15, 90

Placenta previa: cocaine and, 121; tobacco and, 162; heroin and, 163. *See also* pregnancy

Placidyl®. *See* ethchlorvynol

Pneumonia: alcohol and, 39, 61, 66, 188; HIV and, 159; opioids and, 96

Polysubstance use: 113-116; alcohol problems and, 12, 188; assessment of, 113; clinical example of, 116; drug problems and, 15, 117; with methylphenidate, 134; and withdrawal, 113-116, 188

Poppy seeds, enzyme immunoassay and, 25, 26

Porphyria cutanea tarda, hepatitis C and, 154

Portal hypertension. *See* hypertension

Postpartum care, and opioids, 173, 174, 175. *See also* neonates; Pregnancy and Substance Use

Prednisolone, 56

Pregnancy: alcohol and, 30, 161-162, 170, 171; assessment and, 16; barbiturate withdrawal and, 171; benzodiazepine withdrawal and, 171; biophysical profile and, 167; cocaine and, 121, 162-163; disulfiram and, 53, 172; hepatitis and, 155, 169; heroin and, 163; HIV and, 158, 169; methadone treatment and, 94, 172-174; nicotine and, 74, 162, 170-171, 172; opioid tapering during, 88, 172, 174; opioid use and, 172-175; opioid withdrawal and, 90, 91, 114, 165, 172; prenatal care during, 165-167; substance use screening during, 163-165; T-ACE and, 11, 164; tobacco smoke and, 162; urine drug screening during, 165, 166, 167-168; withdrawal during, 15, 170-172. *See also* child protection agency; infants; miscarriage; neonates, withdrawal in; premature labour

Premature labour: cocaine and, 121, 163; opioids and, 15, 88, 91, 163, 172, 174; previous, indicating possible substance use, 164; tobacco smoke and, 162; withdrawal and, 170. *See also* labour

Prescriptions, tamper-proofing, 81

Problem drinking: 3, 8, 12, 30-34, 190; benzodiazepines and, 103; cirrhosis and, 155; comparison with alcohol dependence, 32; defined, 31; hepatitis

and, 56; trauma and, 190; treatment, 32-34, 195-196. *See also* alcohol
   dependence; alcohol problems; alcohol use; drinking and driving
Propanolol, 58, 149
Propylthiouracil, 57
Prozac®. *See* fluoxetine
Pseudo-Parkinsonism, 63
Pseudoaddiction, 86-87
Pseudoephedrine, 132, 133
Psilocybin, 4, 19, 129. *See also* hallucinogens
Psychosis: 16, 99; alcohol problems and, 10, 12, 15, 39; amphetamines and,
   131; anabolic steroids and, 126; barbiturate withdrawal and, 110; benzodi-
   azepine withdrawal and, 15; cannabis and, 14, 186; cocaine and, 14, 120;
   disulfiram and, 52, 53; hallucinogens and, 14, 130
PTU. *See* propylthiouracil
Pyridoxine, 152, 160

Q
Quinolone antibiotics: bupropion and, 73; urine drug screens and, 25

R
Rage: anabolic steroids and, 126; benzodiazepines and, 148
"Rave" parties, 132, 133
Regurgitation, 176, 178, 181
Relapse: to alcohol use, 6, 32, 52, 57, 72; to cocaine use, 15, 119; concurrent
   disorders and, 186; in nurses, 209; to opioid use, 15, 91, 191, 192; in physi-
   cians, 209; during pregnancy, 168, 169, 174; preventing, 197, 198; to smok-
   ing, 68, 69, 70; in Stages of Change model, 200, 201, 204
Renal failure: cocaine and 121; MDMA and, 134; methanol/ethylene glycol and,
   151, 152; prednisolone and, 56
Renarcotization, methadone overdose and, 146
Reproductive complications. *See* infertility; sperm count
Restoril®. *See* temazepam
ReVia®. *See* naltrexone
Rhabdomyolysis: cocaine and, 121, 149; MDMA and, 134; PCP and, 136, 137

Rheumatoid arthritis, 154

Rhinitis, cocaine and, 118

Rhinorrhea, opioid withdrawal and, 15, 90

Rifampin, 159

Rigidity: hepatic encephalopathy and, 59; MDMA and, 133; neonatal withdrawal
    and, 180; PCP and, 136; pseudo-Parkinsonism and, 63

Risperidol, 47

Ritalin®. *See* methylphenidate

Ritonavir, 133

Rivotril®. *See* clonazepam

Rohypnol®. *See* flunitrazepam

S

Salivation, GHB and, 139

SBP. *See* peritonitis

Schizophrenia: 43; benzodiazepines and 103; cannabis and, 123; concurrent
    disorders and, 186; disulfiram and, 53; hallucinogens and, 130

Screening: 4, 9-16; for alcohol problems, 9, 10; CAGE questionnaire for, 11, 18;
    for cannabis, 123; for cocaine 118; for hepatitis C, 154; for HIV, 158; for
    inhalants, 129; for MDMA, 132; mental illness and, 185; nurse responsibility
    in, 5; for OTC drugs, 125; physician responsibility in, 5; before prescribing
    opioids, 79; for STDs, 159; for anabolic steroids, 127; for substance use, 14-15;
    for substance use by adolescents, 18; for substance use by older adults, 17; for
    substance use by women, 18; for substance use during pregnancy, 163; before
    surgery, 188; T-ACE questionnaire for, 11, 18, 164. *See also* assessment; UDS

Secobarbital, 4, 111

Sedative/hypnotics: 4, 102, 143, 145, 165, 188, 190, 203. *See also* antidepressants;
    antihistamines; barbiturates; benzodiazepines; GHB; PCP; SSRIs; tryptophan

Seizures: alcohol use and, 15, 30; alcohol withdrawal and, 35, 38, 39, 40, 44,
    46, 47, 48, 49, 52, 71, 73, 114, 188; amphetamines and, 131; barbiturates
    and, 15, 44, 110, 191; benzodiazepines and, 15, 44, 60, 106, 148, 191;
    bupropion and, 71, 72, 73; cocaine and, 120, 149, 150; disulfiram and, 52;
    flumazenil and, 60, 148; GHB and, 138, 139; haloperidol and, 47; ketamine
    and, 135; MDMA and, 133; meperidine and, 77, 147; neonatal, 91, 176, 180;

suspected overdose and, 141, 142, 144; PCP and, 136, 137

Selective serotonin reuptake inhibitors, 99, 101, 102, 103, 104, 133. *See also* fluoxetine; nefazadone; paroxetine; sertraline; venlafaxine

Sepsis, 144, 160, 176, 188

Serax®. *See* oxazepam

Serotonergic syndrome: dextromethorphan and, 140; MDMA and, 133, 134

Serotonin, 117, 132, 133, 136

Sertraline, 101, 102, 104

Serzone®. *See* nefazodone

Sexual dysfunction, 10. *See also* erectile dysfunction; libido

Sexually transmitted diseases (STDs), 13, 19, 118, 120, 156, 157, 158, 159, 164, 166

SIDS. *See* Sudden Infant Death Syndrome

Sinusitis, cocaine and, 118

6-mono-acetylmorphine. *See* MAM

Sleep apnea. *See* obstructive sleep apnea

Sleep hygiene, 102. *See also* insomnia

Smoking. *See* nicotine; tobacco

Smoking cessation: 31; clinics, 68; counselling for, 7, 67-69, 71, 72; other drug dependence and, 71-72; pharmacotherapy for, 66, 72-75; during pregnancy, 170; strategies for, 7, 68-71; before surgery, 190; weight gain and, 69. *See also* bupropion; nicotine; nicotine withdrawal; tobacco

Social functioning: 2, 3, 4, 10, 14, 15, 16; in adolescents, 19; alcohol dependence and, 32; at-risk drinking and, 31; cannabis and, 123; cocaine and, 117, 118; MDMA and, 132, 133; methadone and, 93; naltrexone and, 97; pregnancy and, 165; problem drinking and, 3, 10, 12, 31, 32, 33

Solvents. *See* inhalants

"Special K." *See* ketamine

Sperm count: anabolic steroids and, 127; cannabis and, 124

Splenomegaly, 16, 23, 54, 55, 154, 155

Spontaneous abortion. *See* miscarriage

Spousal abuse, 3, 10, 12, 14, 16, 165, 204

SSRIs. *See* selective serotonin reuptake inhibitors

Stages of change model, 68-69, 200-201

Standard drink: defined, 30; equivalents, 9

Startle reflex. *See* Moro reflex

STDs. *See* sexually transmitted diseases

Stereotypy, amphetamines and, 131

Steroids. *See* anabolic steroids

Stimulants: 105, 130-134, 184; examples of, 4. *See also* amphetamine; cocaine; MDMA; methylphenidate

Stroke, alcohol and, 30, 64

Subdural hematoma, 40, 62, 143, 145

Substance abuse: classification table of, 4; defined, 2; DSM criteria for, 3

Substance dependence: chronic pain and, 85; DSM-IV criteria for, 1-2; effectiveness of treatment for, 7-8; insomnia and, 103; risk among physicians and nurses, 206; screening for, 79

Substance-induced disorders: 183-186; anxiety and, 98; cocaine and, 119

Substance tolerance: 1; defined, 2

Substance withdrawal: 1; defined, 2

Sudden Infant Death Syndrome (SIDS), 162, 163

Suicide: adolescents and, 18, 19, 31; alcohol problems and, 12, 40; amphetamines and, 131; anabolic steroids and, 126; benzodiazepines and, 108; cocaine and, 15, 118, 119; drug use and, 14, 16; GHB and, 139; HIV and, 159; among nurses, 206; opioid withdrawal and, 91; among physicians, 206; substance-induced disorders and, 185

Sumatriptan, 133

Surgery: 187-192; alcohol and, 7, 66, 187-190; barbiturates and, 191; benzodiazepines and 191; for body packing, 150; hepatic encephalopathy and, 58, 60, 189; naltrexone and, 50; nicotine and, 190; opioids and, 191

Sweating: alcohol use and, 15; alcohol withdrawal and, 13, 38, 40, 41, 42, 44; barbiturate withdrawal and, 110; benzodiazepine withdrawal and, 106; as indicator of substance use problem, 207; opioid use and, 78; opioid withdrawal and, 83, 90; neonatal abstinence syndrome and, 176, 178, 180

T

T-ACE test, 11, 18, 163, 164

Tachyarrhythmias, cocaine and, 120, 149

Tachycardia: alcohol withdrawal and, 15, 38, 19; amphetamines and, 131; barbiturate withdrawal and, 110; benzodiazepine withdrawal and, 106; cannabis and, 124; cocaine and, 149; GHB withdrawal and, 138; MDMA and, 133; opioid withdrawal and, 90; PCP and, 136

Tachydysrhythmias, alcohol and, 63

Tamoxifen, 127

Tamper-proofing prescriptions, 81

Tampering with urine drug screen, 28-29, 165

Teenagers. See adolescents; young adults

Temazepam, 103, 109

Temperature testing in urine drug screen, 28

Testicular atrophy: alcohol and, 54, 65; anabolic steroids and, 126

Testosterone: alcohol and, 65; anabolic steroids and, 127; cannabis and, 123

Tetrahydrocannabinol. See THC

THC: 122; urine drug screen for, 27. See also cannabis

Thiamine: alcohol dependence and, 47; alcohol withdrawal and, 44, 48; coma and, 142; ethylene glycol overdose and, 152; methanol overdose and, 152

Thiocyanates, 162

3, 4-methylenedioxymethamphetamine. See MDMA

Thrombocytopenia, alcohol and, 23, 55, 64, 189

Thrombolytics, for cocaine-induced MI, 149

Thyroiditis, hepatitis C and, 154

Tinnitus, benzodiazepine withdrawal and, 106

Titration: barbiturates for GHB withdrawal, 138; benzodiazepines for GHB withdrawal, 138; buprenorphine, 96-97; flumazenil, 148; methadone, 93, 94-95, 174; for opioid withdrawal, 79, 80-82, 176; naloxone, 146; for polysubstance use, 114, 115

Tobacco: in drug use history, 19; smoke, pregnancy and, 161, 162; smoking cessation and, 67-75; statistics regarding, 6-7. See also nicotine

Tranxene®. See clorazepate

Treatment agreement, 80, 89, 194

Treatment programs: for adolescents, 197; for alcohol problems, 32-33; for alcohol withdrawal, 38-49; for anabolic steroid dependence, 128; for anxiety, 99; for concurrent disorders, 186; driver's license suspension and, 36; effectiveness, 6-8; formal, 195-197; for hepatitis B, 157; for hepatitis C, 155-156; for HIV, 159; for inhalant use, 129; for MDMA use, 133; for medical professionals, 209-210; for neonates, 181-182; for opioid dependence and chronic pain, 87, 88; for opioid withdrawal, 90; after overdose, 141, 143; for polysubstance use, 133; during pregnancy, 165, 166, 168, 173; psychosocial, 32-33; recommending, 199-200, 203; relapse and, 204-205; for smoking, 67-75; testing for compliance with, 23, 33. *See also* halfway houses; mutual aid groups; stages of change

Tremor: GHB withdrawal and, 138; alcohol problems and, 10; alcohol withdrawal and, 12, 13, 15, 38, 39, 40, 41, 42, 44, 188; barbiturate withdrawal and, 110; benzodiazepine withdrawal and, 106; GHB withdrawal and, 138; inhalant withdrawal and, 128; neonatal, 176, 178, 179-180; pseudo-Parkinsonism and, 63

Triazolam: classification of, 4, 103; equivalence to diazepam, 109; risk of dependence on, 105; withdrawal, 108

Tricyclic antidepressants: alcohol and, 185; flumazenil and, 148; insomnia and, 102

Triphasic abstinence syndrome, cocaine and, 119

Tryptophan, 102, 104

Tuberculosis, 159-160

Tubular necrosis, cocaine and, 121, 150

12-Step program, 197-198

2-ethylene-1, 5-dimethyl 3, 3, diphenylpyrrolidine. *See* EDDP

Tylenol®#1. *See* codeine, with acetaminophen

U

UDS. *See* urine drug screen

Urinary retention, opioids and, 78

Urine drug screen: 23-29; for alcohol, 13, 23-25, 27, 36, 144; for amphetamines, 26, 132; for barbiturates, 27, 29; for benzodiazepines, 27; buprenorphine and, 96; for cocaine, 27, 118, 121; counselling and, 200; creatinine in, 28; detection periods, 26-27; for diazepam, 27; driver's license suspension and, 36; for flunitrazepam, 27; for GHB, 27, 138; for heroin, 26; for injection drugs, 29, 118; interpreting, 81; legal consent, 24, 168; limitations of, 26-27;

for MDMA, 26, 133; for methadone, 25-26, 88, 93, 94; for methamphetamine, 26; naltrexone and, 98; neonatal, 167; for nurse treatment, 210; during opioid titration, 80-81; for opioids, 25, 26, 80-81, 86, 89; for overdose, 142, 144; for patients on the ward, 192; for PCP, 26, 137; for physician treatment, 210; precautions, 24; during pregnancy, 165, 166, 167-168; for suspected drug use, 13, 16, 36, 64, 80, 142, 144, 167-168; tampering with, 26, 28-29, 165; for THC, 27, 123. *See also* chromatography; enzyme immunoassay

V

Venlafaxine, 101, 134

Verapamil, 149

Violence, alcohol problems and, 10, 31; cocaine and, 118; drug problems and, 14, 204; PCP and, 136

Vitamin B12 deficiency. *See* B12 deficiency

Vomiting: alcohol use and, 63; alcohol withdrawal and, 15, 38, 39, 40, 41; cannabis and, 122; disulfiram and, 52; GHB and, 138, 139; hepatitis and, 54; methadone and, 95; neonatal, 176, 178, 181; opioid withdrawal and, 90, 147; substance use and, 19

W

Weight gain: nurse impairment and, 207; physician impairment and, 207; smoking cessation and, 69

Weight loss: alcoholic hepatitis and, 54; cocaine and, 118; nurse impairment and, 207; physician impairment and, 207; substance use and, 14, 19; tuberculosis and, 159

Weightlifting, anabolic steroids and, 125, 127

Wernicke's encephalopathy, 40, 47-48, 143

Withdrawal: 1, 2, 15, 16; alcohol (*See* alcohol withdrawal); anabolic steroid, 126; barbiturate, 15, 73, 109-110, 112, 113, 114, 115, 116, 171, 191; benzodiazepine, 15, 60, 73, 100, 105-106, 108, 113, 114, 115, 116, 148, 171, 191; cannabis, 123, 171; cocaine, 15, 118, 119, 171; concurrent disorders and, 186; counselling during, 204, 205; dimenhydrinate, 125; Fiorinal®, 109; GHB, 138; hallucinogen, 130; home treatment of, 49; inhalant, 128; neonatal, 91, 163, 172, 173, 175-182; nicotine, 45, 67, 70, 72, 73, 74, 170,

190; opioid (*See* opioid dependence, withdrawal); following overdose, 141, 143, 146, 147, 148; polysubstance, 113-116, 188; during pregnancy, 163, 170-172, 173, 174; role of nurses during, 5; role of physicians during, 5; substance-induced disorders and, 183, 185

Withdrawal management centres, 49, 195-196

Withdrawal-mediated pain. *See* opioids for chronic pain, withdrawal-mediated

Women: alcohol and, 9, 11, 12, 13, 35; anabolic steroids and, 126, 127; breast cancer risk, 7, 31, 65; breastfeeding, 30, 153, 169-170, 174; cardiomyopathy and, 63; cirrhosis and, 56; drinking guidelines for, 30, 31, 79; lung cancer risk, 7; Pap smears, 159, 166; sexually transmitted diseases and, 159; substance use screening for, 17, 18; tobacco and, 7, 69; treatment options for, 195, 196-197. *See also* fetal effects; labour; neonates; pregnancy

X

Xanax®. *See* alprazolam

Y

Young adults: anabolic steroids and, 127; cocaine and, 120; drinking guidelines for, 31; hepatitis C and, 154; injection drugs and, 154; MDMA and, 132; substance use screening for, 18, 154. *See also* adolescents

Z

Zoloft®. *See* sertraline

Zyban®. *See* bupropion

ISBN 0-88868-413-4

9 780888 684134